Swindler, Spy, Rebel

Swindler,
 Spy,
Rebel

*The Confidence Woman in
Nineteenth-Century America*

Kathleen De Grave

University of Missouri Press   *Columbia and London*

Library of Congress Cataloging-in-Publication Data

De Grave, Kathleen, 1950-
    Swindler, spy, rebel : the confidence woman in nineteenth-century America / Kathleen
De Grave.
        p.   cm.
    Includes bibliographical references (p. 251) and index.
    ISBN 0–8262–1005-8 (alk. paper)
    1. American prose literature—19th century—History and criticism.   2. Swindlers
and swindling—United States—History—19th century.   3. Women and literature—
United States—History—19th century.   4. Alienation (Social psychology) in literature.
5. Swindlers and swindling in literature.   6. Female offenders in literature.   7. Women spies
in literature.   8. Deception in literature.   I. Title.
PS366.S95D4   1995
810.9'352042—dc20   95-10288
                                                                                          CIP

♾ This paper meets the requirements of the American National Standard for Permanence of
Paper for Printed Library Materials, Z39.48, 1984.

Designer: Stephanie Foley
Typesetter: BOOKCOMP
Printer and Binder: Thomson-Shore, Inc.
Typeface: Century Old Style

Images on title page:
Top left: Chicago May Churchill. *Photo courtesy the Illinois State Historical Library*
Top right: A member of the Twenty-eighth Louisiana Volunteer Infantry during the Civil War.
    Photo courtesy Pelican Publishing Company
Bottom: Belle Boyd on tour. *Photo courtesy the Laura Virginia Hale Archives, Warren Heritage
    Society, Front Royal, Virginia*

To Earl Lee
for his intensity and encouragement

Contents

Acknowledgments

As this book has developed over the years, many people have helped me by suggesting sources, talking over ideas, and reading the manuscript with a critical eye. I would like to thank them all for making this project enjoyable and for helping me persist even when the going got rough. In particular, I want to acknowledge the support I received right from the beginning from my dissertation adviser, Gordon Hutner at the University of Wisconsin-Madison, and from my dissertation committee: Susan Friedman, Virginia Sapiro, and William Lenehan. I want to thank them for their encouragement, criticism, and advice. The English department at the University of Wisconsin made my long-distance work as smooth as it could be, and Dean Robert Walter, director of the Axe Library at Pittsburg State University, aided me greatly by allowing me to make copious use of library computers and interlibrary loan. More recently, Steven Meats, chair of the English department at Pittsburg State University, has not only encouraged me but given me direct help by adjusting my work schedule so that I could complete my research.

Many people, becoming intrigued by the idea of the confidence woman, have helped by leading me to obscure sources I would not have found otherwise. In particular, Gene De Grueson, curator of Special Collections at Axe Library, led me to the *Columbus (Kans.) Courier* news entry on Susan B. Anthony and to the Little Blue Books written by Betty Van Deventer. Kathleen Nichols, in the PSU English department, found Harriet Beecher Stowe's *Pink and White Tyranny,* a book I have made a cornerstone of the last chapter.

Family and friends have spent many hours reading the various versions of my manuscript, giving me a chance to deepen and clarify my thinking. I want to give special thanks to my sister Judy De Grave, who brought the eye of a historian to the work, and I want to thank Bonnie Buhrow, Linda Snell, Leanne Snell, Cynthia Bursa Suvak, Liz Zietz, Mary Barnes, and Virginia Green for their reading and commentary. In the last round of work on the manuscript, I have received help from Terri Schmitz, who tracked down some photos, and from a part-time lecturer at PSU, Ted Myrhe, who checked my quotations with precision and speed, an aid I much value.

But above all, I want to thank my husband, Earl Lee. Being an acquisitions librarian for the university, he has kept his eye out for books on a wide range of subjects, from criminology to Civil War stories. He has led me to a wealth of out-of-print texts and has suggested connections between ideas that turned out to be wonderfully fruitful. More than that, he has read and reread my manuscripts, giving encouragement and tough criticism at the same time, arguing me out of shaky ideas and into productive ones. Also, all along the way, he has given me the time and emotional support I have needed to complete the project.

Swindler, Spy, Rebel

1

Confronting the Confidence Woman

We all know at least vaguely about the confidence man—he's a fellow who swindles his way to success. The confidence man is a kind of antihero, like the gambler that James Garner played in the old television show *Maverick* (reincarnated by Mel Gibson in the 1994 movie), or the characters played by Paul Newman and Robert Redford in *The Sting*. The popularity of present-day confidence men partakes of an American tradition that, begrudgingly, admires the criminal who lives by his wits. He is a staple of popular culture, from Brer Rabbit to Bugs Bunny. This fascination with the criminal figure has been a part of American culture for a long time, evident even in the eager popular response to the prison literature of the sixteenth through the eighteenth centuries in England and America, which was written by criminals on their way to the gallows, recounting their exploits and explaining their masterly techniques. H. Bruce Franklin, in *Prison Literature in America*, argues that such crime literature was the precursor to the modern European and American novel. David S. Reynolds shows how the public's admiration for the "likable criminal" burgeoned with the advent of penny presses in the 1830s, causing the appearance of an astonishing number of crime stories and reminiscences about criminals written by the detectives who pursued them.[1]

One such publication was an encyclopedia of crime written in 1886 by Thomas Byrnes, chief of detectives for New York City. In this compendium of criminals

---

1. H. Bruce Franklin, *Prison Literature in America: The Victim as Criminal and Artist*, 124–27; David S. Reynolds, *Beneath the American Renaissance: The Subversive Imagination in the Age of Emerson and Melville*, 169–81.

then at large in America, written for the "prevention and detection of crime," Byrnes describes the modus operandi of almost two hundred criminals of all types, from bank robbers and forgers to confidence men. Among these two hundred, Byrnes describes several women he calls "confidence queens." One of these women is Bertha Heyman, a confidence woman whose territory was Milwaukee, Wisconsin. Byrnes says of Heyman, "She has been concerned in a number of swindling transactions, and has the reputation of being one of the smartest confidence women in America."[2] Bertha Heyman represents a type of woman in nineteenth-century America that has not received much attention, although her male counterpart certainly has. There is, however, much to be said about the "confidence queens" of the late nineteenth and early twentieth centuries, both in how they developed out of American history and culture and in how they then shaped and continue to shape American literature.

Tales of confidence men, real or fictional, are perennial favorites. Readers enjoy watching the confidence man switch from one disguise to another and are even more amazed that he can disguise himself as much by the stories he tells as by the way he looks. He can turn swampland into a paradise and himself into a philanthropic businessman just by the magic of his words. Legends about confidence men came over from England. Some historians say America started as part of a confidence scheme, companies luring immigrants from Europe to these shores with promises of untold riches and limitless opportunity. There is no doubt that early America was populated by criminals, male and female, many of whom made good.[3] The confidence man as an entrepreneur, even if a trickster, is accepted as part of the American psychology. The confidence man is a cynic, at bottom, playing on our ideals. The mixture of cynicism and idealism is as essential to the American tradition as are Franklin and Paine, cynics and idealists both.

An example of how cynicism and idealism interact in a typical piece of literature involving a confidence man is Johnson Jones Hooper's story "The Captain Attends a Camp Meeting," published in 1844. Hooper tells a story about Captain

2. Thomas Byrnes, *1886 Professional Criminals of America,* 200. Of the 200 entries, 19 are about women, the majority of whom were shoplifters, pickpockets, and confidence women.

3. See Walter Hart Blumenthal, *Brides from Bridewell: Female Felons Sent to Colonial America,* 36. Thousands of female felons, including thieves, were transported from England to America between 1619 and approximately 1788. About one-third of a total 35,000 convicts sent to the colonies in that span of time were women.

Simon Suggs, who, needing money to support his wife, goes to a camp meeting, a Bible-banging revival, pretending to be an unregenerate looking for salvation. Through the preaching of the minister and the prayerful urging of the people, Captain Suggs finally, at the right moment, supposedly converts and begins preaching beside the minister. He takes up a collection to start his own church, working on the people's desire to outdo one another in a show of wealth, and then says he must go to the swamp to pray over his mission. His horse awaits him there, and Captain Suggs, laughing, leaves a rich man. The story was quite popular in its day, as much for the admiration readers had for Suggs's ability to rope the people in as for the irreverent comment the story makes on religious pretense.[4]

All this is true for the confidence man, but what about the confidence woman? We might presume that she does not exist, or could not have existed in the nineteenth century, given the social restrictions of the day. Or we might say that if she did exist, she was simply a confidence man in female dress. Certainly, if we go by how little has been written about the confidence woman, we could easily conclude that she has, at any rate, been a very minor phenomenon in American history. But this is not the case. I will show that the confidence woman is not just another confidence man—that her games and disguises, her relation to American culture and to herself, are quite different from his. I will show too that she was a powerful force in her time, especially from the Civil War to the first decade of the twentieth century.

The fact that there has been so little written on the confidence-woman figure in American culture raises an important issue: it is as if nineteenth-century American confidence women have been forgotten. However, what a culture conveniently forgets tells as much about itself as what it self-servingly remembers. Something about the way confidence women related to their culture must have been very disturbing to cause their stories to disappear so completely.

It wasn't that the women were intrinsically uninteresting. Reading about the supposed exploits of criminal confidence women is perhaps even more interesting than reading about confidence men, because their actions come as such a surprise. The confidence game in particular, as compared to other crimes, has an element of humor in it, which makes us enjoy the stories of women

---

4. See Reynolds, *Beneath the American Renaissance,* 86–88, for a discussion of the popular desire to unveil hypocrisy among those wielding religious authority and of the general skepticism among many Americans.

who participate in what Thomas Byrnes calls that "safest, pleasantest, and most amusing" kind of thievery.[5] Even more interesting is the dual attitude that people of the time had toward such women, an attitude reflected in detective reports, newspaper accounts, criminal autobiographies, and fiction. Confidence women inspired, contradictorily, both revulsion and attraction—revulsion against them because they so broke the code that women of the time were expected to live by, and attraction toward the very bravado and intelligence that allowed them to do so.

An example of that dual reaction is the description Allan Pinkerton, the famous late-nineteenth-century detective, gives of Sophie Lewis, a shoplifter, bank robber, and swindler. He wrote that "her hair was black and waving, and her dark eyes were full of expression, and a vivacity that was captivating. . . . [Her face had] a sweetness that was bewitching . . . a beautiful ingenuous face." When he confronted her with her crime, Pinkerton declares that she had an "air of command and dignity." Despite his obvious attraction to Lewis's "vivacity," "sweetness," and "command," however, Pinkerton saw all this as an "outward sham which covered a base and degraded heart."[6] Some descriptions by nineteenth-century observers are more wholeheartedly appreciative, unaffected by the criminal motives of the confidence queens. Thomas Byrnes, for instance, calls Bertha Heyman a "remarkable woman" and "an excellent talker." She succeeded in tricking people out of their money (even in jail she stole $900 from a gullible man) because "she possesse[d] a wonderful knowledge of human nature, and [could] deceive those who consider themselves particularly shrewd in business matters."[7] *Remarkable, excellent,* and *wonderful* are adjectives one normally would not expect a police officer to use in describing the criminals he hunts for, any more than one would expect to hear the words *vivacity, sweetness,* or *dignity.* They indicate that such a criminal has become something more than

5. Byrnes, *1886 Professional Criminals,* 40.

6. Allan Pinkerton, *Thirty Years a Detective: A Thorough and Comprehensive Exposé of Criminal Practices of All Grades and Classes . . . ,* 237–39. Pinkerton seems to have made a composite of several criminal women in his description of Sophie Lewis, but Sophie Lewis is essentially the same as Sophie Lyons, who wrote an autobiography, *Why Crime Does Not Pay.* See Chapter 3.

7. Byrnes, *1886 Professional Criminals,* 200–201. Many of these positive phrases are standard rhetoric for talking about male criminals, too. However, that Byrnes applies favorable male descriptors to a woman who is stepping out of her stereotypical role gives the phrases additional meaning.

just a woman who breaks the law; Bertha Heyman has become instead her alias, "Big Bertha," a character in an American scene, a person of fiction, and Sophie (Lewis) Lyons, née Levy, ultimately creates an official fiction of herself in an autobiography about her life of crime.

This study will look at how confidence women are fictionalized in informal historical accounts and how they create their own fictions in their autobiographies. It will then look at how these images change when they come into the realm of literary fiction. This study is from the point of view of a literary historian: it is a study of the words people use to describe confidence women, rather than a discussion of what the women actually did—for separating fact from fiction requires a different kind of research than I have done here. But a nation's imaginative culture is formed, perhaps, as much by its myths as by its actual history; in terms of cultural imagery, it is questionable whether history and myth can ever be entirely divorced. The focus here will be on how people in the late nineteenth and early twentieth centuries perceived the stories of a few unusual women and how that perception surfaced in literature.

This is not to say that the women I deal with are entirely constructs of the imagination. There is a certain amount of documentary proof that they existed and were involved in some amazing enterprises. However, these pieces of proof are only now being sorted out by serious historians, such as Richard Hall in his study of female Civil War spies, *Patriots in Disguise,* and much work remains to be done. I look forward with great interest to future historical studies of the confidence women that I present here from a literary point of view.

I will proceed to discuss these women with the understanding that I am not documenting the actual histories of the women I have found written about in informal histories, but that I am comparing the *images* that are presented. The women whose personae I will be dealing with are amazingly similar in some important ways—in their use of disguise, their ability to manipulate people's perceptions, their confidence in their own skills, their pleasure in playing the game—and quite dissimilar in others, particularly in their motivations and their ethics. I call these women "confidence women" because they use what are typically understood to be the confidence arts and because they have an assertive attitude similar to that of the well-known confidence man. The reason I hesitate to simply give them this name without discussion is that I understand labeling any human being to be a dangerous thing. Recently some feminist scholars, including Judith Butler, have made the political coercion of such labeling clear: a label both includes and excludes; it sets limits; it reduces the complexity of the human condition to something neat and, most important, manageable.[8] I am fully aware that the women I describe do not fit into any neat categories; there is no clear-cut dividing line between women who are confidence women and those who are not. It is instead like the color spectrum, made up of blurred intersections. Still, the colors—and the confidence women—can be distinguished if one stands far enough back.

Likewise, to consider any time period as a unit, as if it were a chunk of time one could hold up to the light, stable and monolithic, is to be mistaken, to take what is convenient for what is true. The concept "confidence women in the nineteenth century" is therefore a doubly risky one that I will constantly call into question even as I raise points of discussion. Of course, there has already been much said on a companion concept, "the confidence man in the nineteenth century," usually without anyone raising the foundationalist question. Keeping the risks in mind, I will take a look at the definitions various scholars have devised for such men to see if they can help explain the women that detectives in the late nineteenth century called "confidence queens."

Because so much has been written on the confidence man as a literary figure, it would be reasonable to see what sorts of definitions scholars have given the confidence man. Gary Lindberg, in his excellent *The Confidence Man in American Literature,* calls the confidence man a "covert cultural hero for Americans," explaining that he is a rebel against the superficial norms that society accepts, a self-made man who "represents . . . our unofficial reward systems, the strategies that we have for over two centuries allowed to succeed." The confidence man partakes of the "grand promise" of America that anyone can be rich if he has enough ingenuity and daring, and of the faith that Americans can invent a new world if the old one fails them: the confidence man "is at once the celebrant of shared faith and the agent most capable of exploiting it"; he is "a manipulator or contriver who creates an inner effect, an impression, an experience of confidence, that surpasses the grounds for it."[9] This rich definition is especially interesting for its duality: a con man is a creator/exploiter; thus people have a dual response toward the figure. It is also interesting in its emphasis on psychology, that the confidence artist uses effect and impression to wreak his will. Finally, the heart

8. Judith Butler addresses the issues of categorizing women and the reality of "the subject" in "Contingent Foundations: Feminism and the Question of 'Postmodernism.'"
9. Gary Lindberg, *The Confidence Man in American Literature,* 3–4, 7.

of the definition is that the con man is bigger than life, a hero. Lindberg includes such sterling figures as Benjamin Franklin and Thomas Jefferson in his list of confidence men because they are "self-made," obviously expanding the term beyond the idea that a con man is a criminal in the conventional sense.

William E. Lenz in *Fast Talk and Flush Times* takes the idea that the confidence man represents a desire in American culture a step further. He allies the confidence man with the West, which he calls "a psychic landscape, a projection of American hopes and fears." The confidence man—as a literary figure who is associated with the frontier, the "new country"—ultimately "personifies the ambiguities of the new country in a non-threatening form." Lindberg and Lenz differ in their efforts at definition in that Lindberg uses historical figures as exemplars of the confidence man, whereas Lenz tends to focus more on the form the confidence man takes as a fictional character. Lindberg allows his definition to include not only criminals but also boosters, gamesmen, and self-made men. Lenz focuses specifically on the confidence man as a criminal whose "cardinal motive" is "personal profit." Whereas Lindberg's con man can represent American ideals of independence and "self-creation," Lenz's "embodies forces of disorder, transition, and unrest" and ultimately is an ironic figure, a "self-caricature."[10]

In these definitions, the pronoun is securely male—and the men described were typically white males who aspired to the middle class. Most women—white or otherwise—in the eighteenth and nineteenth centuries were not recognized as part of the business world, and in fact historical realities made it very difficult for women to be boosters or self-made women: history has not left us with many stories of female counterparts for Franklin, Jefferson, or P. T. Barnum. The "shared faith" that Lindberg describes is a masculine, middle-class faith in economic opportunity for the man strong and clever enough to take advantage of the promise America offered. Among many nineteenth-century middle-class women, on the other hand, was the shared faith that if a woman were a "true woman," her *husband* would succeed; her role was helpmate, not entrepreneur.

I am speaking here of the cultural ideal, not the reality. In reality, some women were going to the West and taking advantage of the freedom they could find there; other women were fighting to survive in the system of slavery; other, Asian American women were dying in the cribs they had been sold into on the Pacific

10. William E. Lenz, *Fast Talk and Flush Times: The Confidence Man as a Literary Convention*, 1, 15, 20, 2, 1, 7–8.

seaboard; still others were burying their children along the Trail of Tears, and the list goes on. According to the ideal, women were domestic and submissive and happy to be so. In familial reality, many women came to see that submission to their husbands brought ruin to themselves and their families, not success. In the ideal, women created a haven for men at home. In economic reality, many women, especially as widows, were entrepreneurs running businesses as diverse as millinery shops and sawmills. Overall, a significant proportion of women in the real world could not or did not want to fit the ideal of the "true woman" because they were not middle class; they were ex-slaves or Native American or part of the huge underclass of American society.

Even though the true woman ideal was not the reality for many American women, the true woman myth affected the entire culture, making people believe that any other kind of woman was something less. Obviously, a cultural myth can have a far-reaching effect. As both Lindberg and Lenz agree, American literature and culture have been affected by the larger *myth* of the confidence artist, not just the bare reality. However, the error of the myth they describe is that the confidence artist is by definition male.

The fact is, there is a confidence-woman myth, too, although it has not been much discussed. In representations of such women in the nineteenth century, the myth generally consists of these elements: confidence women are grand deceivers; they use psychology to outmaneuver their opponents, and often that psychology involves manipulating the perception of their own "beauty" or "sweetness"; confidence women are bigger than life—smarter, tougher, more easily amused, less confined by convention—often less conventionally moral than other women; they take bigger risks and often end up with bigger consequences, good or bad. We recount the myth ostensibly so that we will be shocked by such women who overstep their "rightful place" in society. But the mythic narrative openly admires these women all the while it excoriates their "wicked hearts."

However, this discussion has so far focused just on the myth, not on an entire definition, which we can attempt by comparing the historical confidence women of various sorts who contributed to the myth but were of much less legendary size. As I try to define the similarities among these real women, I will take into account Lindberg's insight that the confidence game involves a manipulation of belief, creates an impression of confidence in something that is not there. My definition will allow, as does Lindberg's, for categories of confidence women who are not criminals out only for "personal profit," as Lenz put it. But like Lenz's definition, mine will look for the "disorder, transition, and unrest" that underlies the image of the confidence woman. On the other hand, I will ask whether the confidence-woman image is "self-caricature," as Lenz's confidence-man image is, or rather self-discovery.

A quotation from an autobiography by a turn-of-the-century confidence woman will begin to shape the definition. May Churchill Sharpe—"Chicago May"—said of herself as a criminal confidence woman, "I was always quick-witted. . . . I never hunted with the pack. This may have been because I was proud of my ability and thought most other crooks were not my equal. I worked hard to make myself a master workman."[11] The tone here is serious, as Churchill transforms herself into her mythical persona, Chicago May. Confidence women, or at least the mythic figures they self-created, first and foremost had confidence in themselves, a sense of their ability to independently confront their world. This in itself is an important difference between these women and the womanly ideal that was just beginning to lose force in the latter part of the century—an ideal they actively rebelled against. These confidence women set goals for themselves and allowed themselves styles of action not condoned by the greater society. Certainly many women who were not confidence women were likewise choosing their own lives, by becoming writers, by moving west and becoming ranchers, by beginning the women's movement in labor organizations and in social reform. But confidence women took this element of choice to an extreme. They became criminals or adventuresses, spies, and soldiers. Their pride in their own personal abilities was at the center of who they were.

As a clarifying contrast, one might look at the middle-class women who became a particular kind of shoplifter—people we might mistakenly include in the same criminal category as confidence women—in the same time period. Elaine Abelson in *When Ladies Go A-Thieving* argues that middle-class women shoplifters were a logical result of the consumerism of the Victorian era. Shopping became woman's work; shoplifting was that role carried to excess. To avoid calling female shoplifters thieves, society's officials labeled them "kleptomaniacs"—their crime was turned into a "typically female" disease. The middle-class shoplifters Abelson describes were certainly thieves, but they were not confidence women. This is evident in the quotation she gives from one Boston woman who, sobbing, says "she could not resist the temptation to steal" and that she considers herself "disgraced." Chicago May, on the other hand, claimed, "I

11. May Churchill Sharpe, *Chicago May: Her Story,* 13–14.

have never suffered from qualms of conscience. I have had no regrets—except when I was caught. I am not really sorry I was a criminal." Thomas Byrnes, too, is quite clear about the difference. He describes the professional criminal shoplifter—a subcategory of confidence woman—as "she of the ready fingers and fluent tongue," not of the same type as the "kleptomaniac," with "her frightened glance, her sneaking attitude."[12] His language shows his appreciation of the one and his scorn for the other.

In addition to her supreme self-confidence, a confidence woman has a certain joie de vivre and often a sense of humor, or at least this is how she is shown and shows herself. This is in line with Lenz's depiction of the literary confidence man as a comic figure—the "tightly controlled" comedy, he says, dissolves "the spectres of ambiguity, immorality, and betrayal" the stories raise.[13] There is pleasure for the confidence artist in exposing the falsity of a myth. For the confidence man, it is the myth that hard work and morality will overcome all obstacles. For the confidence woman in the nineteenth century, it was the myth of sincerity, purity, and domesticity surrounding the image of the good and happy woman. There is also a joy in creating a specific image that corresponds perfectly with society's expectations and then shattering it ourselves. An example of this *jouissance* is Sophie Lyons's description, in her autobiography *Why Crime Does Not Pay*, of how she distracted a bank clerk as she made a preliminary assessment of the job: "Alas! how well I remember how that vain old man enjoyed his innocent flirtation." Lyons gives the story in great detail, relishing every moment.[14] We see in her description her enjoyment of her own actions and her delight in shattering the "pretty widow" image she had so carefully constructed. We also see her creating herself as a mythical persona.

The construction of images is an integral part of what a confidence woman does, for the heart of a confidence game lies in its dishonesty, its deception, its pretense of innocence. Like the confidence man, the confidence woman manipulates people's impressions. The difference lies in what she creates an impression *of.* Typically, the confidence man has something to sell—a lame horse,

12. Elaine S. Abelson, *When Ladies Go A-Thieving: Middle-Class Shoplifters in the Victorian Department Store,* 3–12, 16; Sharpe, *Chicago May,* 12; Byrnes, *1886 Professional Criminals,* 31–32. Whenever I speak of shoplifters from this point on, I will be referring to those who shoplift as a criminal trade. I will use the term *kleptomaniac* or make some other designation if I mean shoplifting in the other sense.

13. Lenz, *Fast Talk,* 21–22.

14. Sophie Lyons, *Why Crime Does Not Pay,* 30–31, 33–34.

swampland, snake oil, or stock in a nonexistent company. The confidence he raises is twofold: confidence in himself and confidence in the product he is selling. The confidence woman, on the other hand, usually has no product but an image of herself. She manipulates the stereotypes of women, playing a stereotype out, selling the image, then laughing when the game is over, having caught people by surprise. In this way, the confidence woman is certainly not a "covert cultural hero"; rather, she "embodies disorder." She does not celebrate the ideal; rather, she rebels against it, showing how hollow it is.

In essence, the confidence woman, like the confidence man, uses disguise, deception, and manipulation to get what she wants, and, as with him, an aura of comedy surrounds her. She, like the confidence man, is a storyteller, has a gift for making people believe—whatever she wants. But there the similarity ends. Because women, especially in the nineteenth century, are not perceived as having the same access to goods and financial power as men, the stories a confidence woman tells are substantially different from the confidence man's stories. Whereas the confidence man typically tells a story about a thing—a product, a commodity, an organization—the confidence woman most often tells a story about herself, a story built out of the stereotypes about women that prevail at the time. And her story is often told in pantomime rather than in words—she uses tears and golden smiles as her "fast talk."

Several good examples of the kinds of stories a confidence man most often tells appear in Herman Melville's *The Confidence-Man:* a man in a gray coat tells a story about an asylum for Seminole widows and orphans; a man in a traveling-cap tells a story about stock in the nonexistent Black Rapids Coal Company; a man calling himself an agent for the Philosophical Intelligence Office says he has boys for hire; and the herb-doctor sells his Omni-Balsamic Reinvigorator, his Samaritan Pain Dissuader, and his boxes of Natural Bone-setter Pills. For the confidence man, there is an interplay between the commodity and the salesman. The customers begin to have confidence in the item for sale when they gain confidence in the salesman. Likewise, the more enamored the customers become of the commodity, the readier they are to have confidence in the man. In effect, the confidence man and the commodity he sells gain stature from each other. Melville makes it clear through the failure of the Cosmopolitan and the man with the weed that people will seldom put confidence in a man if he does not have a reasonably credible product for sale.

Confidence women, on the other hand, typically do not have a separate com-modity for sale. Rather, if they are selling at all, they are selling an image of themselves, but not for a direct monetary price; their financial gain comes about more indirectly. That in a patriarchal and capitalist society women will be items of exchange is an idea well argued by Karl Marx, Thorstein Veblen, Simone de Beauvoir, and Luce Irigaray, thinkers spanning the nineteenth and twentieth centuries. That in such a society women would turn capitalist and bring themselves to market is an idea not so often explored. Irigaray, in *This Sex Which Is Not One*, states that in a capitalist, patriarchal society "commodities should never speak, and certainly should not go to market alone. For such actions turn out to be totally subversive to the economy of exchange among subjects," since the subject/object dichotomy underpins the ethic of that exchange.[15] Yet that is exactly what many confidence women do—go to market alone, or, conversely, take themselves off the market entirely. Perhaps that is why the confidence woman has not been much discussed: perhaps she is too subversive to handle. The confidence man is subversive too, in his cynicism. But cynicism in women has a different effect. Karen Halttunen, who has studied the confidence man and some forms of the confidence woman in nineteenth-century America, suggests that women were ideally expected to be "transparent," sincere, and trusting, much more than men were, since men had to be able to deal with the hard world of the marketplace. If *women* were cynical and wore disguises in order to deceive, then what was left to trust?

It is necessary to remember that the role of "woman" is itself a masquerade played by individual females, as anyone knows who has heard a mother tell her daughter to disguise her intelligence, wear appropriately feminine attire, and smile a lot if she wishes to strike a man favorably. Mary Murphy recounts, in her study of prostitutes on the frontier, how in Butte, Montana, in the late 1800s, the city elders made it clear that the idea "woman" was not a biological definition but a social construct when they made it illegal for "lewd females" to swear in the presence of women.[16] "Womanliness" is a sex role, with definite rules for the actress to follow, including that she be "sincere." How the confidence woman's act differs from this more mundane masquerade becomes quite complicated, but the essential difference—and it is a big one—between any woman playing her socially assigned role and the confidence woman is that the con woman writes her own script.

15. Luce Irigaray, *This Sex Which Is Not One,* 158.
16. Mary Murphy, "The Private Lives of Public Women: Prostitution in Butte, Montana, 1878–1917," in Susan Armitage and Elizabeth Jameson, eds., *The Women's West,* 195.

Most women at some time in their lives play a role—a sex role—in their personal drama, the script of which is generally written by someone else: society, tradition, upbringing. For the most part, women are unaware that they are playing a role at all, being so well trained from childhood. Such women are not confidence women. The confidence woman is very much aware of what she is doing; she is both playwright and actress, at least during the span of the game, perfectly capable of changing the story line and the role assigned. Hers is, perhaps, a play within a play, and her control of the stage and the other participants goes as far as her story-making can take her. One of the most common stories confidence women tell about themselves is that they are innocent and naïve and thus in need of protection ("protection" translating into money if they play the game right). The story is frequently wordless, composed of looks and tears. The woman sells her helplessness, playing on her victim's stereotypes.

Some confidence men, too, tell stories about themselves without reference to a separate product, and in this way they overlap the definition of the confidence woman. Melville gives an example of this kind of story in the case of Black Guinea, one of the disguises of the nameless confidence man—in this instance the confidence man pretends to be a black, crippled beggar; he sells the image he creates of himself, sells his condition. The man with the weed similarly tries to sell an image of himself as someone who is destitute but worthy, just as Simon Suggs at the camp meeting creates the image of himself as a sudden convert full of missionary zeal. Such strategies by confidence men, however, are relatively infrequent. Likewise, some confidence women overlap the definition of the confidence man by telling stories about a product other than themselves. Sophie Lyons and Ellen Peck, both confidence women, at one point—so Lyons tells us in her autobiography—teamed up and repeatedly sold rented pianos for as much as they could get, selling the same piano several times in one afternoon.[17] They experienced the interplay of product and saleswoman in the way confidence men usually do, but their scheme was not typical of the games they or other con women usually played. I use the term *game* advisedly, because confidence women often did consider their manipulations to be as enjoyable as a round of chess, needing a similar kind of forethought and intuitive understanding of an opponent's next move—although the con woman's games were usually less sedate.

Confidence women who sell an image of themselves at market—as helpless, vulnerable, naïve—put on the disguise of womanliness, femininity. They play

17. Sophie Lyons, *Why Crime Does Not Pay,* 116–17.

the sex role to perfection. Their immediate goal is sometimes a direct payoff, sometimes blackmail, often diversion so that spying or a robbery or an escape can go on behind the victim's back. On the other hand, confidence women who take themselves *off* the market put on the disguise of masculinity by dressing like men, or make their commodity value extremely low by dressing like beggar women or other women of classes normally discounted by the society in question. In either case, I will argue, the final, if unconscious, aim of the confidence woman is to step outside her restrictive role as commodity and achieve a personal sense of selfhood, no matter how socially unacceptable that self might be— not a final aim of most confidence men, who were already considered subjects in the exchange economy.

The confidence woman, then, is a subversive element in a society that has constructed its images of women very carefully. In *Confidence Men and Painted Women,* Karen Halttunen discusses the image of sincerity that nineteenth-century American women worked hard to construct and the contradictions that lie in working to appear as if one is "true." But she separates the "painted woman" from the confidence man by focusing on the women in middle-class society who could "manipulate facial expression, manner, and personal appearance" either "in a calculated effort to lure the guileless into granting them confidence" or with the more innocent aim of demonstrating their middle-class status. Halttunen argues that "under the powerful sway of fashion, society was being transformed into one great masquerade."[18]

One might be tempted to speculate, then, that all women who had to survive in a hypocritical society were confidence women. But this is not the case. One cannot be a confidence woman by default; women who are confidence artists choose to be so and consciously calculate their dishonesty. Halttunen's middle-class women were not making bold statements of personality; they were participating in a group action, a tacitly acceptable deception that was too widespread to be subversive. However, I do want to follow Lindberg's lead and open the definition of the confidence woman beyond criminality. For there were other women besides criminals who manipulated the stereotypes of women with a certain joy and who found their self-definition in doing so.

18. Karen Halttunen, *Confidence Men and Painted Women: A Study of Middle-Class Culture in America, 1830–1870,* xv, 65–66. Halttunen's study deals with a class of women different from most of the confidence women I have found. The manipulations of these women are of the sort used by the group I call "everyday pretenders."

One group includes adventuresses, who were perhaps unethical but who did not break the law. Such women manipulated people for profit or for the sheer pleasure of control. Fortune-tellers, quack doctors, gold diggers, and fortune hunters all fall into this category. An adventuress like Tennessee Claflin, who claimed she could cure cancer and reaped great profits until she was run out of town, is not the same as an adventurer like Annie Oakley, who built her reputation on real prowess. The women I call adventuresses were grand deceivers, but they were not outright thieves, as the criminal confidence women were. A gold digger persuades a man to give her money; a criminal confidence woman tricks or extorts the money out of him. Adventuresses are the kind of confidence women who most often appear in nineteenth-century fiction. Another group of confidence women includes women who were soldiers and spies. These women, too, used deception and disguise to achieve their purposes. S. Emma Edmonds dressed like a man and joined the Union Army, keeping up that disguise for over a year. She also spied for the Union by, in one instance, disfiguring her face and dressing like an Irish peddler woman; in another, she disguised herself as a black man so she could slip behind enemy lines and listen to the officers talk while she poured their water. What criminal confidence women and adventuresses did for profit, soldiers and spies did for a cause. The autobiographies of the soldiers and spies have striking similarities to those of criminal confidence women, although their motives were vastly different. All these kinds of confidence women exude a self-confidence and delight in life that is refreshing; they exhibit an ability to analyze the roles women play, showing a certain understanding of human psychology; and they dare to manipulate those roles for an ulterior purpose in an intelligent, calculating way.

Obviously, I appreciate the confidence-woman myth in much the same way some nineteenth-century observers did and in much the same spirit as contemporary literary historians appreciate the confidence man. Likewise, my admiration, like theirs, is heavily tinctured by my repugnance for what many of the confidence women actually did. It is interesting that the myth of the confidence artist typically glosses over the pain caused by the deception, the deleterious psychological effects on the victims. It points out the comedy, but not the sordid lifestyles and the skewed sense of community and ethics that goes with them. The dual reaction of attraction and repulsion is perhaps one of the underlying fascinations of the figure; the confidence artist—like the trickster figures in Native American legend—takes everything, good and bad, to an extreme. But that is how myths are made.

I limit my definition of the confidence woman essentially to those women who define themselves by their ability to manipulate and deceive. However, certain other women might fruitfully come into the analysis, too: for instance, those who play a confidence game only once in their lives to escape some terrifying situation—those whom I call "escape artists." They might illuminate confidence women, by contrast, with the limits beyond which they are unwilling to go. Likewise, those women who use many of the strategies of the confidence woman but who do not escape or undermine the womanly role in so doing can make it clear that the confidence-woman figure is indeed a separate type, of a category far beyond what I call the "everyday pretender."

Raising the question of who the confidence woman is brings with it several other issues that will be dealt with in the following chapters. The most complex is the issue of criminality itself and how women's crime was viewed in the nineteenth century. More quickly dealt with are the issues of transvestism—asking whether cross-dressing is a form of the confidence game—and passing—asking whether a black woman who passes for white or a lesbian woman who passes for straight is a confidence woman. Considering these issues will help clarify the uses of confidence women in fiction.

My analysis of the confidence-woman figure will be an analysis of the construction of a myth. First, in Chapters 2 and 3, I will give some historical context and consider historical confidence women as documented in informal histories, police accounts, or autobiographies, always with the caveat that this "documentation" is itself suspect, involved in the creation of the myth even as it purports to be "real." Chapters 4 and 5 consider how the confidence woman appears in two different forms of discourse: autobiography and fiction. It is instructive to see how the image of the confidence woman changes in the shift from (relative) nonfiction to fiction. In Chapter 6, I will look at how some nineteenth-century women writers used the confidence game as a narrative strategy, hoping to trick their readers into the text and to awaken a subversive attitude toward their society. Finally, Chapter 7 discusses how the discourse concerning the confidence woman has undergone a considerable change in the twentieth century.

2

The Confidence Woman in Context

We easily recognize the confidence women in other literatures: the ancient Sheherazade, Chaucer's fabliaux women, Shakespeare's Portia and Rosalind, Defoe's Moll Flanders, Thackeray's Becky Sharp, de Staël's Corinne. Types of confidence women abound in history also, especially women who dressed like men in order to serve as soldiers, pirates, or doctors, or sometimes simply to own property: Catalina de Erauso, Christina de Meryac, Christian Davies, Mary Read, Anne Bonny, Mary East, Mary Anne Talbot, Hannah Snell, Annabella Parsons, Dr. James Barry, Catherine Coombs, Nadezhda Durova.[1] But when we try to recall the confidence women in our American history and literature, the names and the stories do not come so easily. This is perhaps in part because confidence women did not come on the scene, historically or in written texts, with any force until the late nineteenth century and then took so many different forms that they could not be recognized as a single type at the time. Confidence women were swindlers, blackmailers, pickpockets, or experts at playing elaborate cons like the "badger game." Sometimes a confidence woman was a "financier" like Sophie Beck, who, according to some reports, set up a

---

1. For these stories many sources are available. See Antonia Fraser, *The Warrior Queens;* Marjorie Garber, *Vested Interests: Cross-Dressing and Cultural Anxiety;* Reay Tannahill, *Sex in History;* C. J. S. Thompson, *The Mysteries of Sex: Women Who Posed as Men and Men Who Impersonated Women;* and Julie Wheelwright, *Amazons and Military Maids: Women Who Dressed as Men in the Pursuit of Life, Liberty, and Happiness.* For the Nadezhda Durova story, see Nadezhda Durova, *The Cavalry Maiden: Journals of a Russian Officer in the Napoleonic Wars.* For American women cross-dressers, see Richard Hall, *Patriots in Disguise: Women Warriors of the Civil War;* Jonathan Ned Katz, *Gay American History: Lesbians and Gay Men in the U.S.A., A Documentary History;* and Oscar A. Kinchen, *Women Who Spied for the Blue and the Gray.*

lavishly furnished false-front company, sold worthless stock, and made off to Europe with $2 million. Many times confidence women were not criminals but adventuresses, staying just this side of the law, a form of confidence woman we most often find in literature. A different brand of confidence women were spies during the Civil War, using disguises and ruses to complete their assignments, or were soldiers, staking their success on being taken for men. Despite her many different forms, however, the confidence woman is in many ways a singular type apart from other female characters and historical figures.

The vast majority of American confidence women about whom I have found written records lived, or were written about, between the Civil War and World War I. Although the conditions that led slave women to use their confidence skills were different from the forces behind urban swindlers, and different again from the forces that led other women to become spies, the fact that all these forms appeared at about the same time suggests that the second half of the nineteenth century was an unusually fertile time for American women to manipulate their environment by deceit. One of the questions that needs to be answered is why that was so.

One obvious reason for the flourishing of the confidence woman in America from the 1860s to the early 1900s was the rise of cities. As Daniel Defoe made clear in his picaresque tale of the eighteenth-century confidence woman Moll Flanders, a densely populated city allows a woman to pick pockets or shoplift without much chance of detection. The social and physical restraints normally put on women in small towns were absent in the city, at least for lower-class women, many of whom were immigrants, and often "honest" work was hard to find or was ill paying. But poverty itself does not explain the confidence woman. May Churchill, for instance, married into the wealthy New York Sharpe family in the 1890s. She had the option of living with her husband's family in a beautiful home with servants and fine china. But instead, after some rough times with her husband, she struck out on her own, saying, "I'm for myself. I want to risk myself in the world. The thought of having security annoys me."[2] She was careful, of course, to take enough of her ex-husband's money with her to live well as she began her career as a confidence woman in earnest, and she went on to become "Chicago May," the celebrated "Queen of the Badgers." Being "for oneself,"

2. Quoted in Jay Robert Nash, *Look for the Woman: A Narrative Encyclopedia of Female Poisoners, Kidnappers, Thieves, Extortionists, Terrorists, Swindlers, and Spies from Elizabethan Times to the Present,* 81.

wanting to take risks, is a part of the psychological make-up of many of the confidence women of the late 1800s, as it is today. But this psychological drive is not enough to explain the upsurge in the number of confidence women during and after the Civil War. It was necessary that the culture allow a woman like May Churchill a certain amount of freedom in order for her to be successful in the confidence arena, and that freedom was more prevalent in the cosmopolitan atmosphere of cities. Confidence women arose in full force in the years of accelerated change at the end of the nineteenth century.

I will later examine in detail the historical conditions that encouraged the number of confidence women to rise in the second half of the nineteenth century, but at this point it is necessary only to understand that one of the most important forces behind this rise was the conflict in the late nineteenth century created by the convergence of a restrictive stereotype, a harsh reality, and a new potential. Just as the confidence man appears on the edge of the "new country,"[3] no matter where it might be, so the confidence woman appears on the leading edge of what Susan P. Conrad calls new "countries of the mind."[4] Because women could imagine their own freedom, they could see their restrictions clearly; they could see that the old stereotypes had to be broken before a new relationship between women and society could prevail. In 1845, Margaret Fuller had articulated that necessity in *Woman in the Nineteenth Century,* but it would not be until major changes occurred in the economy and women like Elizabeth Cady Stanton and Ernestine Rose effected real change in the legal structure that the new relationship would become a reality. It was during those years of change, of open rebellion on the part of some women and fearful holding back on the part of many others, that the confidence woman held sway. A covert rebel, she appeared to bend to traditional roles but in fact used the roles as a disguise for a purpose that was as nontraditional as the most open rebel's would be, subverting and sabotaging the established order by the very nature of her enterprise. The confidence woman was a transitional figure, growing out of the social conditions of the past and pointing toward a new relationship in the future. It was in the transition from "true womanhood" to the "new woman" that the confidence woman reigned.

One of the most important reasons that confidence women became so prevalent in the late nineteenth century is the strong tendency of people living in

3. See Lenz, *Fast Talk.*
4. Susan P. Conrad, *Perish the Thought: Intellectual Women in Romantic America, 1830–1860,* 96.

the Victorian era to see women in rigid stereotypes. A con artist like May Churchill used this tendency to her advantage, acting the "womanly" role to disguise her true purposes. Stereotypes of women were so strong that people found it hard to believe such confidence women even existed. However, America had always been a country that harbored female criminals, whether the general populace admitted it or not. Walter Hart Blumenthal, in *Brides from Bridewell: Female Felons Sent to Colonial America,* discusses the historical records that show that hundreds of women were deported from England to Virginia alone in the seventeenth and eighteenth centuries. Among these women were some confidence women. Elizabeth Grieve, for instance, was transported for "defrauding divers persons in England under pretence of procuring them places under the Government." Blumenthal gives details of the especially interesting case of Sarah Wilson, who, after being deported from England, "assumed the title of Princess Susanna Caroline Matilda, declaring herself a sister of the Queen." She had in fact been maid of honor to Queen Charlotte, so she knew how the royalty carried themselves and how they spoke. Wilson had some clothes from her days as maid of honor and, according to a *London Magazine* story of 1773 quoted by Blumenthal, she went from mansion to mansion in South Carolina, "making astonishing impressions in many places, affecting the mode of royalty so inimitably that many had the honor to kiss her hand." She succeeded in eliciting "substantial loans" in exchange for promises of promotions and careers. Finally, Wilson's indenture master caught up with her, and the spree was over. Blumenthal suggests that the criminal women of the colonies passed down "an abiding insurgence" to their children, helping to bring on the revolution.[5] America seemed to be a natural environment for con women, both historically and in fiction. Defoe quite rightly shows Moll Flanders at the end of her career in England being exiled to America; Arthur Conan Doyle was also perceptive in imagining that one of the only two people who ever outsmarted Sherlock Holmes was an American actress (Irene Adler in "A Scandal in Bohemia") who saw through his disguise.

But all this will need much discussion. To put American confidence women—figures who cut across the boundaries of race, class, and ethnicity—in context, I will first look at the mythical tradition they grew out of and then consider the forces of time and place that seem to have fostered their burgeoning in the cities of the late nineteenth century.

5. Blumenthal, *Brides from Bridewell,* 58–60.

Silencing the Confidence-Woman Myth

The fact that so little has been said about the confidence woman is evidence that the old prejudices still have power. Although late-nineteenth-century America saw the flowering of the confidence woman, in fact she has existed in many ages and in many cultures. Whenever the reigning ideology concerning women has been at great variance with the reality, and whenever there has been a simultaneous sense of potential freedom, the confidence woman has arisen.

The urge to deny the confidence woman is likewise not new. It is as old as the Sheherazade legend, part of the oral tradition of the Middle East, written down in Arabic in the tenth century and translated into its most celebrated English version in 1885 by Sir Richard Burton. Burton's spelling of the name is Shahrazad, and the difference in spelling makes an important point; the old Shahrazad is very different from the Sheherazade we know in the legend today. Burton's translation tells the story of Shahrazad's heroism as it was given in the old texts, but in his footnotes he tries to redefine what she does, to reduce her unique personality and genius to the stereotype of the designing, deceiving woman. The Sheherazade we are told about when we are children, a woman who fearfully tells stories night after night in order to save merely her own life instead of the lives of thousands, a woman whose physical beauty charms the king as much as her clever words do, bears little resemblance to the actual Shahrazad of the *Arabian Nights*. The transformation of Shahrazad into Sheherazade is one of the oldest examples of how the confidence woman as heroine has been silenced.

It has been a central tenet of misogyny that women deceive because it is their nature to do so. Late-nineteenth-century and early-twentieth-century psychology, following the lead of Caesar Lombroso, the father of female criminal psychology, is replete with explanations of women's innate tendency to lie. Women are likened to children or to primitives who lie because they are selfish and not "morally" developed. Despite its supposedly scientific language and discussions of brain size and phrenology, such a psychology develops out of the older misogynist tradition that women do not have souls, are incapable of reason, and therefore are inferior to men, just as men are inferior to God and the angels. That new "scientific" psychology explains that for the same reason that women lie, they cannot be great criminals. Lombroso and G. T. W. Patrick, a disciple, claimed that women do not have the inventive powers, the forethought, the daring, and the persistence a true criminal needs to be successful. Women are, the psychology goes, occasional criminals, lying and deceiving on the whim of the moment only. According to nineteenth-century psychology, as I will show in detail in my analysis of criminal confidence women in Chapter 3, a confidence woman could not exist.

Recently, French feminists have transformed the stereotype of the deceptive woman into an affirmation of woman's plurality. Luce Irigaray puns in the title of her book *This Sex Which Is Not One,* showing how women are not one but two, or more than two; she argues that women can understand life from many points of view, including contradictory ones, and that this pluralism is women's strength. From this point of view, the confidence woman's versatility and vitality take on a new significance, representing the multiplicity that makes women strong. American feminists are more likely to discuss the social conditions that foster deceptiveness in women. Karen Halttunen shows how the "cult of sincerity" encouraged women to lie. In her *Confidence Men and Painted Women,* Halttunen describes white middle-class women in mid-nineteenth-century America as deceitful women playing the game of upward mobility. The "cult of sincerity," she says, caused women by its very potency to be insincere, to feign tears and helplessness as they manipulated the social situation to their advantage. Adrienne Rich explains that the lie was one of the few sources of power women had in a society that created for them sexual roles that denied their humanity: when the prevailing "truth" is in fact a lie, "lies" can approach the truth.[6]

Confidence women have an assertive attitude toward life and strong confidence in their own skill. They choose from the outset the power of lies; they decide to "manage" things, and they do so with a fair amount of success. This attitude and subsequent action are extraordinary in a society that labels women as weak, dependent, and passive. To a certain extent, it does not matter whether individual confidence women are motivated by a desire for money, for glory, or for survival. What is important is that they recognize that they *have* a desire of their own and then act on it. This is in sharp contrast to the more typical female response of participating in, as Teresa de Lauretis might say, the male desire— the desire to transform woman into the other—instead.[7] The confidence woman is characterized by both strength and perversity. The complexity and multiplicity of the confidence woman's image are what hold such fascination for us.

6. Adrienne Rich, *On Lies, Secrets, and Silence: Selected Prose, 1966–1978.*
7. De Lauretis, "Desire in Narrative."

By looking at the legend of Shahrazad the storyteller, a confidence woman who has reigned in people's imaginations for centuries, we can begin to clarify who the confidence woman is, why her image holds such power, and how she has been muted and sometimes silenced. Shahrazad stands as the reverse of the woman in the harem, the prisoner of male desire, for she acts on her own desire—to save the women of her land from slaughter and to bring order back into the kingdom by bringing the king back to sanity—and she transforms her husband's desire as well. From desiring a generic virgin for his bed and then desiring her death in the morning, the king comes to desire one particular woman, Shahrazad. She achieves her own desire by making him see one woman as human.

The Shahrazad legend as it has come down to us in Burton's translation makes a feminist statement despite Burton's effort to subvert it in his footnotes. King Shahyar, king of the kings of the Banu Sassan, has discovered that whenever he leaves his palace, the queen and his ten concubines have a sexual tryst in the garden with his male slaves. This is such a shock to his self-image as supreme ruler that he and his brother, who has also been cuckolded, go in search of one man who has managed to keep his women faithful. Their search ends when they run into a powerful genie and his female slave. They discover that even he cannot control his concubine, for as the genie sleeps, the woman forces the two men to have intercourse with her on the threat of awakening the genie and setting him upon them. Although Burton translates the Arabic tale precisely, in his footnotes early in the story, he provides the obvious misogynistic interpretation of the queen's actions and the actions of the genie's slave—the same interpretation King Shahyar and his brother make—that all women are unfaithful, deceitful, and creatures of lust, no matter how powerful their masters might be. However, the legend itself—even as Burton translates it—makes clear that the point is not that the women are unfaithful but that this is the only form of resistance they can manage to their imprisonment. The genie's concubine is, in fact, his slave, abducted by the genie on the day of her wedding. This genie, a "malignant being, hostile and injurious to mankind," as Burton defines for us in a note, locked her in a sea chest with seven locks and kept her imprisoned at the bottom of the sea. When and only when he wanted her for his pleasure, he would allow her out of the chest. His purpose in locking her up so securely was to keep her "chaste and honest, quotha! that none save himself might have connexion" with her. There is a symbolic relationship between the sea chest and the harem, and there is a more general relationship to the condition of all women in the repressive

Arabic society. Neither the king, his brother, nor Burton questions the humanity of imprisoning women. In fact, Burton says in his note on the king's going back and slaughtering his queen and concubines that "one can hardly pity women who are fools enough to run such risks."[8] The legend itself, however, focuses on just that issue. The genie's slave forces the two men, as she has 570 others, to cuckold the genie, not out of lust but as an act of rebellion.

The genie's slave and the king's wife and concubines fail in their resistance, however, since they do not overturn the cultural expectation. Like the designing woman and the "painted woman" that Halttunen describes, the women in the first part of the Shahrazad legend stay within the cultural stereotypes even as they resist their condition. The result of this failure is a terrible retribution against other women. The king had told his brother early in the story that if he were to discover his own wife being unfaithful as his brother had, he "would not have been satisfied without slaying a thousand women and that way madness lies!"[9] When Shahyar does so discover his wife and concubines' unfaithfulness, his mania exceeds even his own expectations. To ensure that he will never again be cuckolded in his own palace, he orders his chief wazir to slay each new wife on the morning after the wedding night. For three years, the king weds a virgin every night and has her executed before breakfast. Finally, because his subjects leave the kingdom in a frenzy to save their daughters, there are no virgins left, and all is chaos.

It is only at this point, when the kingdom is almost in ruins and over one thousand women have been slain, that Shahrazad enters the story. Being the daughter of the chief wazir, the executioner himself, she has been counted off limits, even though she and her sister Dunyazad are virgins and are of age. However, Shahrazad demands that her father allow her to be the king's next bride. Like the genie's slave, she forces an action to ensue, but her resistance will be of quite an unexpected type. When her father asks her why she wants to court her certain death, Shahrazad says that her purpose is to stem "this slaughter of women" and "to save both sides from destruction." She says she will "be a ransom for the virgin daughters of Moslems and the cause of their deliverance from his hands and thine."[10] This "and thine" suggests that the

8. Richard F. Burton, trans., *Tales from the Arabian Nights: Selected from the Book of the Thousand Nights and a Night*, 11, 13, 14.
9. Ibid., 8.
10. Ibid., 15.

madness extends beyond the king, as a general madness of the society that is responsible for this holocaust.

Burton speculates in his footnote to the scene that Shahrazad intends to murder the king, but there is no indication of that in the legend itself. The ransom will be Shahrazad's stories, not her life or the king's. She dares to marry the monster in the confidence that she will be able to tame him with words. The idea that words, fictions, can be a ransom, can free the prisoners, is appropriate to a discussion of the confidence woman in the nineteenth century. Ellen Craft ransomed herself from slavery by creating a fiction; women writers ransomed womanhood in their books, in what Cathy N. Davidson calls a "quiet revolution."[11] For the confidence woman, words and the fiction they create are her best disguise. Understanding the relationship of women to the word is crucial, for the word is often the sole power of women, in an otherwise powerless condition, to shape their world. That women's power comes through words implies many things about women: that they have intelligence, a strong will, knowledge, foresight, imagination, and tact.

The *Arabian Nights* legend is explicit about Shahrazad's genius, about why she will succeed using the power of the word where the other women have failed in their attempts to use the power of the body. Shahrazad, according to the legend, is well known as a scholar; "indeed it was said that she had collected a thousand books of histories." She knows poetry by heart, knows philosophy and science; "she was pleasant and polite, wise and witty, well read and well bred."[12] This description of Shahrazad is a good description of the boldest confidence women, for whom politeness and breeding are often part of the disguise. Historical confidence women, of course, do not live up to the ideals of altruism, courage, and wisdom created by the legend, but the configuration of attributes is the same.

Interestingly enough, in Arabia at the time the legend takes place there was an analogue to Shahrazad and the confidence woman: the slave singer. The slave singer was usually a foreigner captured in war and typically "self-possessed, exquisite, highly trained, cultured." The slave singer would "ravish the gentleman" who owned her "with her wit and beauty" and in the process get his money. According to the poet-scholar Djahiz, the slave singer "uses treachery and cunning to exhaust her victim's fortune." She sounds very much like the criminal confidence women of the nineteenth century. It is significant, for her time as well

11. See Cathy N. Davidson, *Revolution and the Word: The Rise of the Novel in America.*
12. Burton, trans., *Arabian Nights,* 15.

as that of her nineteenth-century successors, that the motivation for the "treach-ery and cunning" was to amass a fortune great enough to buy her own freedom.[13]

One of the key attributes of confidence women is their supreme confidence in themselves. Such women enjoy their own strength and intelligence; when the motivation is altruistic, as it is in Shahrazad's case, they often have an almost military fervor about their actions. Shahrazad will not let her father say no. Furthermore, like all good con women, she prepares her plan well ahead of time. She secretly instructs her sister to come to her when she is summoned, which Shahrazad plans as her last request. It will be Dunyazad who asks her sister to tell a tale; Shahrazad will not depend on the king to do so. But it will be he who will call off her father, allowing her to live another night in order to bring the story to an end.

For 1,001 nights, Shahrazad's scheme works; each morning at dawn she leaves her story hanging, and she and the king sleep into the day "in mutual embrace." Each night, the ever-present Dunyazad asks for a story even better than the last one, once the king's curiosity about the previous story is satisfied. Shahrazad tells one story for almost every woman the king has killed, a one-for-one ransom. After three years of listening to Shahrazad every night and holding her in his arms every morning, the king's insanity is cured. By treating Shahrazad as a human being and coming to see her as one, the king has found a woman he can trust and respect. Order is restored to the kingdom, the prisoners are symbolically freed, and the king, the monster, regains his own humanity.

The confidence woman as one who heals a sick society, one who restores order, is a motif that sometimes appears in fiction written by American women in the nineteenth century. This motif transforms the destructive actions of a "Chicago May" into the constructive breaking of the imprisoning stereotypes implied by her very existence. Shahrazad does not in reality free Moslem women from the restriction of purdah any more than Louisa May Alcott's Jean Muir in "Behind a Mask" really makes men and women better, although the characters in the novella find renewal through their relationships with her, but just having such heroes in our imaginations is a step toward real change.

Therein lies, on the one hand, the purpose and, on the other hand, the danger of denying these fictional types. Shahrazad has been silenced by her reduction to Sheherazade, a seductive woman whose stories magically charm the king as she tries to save her own life. Sheherazade is a combination of the female stereotypes

13. Tannahill, *Sex in History*, 235–56.

of the seducer, the witch, and the victim, whose purpose goes no further than staving off violence against herself. This silencing of Shahrazad's true character in our culture is clear in John Barth's National Book Award–winning *Chimera*, which serves as a symbol of the way the confidence woman has been eradicated from our memories. In Barth's rendition, Shahrazad, now Sherry, tells her stories in order to save her own life as much as from any desire to rescue her sisters, and the stories are not her own, but are given to her by a man, presumably no less than Barth himself, whose pen is a magic wand. Sherry offers sex in return for the stories the man gives her, offers to be his concubine. Barth co-opts Shahrazad's feminism by refusing such a crass exchange. Shahrazad was an independent woman of vast knowledge and great daring. Sherry cannot do anything without her male support; when she finally considers an action of her own—to bind the king to the bed and "cut his bloody engine off and choke him on it"—it is to reenact the dehumanizing violence and torture that the legendary Shahrazad fought against. Similarly, Dunyazad is transformed from a confederate in the effort to free the prisoners into a captive voyeur who ultimately becomes the center of the story, the ideal woman: an expert at sexual play. The legend of Shahrazad is both an ideal and a warning; the travesty of the Shahrazad character in our modern memory suggests that the confidence woman, or her positive characteristics at least, will be lost to our imagination unless we actively search her out.

If we understand the confidence woman as a storyteller, especially one who tells a story about herself, we can pull together a few of the various forms the confidence woman takes: women who pretend to be men, women who pretend to be naïve, women who pretend to be prostitutes, women who pretend to be rich, or, as in Shahrazad's case, women who pretend to be afraid for their lives. In all cases, the story hides a purpose the listener would little expect. Shahrazad is the ideal storyteller in that she tells multiple stories, one of which ends up being true; the story behind her stories, the true story she tells about herself, is that she is human and capable of faithful love. When the king finally hears her, the other stories can stop and Shahrazad needs to be a confidence woman no longer. In nineteenth-century America, that subtext to the confidence women's stories about themselves, the text that asserted their humanity, was too seldom heard.

Although we do not hear much in the late twentieth century about nineteenth-century confidence women, by the early twentieth century, certain writers were relatively outspoken about the confidence women of their own time. Criminal confidence women like Sophie Lyons and Chicago May published their autobiographies, and Edith Wharton told her stories about confidence women in high society. In the 1920s, Betty Van Deventer wrote a paperback, pocket-sized book for the Little Blue Books series that explains how a certain type of confidence woman operated. She calls this kind of confidence woman a "gold digger," a type I place in the adventuress category; the publication is called *Confessions of a Gold Digger,* for Van Deventer professes to be a gold digger herself.

Van Deventer considered gold digging—a woman getting money out of a man—to be one of the few "businesses" open to women. "Gold digging is merely a modern business method," she explains, comparing it to a merchant's outwitting his opponent in trade. Gold digging, a confidence game, is not just a manifestation of capitalist cunning; it is also a manifestation of the war between the sexes, "for man and woman are opponents in this economic era." Van Deventer describes the techniques a gold digger uses—obvious extensions of the commonly acknowledged "feminine arts." In what Van Deventer calls the "Timid Technique," a gold digger makes her eyes big as she tells a man how weak she is. Her object is to flatter the man's ego and simultaneously arouse his pity, for "pity proves akin to his pocketbook." Van Deventer makes it clear that the "womanliness" that gets a man to hand over his money is an act, carefully costumed and "staged": "Genteel shabbiness often moves the most hard-hearted of men to tears." However, Van Deventer does concede that "many, many girls gold dig and refuse to admit it, even to themselves." She argues that married women are gold diggers, manipulating their husbands by playing the wife and mother role, and that this form of gold digging is "socially accepted" as part of the female condition. Van Deventer reveals one manipulation she ostensibly used as a confidence woman that resembles the manipulations some women use in their everyday lives: "I always listen with almost reverence to any opinion which a man states, no matter how silly or erroneous I may know it to be."[14]

However, Van Deventer insists that the professional gold digger is not an ordinary woman but an artist who will be more successful as she develops more techniques. What some women do out of habit, confidence women do as a creative act, with humor and a cynical awareness of the implications. Van Deventer's differentiation between the everyday deceptions that some women practice because of the restrictions of a patriarchal society and the art of the professional gold digger underlines the idea that a confidence woman is a breed apart.

14. Betty Van Deventer, *Confessions of a Gold Digger,* 30, 7–8, 6, 26, 13.

Van Deventer's assertions are a good example of the unreliability of many of the "memoirs" I will be using, for there is reason to believe that Van Deventer was a writer and a friend of writers, not a "gold digger" as she styles herself. However, the truth or fiction of her descriptions is not the issue. The images had power to influence people's perceptions whether they were "true" or not, especially when the readers of the Little Blue Books had a willingness to believe. Whether Van Deventer did in fact "gold dig" is a matter for historians to determine. I am interested in what she *says* she did. In her list of gold-digging "techniques," she describes one that she says she preferred to use—the "Coup D'Etat Technique." According to her own statement, she brought in a good wage working only a few hours a day by flattering men into giving her inside tips on the stock market. She played the naïve woman, awed by the man's insights, asking ingenuous questions until she heard the information she wanted. Then she went to her broker and made a killing. Other women, Van Deventer says, are content with "the lunches, the theater tickets, books, and small fry." She "prefer[red] to profit enough from larger coups to be able to afford these small luxuries at [her] own convenience." Whether the women content with "small fry" are confidence women is debatable. Certainly they are not unusual or imaginative enough to fuel the confidence-woman myth. Van Deventer makes the same distinction when she says, "Although there is a little gold digger in every girl, the really proficient gold digger is made, not born."[15]

Unlike Van Deventer's gold diggers, some confidence women veil their status as a commodity rather than enhancing it. Typically these women, however, are not criminals like Chicago May or adventuresses like the gold diggers. They are women who play a confidence game for some motive other than profit, women like Ellen Craft, who escaped slavery by dressing like a middle-class white man. She used disguise to evade the "womanly" role—and the class and racial restrictions—society had predetermined for her. Such women, even though they do not consider themselves a commodity, tell a story about themselves just as their profit-minded sisters do and use this deception to achieve their ends.

The confidence women of the nineteenth century come to us in the twentieth century only through the printed page, with all the limitations that implies. The historical records are for the most part accounts of confidence women written by police detectives, sensationalist and informal historians, and the confidence women themselves; all these sources bring "history" very close to

15. Ibid., 10–12, 6, 13–14.

fiction. Events in a con woman's life are carefully selected, then exaggerated or underplayed in order to advance the author's thesis. Therefore, I look at these historical accounts as unreliable sources of information, but interesting and illuminating as fictional texts nonetheless, keeping in mind that the fictions a society creates are as influential as actual events.

One of the most powerful stories that the general culture in the nineteenth century believed about women was the stereotypical story that women are more primitive than men, that they were not as able to keep up with the rapid changes that were happening all around them. That this stereotype was forceful is evident in the writings of Henry Adams, a representative thinker at the turn of the century. Adams tries to define womanhood in his autobiography *The Education of Henry Adams* by mythologizing women, calling them the "Venus" of natural passion or the "Virgin" of spirituality, static forms that are immutable and therefore tragic, as he saw it, for woman could not change with the forces of history. While the world would move on and men would change with it, Adams believed that "woman would swim about the ocean of future time, as she had swum in the past, with the gar-fish and the shark, unable to change."[16] His division Venus/Virgin is the old one of Magdalene/Madonna, whore/angel, although his explanation of how the two forms of womanhood have shaped history is new. Adams was expressing an idea that has had immense power in the American imagination both before him and after: Beatrice Rappaccini had to face the dual stereotype, and so did Lady Brett Ashley after her. It was seeing womanhood as either Virgin or Venus that made real women invisible.

Adams was aware of the real women, the "myriads of new types" of women in the 1890s, the "telephone and telegraph-girls, shop-clerks, factory-hands, running into millions of millions," but they mystified him, and he presumed that they mystified everyone else too, including women themselves. Adams believed that "the American woman had no illusions or ambitions or new resources, and nothing to rebel against, except her own maternity; yet the rebels increased by millions from year to year till they blocked the path of rebellion." Those millions of rebels were an enigma to Adams and the men and women he spoke for because he was blinded by the stereotypes he had put his faith in; he could not see American women. Nor could he hear them. In one instance, Adams records that he sat next to a typical "unthinking" woman at a dinner party who answered his query why the American woman has failed, "Because the

16. Henry Adams, *The Education of Henry Adams: An Autobiography,* 448.

American man is a failure!"[17] Adams presumed the woman was unaware of the meaning of her own words, but in fact it was Adams who did not understand; he missed the irony in the reply, the woman's comment on his failure to see her. He did not understand that the failure was a failure of perception. Edith Wharton, however, understood. She knew what illusions and ambitions urged on an Undine Spragg. Before Henry Adams, Nathaniel Hawthorne understood that what women like Beatrice Rappaccini and Hester Prynne had to rebel against was a failure of perception. But Henry Adams, that representative man, did not understand.

In the 1990s, Adams's dichotomy still has power, enough so that a popular novelist has felt the need to combat it. Florence King in *The Confessions of a Failed Southern Lady* argues that there has always been a third type of American woman that people like Henry Adams ignored. In addition to the Venus and the Virgin, who Adams says are both eternal victims, "victim to a man, a church, a machine,"[18] is the Virago: the woman of power who refuses to be a victim and simply goes her own way. Nineteenth-century literature written by women and by some men is filled with Viragoes: hardworking women, pioneering women, women who coped. My contention is that out of the dialectic of reality and stereotype, of Virago and Virgin/Venus, came a "new resource": the confidence woman. Women of power who found themselves invisible sometimes used one stereotype or the other to open a path for themselves. These were rebels beyond those shop girls and telephone workers that mystified Henry Adams so.

By answering the question of why confidence women would come to the fore in the late nineteenth century, we also partially answer the question why they had to be silenced. An understanding of womanhood so interwoven with the American culture as the Virgin/Venus stereotype could not be undermined without creating a frightening insecurity. Apparently, it seemed safer to pretend that confidence women could not exist than to face them. One way to mitigate the reality of confidence women was to dilute the image, turn it into a stereo-typical form: the designing woman. A designing woman does not question the status quo of gender, race, or class; therefore she does not present much of a threat to the system. An example of a designing woman is the Marquise de Merteuil in *Les Liaisons dangereuses,* that eighteenth-century study of a woman out for revenge and self-satisfaction. Although the Marquise is remarkable in her

17. Ibid., 445, 446, 442.
18. Ibid., 447.

subtlety, she merely plays out the misogynistic stereotype. Whereas confidence women approach their deceptions as an entrepreneurial device or for some semi-altruistic or self-preservationist reason, designing women like the Marquise have as their purpose interpersonal—usually sexual—relationships alone, seeking marriage or reputation or a lover's revenge. Reducing the confidence woman to the designing woman is one way of silencing her: it trivializes her nature and tries to trap her within the accepted stereotypes.

In nineteenth-century America, the idea that women would be "designing" made a lot of sense, because women's whole lives were tied up with men. They were men's property by law and by custom—under the "femme couverte" construction of the marriage laws, married women did not exist legally, and before marriage, women were considered to be the property of their fathers. Women naturally focused on their emotional attachments; they were not supposed to even dream about seamy business transactions. Certainly, property by definition should not sell itself or anything else; for a woman to use the strategies of the marketplace, to deceive and manipulate like a Wall Street entrepreneur, would have been intolerable. In the nineteenth century, the "shared faith" about women was that they had a separate sphere and were constitutionally unable to handle the stresses and demands of the marketplace. Therefore, when a woman played a confidence game, she was neither hero nor celebrant, but rebel, for she disrupted the same system the confidence man embodied. The confidence women's strength and versatility undermined the belief in women's basic weakness and eternally unchanging nature. The confidence women's perversity undermined some men's and women's equally strong belief in women's moral superiority.

But the culture's pretending that confidence women did not exist only abetted their disguises. Despite their being silenced, the confidence women's rebellious activity was not stopped. The criminal confidence women who plied their trade in the big cities built America as surely as did the bunco men and the land speculators. The confidence women who tricked and spied upon the enemy during the Civil War were perhaps ladies before and after they played their parts, but they were amazingly unladylike in performing their roles. These women broke the social code by being aggressive, far-thinking, adept, and strikingly imaginative. They broke it too by showing a genius for criminality, a genius not thought possible in women. Even more, they broke the social code by succeeding. A faith very similar to the one Gary Lindberg shows the confidence man to uphold through his actions—the faith in the self-made man—is the faith that the confidence woman breaks. In the nineteenth century, women were to be in effect man-made. By becoming self-made women, they broke that faith. To assert the self, as the confidence woman had to do, was the ultimate rebellion. For this reason, the disorder embodied by the confidence woman in the nineteenth century was much more dangerous than the disorder the confidence man symbolized.

A confidence man, then, is a cynical actor within society; a confidence woman, on the other hand, is a rebel purposely acting against social norms. However, confidence women were not "revolutionists," to use the distinction between rebels and revolutionists that Erich Fromm explains in an essay on disobedience written in 1963. A rebel disobeys out of "anger, disappointment, resentment," whereas a revolutionist acts "in the name of a conviction or a principle." Women like Elizabeth Cady Stanton and Alice Paul were revolutionists, working for the suffragist cause; women like Sophie Lyons, Ellen Peck, and Chicago May had no revolutionary principle. They were not out to change society; they just wanted to use society's prejudices and blindnesses to their advantage. In the process, however, they disrupted those very prejudices by acting in a way that demonstrated how invalid the stereotypes were. Lindberg calls the confidence man a hero rather than a rebel because he embodies the beliefs that lie behind the ideal of the self-made man. But confidence women embody the very opposite of the womanly ideal. William Lenz explains that the confidence man in literature lets us laugh at ourselves rather ironically, because we admire the con man's skill even as we recognize that he represents "disorder." Confidence women, on the other hand, elicit a much more nervous laughter, because they make it clear that the false ideal will have to change. According to John Blair, in the twentieth century the confidence man as a literary figure has changed from a devil into a god, for the new con man, like the "fool" in Shakespeare, reveals truth under falsehood, reality under pretense.[19] Perhaps in a similar way, our view of the role of the late-nineteenth-century confidence woman must also change. We must return to the old myths to understand the truth that is told beneath the lies.

Where the Confidence Woman Appears

Many of those who have examined the confidence man sum up his rise in the words of Captain Simon Suggs, "It is good to be shifty in a new country." The

19. Erich Fromm, "Disobedience as a Psychological and Moral Problem," 18–19; John G. Blair, *The Confidence Man in Modern Fiction: Rogue's Gallery with Six Portraits*, 124.

confidence man is a phenomenon of the expanding nation, to be found on the edge of the frontier as it moves farther and farther west and to be found in the cities as they grow, when boundary lines between the classes are less clear. The duke and the king in Mark Twain's *Huckleberry Finn* work their schemes on the Mississippi River, the legendary boundary between East and West; Augustus Baldwin Longstreet's con man of "The Horse Swap," who put burrs under a horse's saddle on top of its saddlesores in order to make the horse look lively and make a better trade, inhabits the Old Southwest, before "civilization" takes hold; Melville's confidence man plays his games on board the *Fidèle*, with its fragile social structure easily thrown into chaos. The confidence woman, on the other hand, does not often appear on the frontier. She needs a relatively rigid social structure in which to tell her stories, for often her scheme depends on people's assuming she fits some stereotype of womanhood. For that reason, one most commonly finds the confidence woman in a city that has reached some maturity and in the South, where several forces came together to foster the confidence arts. One does not so readily find the confidence woman in the West or in the rural Northeast, where the stereotypes about women were broken down by the necessities of living.

Because the West—an area whose boundaries changed radically between the Civil War and the end of the century—was relatively unstructured and allowed a certain freedom, most women there did not have to play games to express their adventurous spirit or to move ahead. Women could, for instance, be independent homesteaders, especially after the Homestead Act of 1862. Not only "girl homesteaders" but also divorced and widowed women, many with children, saw homesteading as an adventurous and economically sound alternative to living in cities. Katherine Harris, in her recent study of northeastern Colorado in the late nineteenth century, explains that "the elevated status and autonomy of this very visible group in the local female population served as an inspiration to all women and especially to girls."[20]

Married women living in new towns, on the other hand, could combine their talents and belongings and start community projects, like a town library. Even though the town aldermen eventually took the credit, there was a sense of

20. Glenda Riley, *The Female Frontier: A Comparative View of Women on the Prairie and the Plains,* 134; Katherine Harris, "Homesteading in Northeastern Colorado, 1873–1920: Sex Roles and Women's Experience," in Armitage and Jameson, eds., *The Women's West,* 175.

accomplishment in the action. On the farm, husband and wife were a single unit of production; there was no secondary, "merely" domestic sphere for the woman. In fact, Harris shows that men and women often shared roles on the frontier, leading to "the development of unfamiliar skills, especially among women." Furthermore, Elizabeth Jameson, another historian who has looked at how women lived in the Far West, argues that the "true womanhood" ideal of the eastern, middle-class, native-born woman did not have much influence on the women pioneers, many of whom were immigrants from very different cultures, unable to read the prescriptive literature that had such power in the East. Some women in the West also found an outlet for their strength and intelligence in the campaign for universal suffrage. They won the vote in the territories as early as 1869 and 1870, and in Colorado and Idaho in 1890. By 1914, ten western states had female suffrage, but only one eastern state did.[21] Many women in mining towns ran boardinghouses, did laundry for pay, and participated in strikes with the men by yelling, throwing stones, and defending their homes against the militia. In the West, there was typically enough real opportunity for women and enough real sense of worth from their activities to preclude the need for confidence games.

Among Native American women the situation was similar, according to Sylvia Van Kirk. Native American women played a productive part in their societies that was not relegated to a domestic sphere separate from the men's; they made moccasins and pemmican essential for the men's hunting trips, collected the materials for repairing canoes, hunted small game, and made clothes, all central to the Native American economy. Also, autobiographies of Native American women stress "the connectedness of all things, [the] personal life flow."[22] It was the community that counted, rather than the individual. This cultural value system, coupled with the economic arrangement in which women played an important part, seems to have virtually eliminated the confidence artist from that segment of western women. Even during assimilation in the late nineteenth century, the tradition of straightforward dealings carried through. Sarah Winnemucca Hop-

21. Harris, "Homesteading in Northeastern Colorado," in Armitage and Jameson, eds., *The Women's West,* 169; Elizabeth Jameson, "Women as Workers, Women as Civilizers: True Womanhood in the American West," in Armitage and Jameson, eds., *The Women's West,* 147, 155.

22. Sylvia Van Kirk, "The Role of Native Women in the Creation of Fur Trade Society in Western Canada, 1670–1830," in Armitage and Jameson, eds., *The Women's West,* 55; Gretchen M. Bataille and Kathleen Mullen Sands, *American Indian Women Telling Their Lives,* 8.

kins, a Paiute woman who had received a white woman's middle-class education and who acted as go-between for her tribe and the government officials who ran the reservations her tribe lived on, did not play games, although she would have had ample opportunity to do so. In her entire autobiography, the only mention of a ruse comes in her description of the part she played in the Bannock War. But war, as I will explain later, is a special situation, an especially fertile one for confidence games.

In addition to the positive forces that helped make confidence games for women less necessary in the West, there are indications that negative forces also militated against them there. One forceful indication is the kind of fiction that was being produced by women living in the West. Although fiction cannot replace historical documents, it can be useful in suggesting routes for further investigation. Caroline Kirkland, for instance, who pioneered in Michigan when it was part of the West, describes in her fiction a life of isolation and drudgery, wives and daughters trying to survive in the midst of mud and petty rivalries. There were confidence men enough, according to her stories, in the form of land speculators and roadside showmen, but she describes no confidence women. Mary Catherwood likewise wrote about the frontier that bordered on Canada, telling the stories of many stoic women who succeeded through persistence and courage, but the only woman in her stories who plays a game of deception is Marianson, in the story of that name, but like Hopkins, Marianson plays her game only in wartime. The image that Alice Cary uses to describe a scene in one of her most powerful Clovernook stories sums up the negative forces that could well have worked against the confidence woman in the West: she describes a dreary cabin in Ohio, lorded over by a fanatical man, in which seven sisters knit seven stockings night after night, their faces hard, their lives empty, their imaginations dull.[23] Certainly women in the cities lived desperate lives, too, but there is a huge difference between being desperate alone with just one's own family, no one else for miles around, and being desperate in the midst of an anonymous population offering an easy opportunity for crime.

However, as the locations of these three sets of stories indicate, the "West" is a shifting locale. By the time the West had become the Far West late in the century, and by the time even Colorado and Nevada were on the brink of being fully "civilized," there was perhaps more inducement for women to use their confidence skills. Such is the impression, at least, given by two writers of the

---

23. See Caroline M. Kirkland, *A New Home—Who'll Follow;* Mary Hartwell Catherwood, "Marianson"; and Alice Cary, "Uncle Christopher's."

fading West, Bret Harte and Willa Cather. In the story "An Ingenue of the Sierras," in which Polly Mullins dupes the men with whom she rides on a stagecoach, Harte creates a full-fledged confidence woman. Polly plays the part of the innocent young girl, rebelling against her unyielding father in order to marry her true love. In other words, she plays the romantic heroine stereotype, using tears and feigned naïveté to gain the men's confidence. The truth of the matter is that she and her confederate have stolen a wealth of gold, which she hides under a wedding dress and trousseau (also stolen, by the way), an appropriate symbol for the kind of game she plays.

Cather's novels give a clear indication of how the progression from an un-settled West to a West verging on civilization might have affected the kinds of women living there. In *O Pioneers!* Alexandra Bergson's "mind was slow, truthful, steadfast. She had not the least spark of cleverness." She succeeds on the Nebraska prairie because she is willing to work hard, to listen to those who have more experience than she, and to take a risk based on her love for the land. Her battle is with the land, not with men, and she can find fulfillment through it; therefore, she does not need to learn confidence skills. Likewise, Thea Kronberg in *The Song of the Lark* does not have to be a con woman to succeed, although some critics have suggested that she uses people and then discards them as her career develops. Fred Ottenberg, another character, remarks, too, that she always seems to have an "ulterior motive."[24] But Thea does not become a confidence woman; instead, she is able to leave the West and achieve her desire in Chicago, New York, Europe, ever farther east. Mrs. Forrester in *A Lost Lady,* however, is a confidence woman. She wears a droll smile and dresses just elegantly or nonchalantly enough to be thought charming by everyone, from rude lower-class boys to railroad magnates. When Mr. Forrester dies, leaving her in relative poverty, Mrs. Forrester knows exactly whom to play to get enough money to begin again. That she can successfully manipulate her old admirer Ivy Peters, representative of the unscrupulous entrepreneurs sullying the purity of the Old West, is evidence that she is a confidence woman—unscrupulous—herself. She dies the rich wife of a South American baron, the star of eastern high society. Mrs. Forrester is not a confidence woman who flourishes on the leading edge of the frontier; rather she is a sign that the untamed West has died. She does not fight the land, does not live in mud and dreariness. When her life threatens to turn into the kind of life Kirkland and Cary describe, she uses all her skill to get out of it.

24. Willa Cather, *O Pioneers!*, 35; *The Song of the Lark,* 315.

Using fiction to discuss historical periods has its limits, however. If we consider the stories that Harte and Cather have written, it appears that when a confidence woman does show up in the West, she is merely a transplant from the East, not really a new type. But their fiction was perhaps influenced by the eastern confidence-woman myth. The only way to determine more certainly whether confidence women *did* appear in the West would be to do more historical study, focusing directly on the issue. The prostitution in mining towns would seem to be a rich field for investigation, although everything I have read by those who have done historical research on it suggests that most of the prostitutes in the West were businesswomen or victims of trickery themselves, not confidence artists.

In the big cities of the East, however, new types of confidence women were being created by the changing social conditions. Lower-class women living in the cities quickly discovered that the true womanhood ideology translated into poverty and grueling, ill-paid work; this realization gave them an incentive to find alternative ways to succeed. Some women became pickpockets, shoplifters, or blackmailers, all professions that require confidence arts. Also, stereotypes rigidified more quickly in the big cities than on the frontier. To show how the change from frontier to city led to the rise of the confidence woman, I will discuss her birth in one particular city: Chicago. In 1940, Herbert Asbury wrote an informal history of the underworld of Chicago that supposedly traces the development of the city and its criminal elements from its beginnings. His history gives a possible explanation of how and when confidence women came on the scene in the East.[25]

In 1812, Chicago was an Indian trading post on the frontier. There were neither confidence men nor confidence women there at the time, according to Asbury, but by 1834, shortly after a canal was dug to connect Chicago's rivers with the Mississippi River, the first confidence men had arrived. They were the land speculators, preparing to sell tracts of land at extravagant prices to the immigrants who would be flocking to Chicago by 1835. The gamblers came next, when the population was about 4,000, and with them the first prostitutes. However, these prostitutes were probably not confidence women, if they followed the patterns of prostitutes in frontier towns. They would advertise themselves by

25. Herbert Asbury, *Gem of the Prairie: An Informal History of the Chicago Underworld.* I use such informal histories for this kind of discussion because more rigorous histories do not deal with confidence women. Perhaps this implies that Asbury's descriptions are suspect; but the implication could as easily be that professional historians have not yet discovered this fertile subject.

standing in their doorways in various modes of dress and undress. In a land where there were so few women, prostitutes could make a reasonable living by being straightforward entrepreneurs. As the population grew and prostitutes lived in small "houses," the women would use their "feminine arts" to lure men away from the competition, but this still is not a confidence game except in the mode of an everyday pretense. When the population reached 93,000, in 1857, the first of the lavish houses of prostitution were built, houses for which Chicago was to have renown. Now there was immense competition and money was flowing. It was in these houses that the con games proceeded.

It was also in 1857, Asbury tells us, that a particular kind of confidence woman appeared: women like Mary Hill. She and her husband, John, "are said to have been the first persons in Chicago to work the badger game," a ruse in which a woman lures a man to her room, where they are soon "discovered" by her confederate, playing the angry husband. Extortion ensues. As the city grew, the number of criminal confidence women drastically increased. Mary Hodges, for instance, became rich by shoplifting and picking pockets—two occupations that in the hands of professionals involve a good deal of subterfuge—between 1861 and 1871, when the population rose to 300,000. Mary Brennan ran "a thieves' school for girls" during the same period, and Mollie Holbrook, a prostitute in a well-known house, "organized her fellow harlots into a band of pickpockets and shoplifters and was using the bagnio as a warehouse for stolen goods." It is interesting to note that that same Mollie Holbrook later ran an assignation house in which "she fleeced a rich western man out of $25,000 with the badger game."[26] The stories such women tell about themselves vary. The pickpockets tell a story of innocence to make their victims unwary; the badger artists present themselves as sexual playmates, although Asbury implies that the confederate usually intervenes before the victim goes very far. Obviously, these kinds of confidence women are a far cry from the altruistic Shahrazad and Alcott's polite Jean Muir. But they are types that have to be reckoned with.

A more complicated kind of confidence game, quite a bit seamier than picking pockets, is the panel house. A panel house is a particular kind of house of prostitution that can exist only in a big city, where there are many legitimate houses of prostitution to camouflage it. The first recorded panel house in Chicago, Asbury says, did not appear until 1865, after an influx of prostitutes during the war, but by 1890 there were at least two hundred panel houses on record there.

26. Ibid., 53, 63, 99, 100.

The panel house uses prostitution as a decoy for its real business: robbery. A supposed prostitute brings her customer to her room, arranged so that the only place the man can throw his clothes is on a chair near a wall or closet. When he is otherwise engrossed, another woman or man behind the wall in a secret room opens a hidden panel and goes through the man's pockets. Asbury cites Moll Hodges as the creator of this game. It could be quite lucrative; Asbury estimates that $1.5 million was stolen in panel houses in Chicago in 1896.[27]

Another type of confidence woman that sprang up in Chicago was the "strong-arm woman," who typically worked in tandem with another woman. One woman would lure a man into an alley, presumably for sexual purposes; the other woman would jump on him so that the first one could take his money. According to Asbury, "The most dangerous of the strong arm women were Flossie Moore and Emma Ford, both of whom were expert pickpockets as well as gifted stick-up artists and panel-workers." Between 1889 and 1893, Moore, a black woman, stole over $125,000, according to Asbury, and was known to flaunt her wealth because money came to her so cheaply.[28]

Even though a dense population fosters the development of confidence women, Asbury claims that the rash of con women in Chicago subsided in the first decades of the twentieth century, when police corruption began to be controlled and when the red-light districts were closed, ending the era of the sumptuous houses of prostitution and their shadows, the panel houses. This was the same time in which women were discovering other, legal avenues to financial security, especially during World War I, when women took over many of the jobs formerly held by the men who had gone to war.

Chicago was not the only city with confidence women, and Asbury is not the only one who has written about them. In New York City, the numbers and kinds of criminal confidence women were similarly large. Thomas Byrnes, the New York detective, describes female pickpockets and shoplifters in New York in the 1880s in great detail. He also talks about women who outsmarted other criminal types, such as bogus diamond salesmen and dishonest stockbrokers. Women who pretend to have lost their car fare, fraudulent female divorce detectives, and blackmailers are all types of criminal confidence women spawned by the big city.[29]

27. Ibid., 125.
28. Ibid., 128, 129.
29. See Byrnes, *1886 Professional Criminals,* for detailed discussions of each kind of confidence scam.

High society was also fertile ground for confidence women. One surprising kind of high-society confidence artist was the woman who would bring affluent men to her own rich home to give them "tips" on business deals she had a personal interest in. Her charm would go far to convince her guests to pay for the tips extravagantly.[30] European high society provides more than its share of confidence women in novels by American authors. Alcott's Jean Muir and V. V., two of her strongest confidence women characters, are European, as are Henry James's Madame Merle, Madame de Vionnet, the "countess" in "Four Meetings," and Kate Croy, all arguably literary versions of the confidence woman.

The other main region in which the confidence woman appears is the South. Southern cities, like New Orleans, would of course harbor criminal confidence women similar to those in northern cities, although they also had some unique types, like the voodoo queens in the French Quarter of New Orleans,[31] but much of the South remained rural long after the North had become effectively urbanized, causing the confidence woman to take a distinct form there.

As on the frontier, there were many conditions working against the southern confidence woman. Women who were farmers and women who ran plantations did not suffer the sense of economic worthlessness many wives of wage earners did, since the farm and plantation still worked on the old system. Ladies of leisure were infrequent, according to Anne Firor Scott in her classic study of the southern lady: "Fine ladies thought nothing of supervising hog butchering. . . . they made their own yeast, lard, and soap, set their own hens, and were expected to be able to make with equal skill a rough dress for a slave or a ball gown for themselves." They had to supervise slaves, do medical duty, act as judge, and supervise the planting when the husband was away, all work of obvious value to the woman herself and to her society.[32] In addition, before the war southern women were immersed in the patriarchal ideology necessary to rationalize the slave system. They for the most part internalized the requirements of Christian submission, often berating themselves in their diaries for their inability to live up to their own Christian ideals.

Psychologically and socially, then, the South did not foster confidence women. However, there were at the same time several forces working in the opposite

30. Thomas Byrnes, *Darkness and Daylight in New York: Criminal Life and Detective Experiences in the Great Metropolis,* 722.

31. Herbert Asbury, *The French Quarter: An Informal History of the New Orleans Underworld,* 188–205.

32. Anne Firor Scott, *The Southern Lady: From Pedestal to Politics, 1830–1930,* 31, 37–38, 34.

direction; one was the stereotype of the "lady" itself. Despite her hard work in real life, plantation wives and daughters were expected to live up to the image of the submissive, self-denying, well-read, and elegant woman. The southern lady never loses her temper, even in her own defense; she is the true woman taken to an extreme. Such a tension between the accepted image of womanhood and the reality of work and continual child-bearing—for many southern women had as many as sixteen children, a situation seldom met with in the North due to the growth of the cities and the wage economy, in which children were not an asset—brought about a low-key sort of con game. Women were expected to "cover up their [husbands'] indiscretions" and were expected to play the gentlewoman when there were guests, telling a story about their lives that was far from the truth.[33]

In the literature of the South, often enough the reality was hidden, helping to create the southern lady image. Stowe did as much to give that image credence as anyone, although she cast the "lady" in a negative light. It is in women's private diaries that the everyday pretense comes to light. Madge Preston, a gentlewoman from Maryland, details how she manages the farm, the orchard, and the house while her husband is gone for long periods of time working at politics and his law career. Her particular game was to cover her husband's brutality and infidelity when he was home, in order to create the aura of the perfect home and marriage. It is interesting that Sarah Grimké states in one of her "Letters on the Equality of the Sexes" that wealthy women "are frequently driven to use deception, to compass their ends. They are early taught that to appear to yield, is the only way to govern."[34] This explicit reference to the manipulation performed by many women in the South is made by a woman raised in the tradition of the southern lady, making it evident that these women were aware of what they were doing. But such a common practice of deception is quite different from the deceptive arts used by confidence women, and it is illuminating mainly for its contrast: southern ladies who deceived their husbands lacked the bravado and the humor of most confidence women; certainly their deceptions were not conducive to the development of a sense of self, for they played into a tradition instead of against it; their purpose was to uphold the tradition and still get what

33. Ibid., 42, 15.
34. See Virginia Walcott Beauchamp, ed., *A Private War: Letters and Diaries of Madge Preston, 1862–1867;* Sarah M. Grimké, "Letters on the Equality of the Sexes and the Condition of Women," 47.

they needed, not to scorn the tradition as they made use of it. Southern ladies were everyday pretenders, not of the same category as the blackmailers and fraudulent "heiresses" of the North. Perhaps one reason the rigid stereotypes of the South did not lead women into the confidence arts is that the stereotypes were excessively strong. Just as the true woman ideal in the 1830s militated against the confidence game, so did the ideal of the southern lady. In the North the psychology of change, of possible liberation, had begun to gain momentum. This was not so in the South until after the war, when change slowly began.

As southern cities began to grow after the war, northern criminal confidence women and adventuresses came to the South. In fiction, we get intimations of the arrival of the confidence woman: Artemus Ward's "tragic octoroon" was a confidence woman of the South, and John William De Forest tells the story of an adventuress in New Orleans in *Miss Ravenel's Conversion from Secession to Loyalty*. The war's effect was not limited to the transformation of an agrarian society into an urban one; it also affected women psychologically. Scott tells us how, during and after the war, the refugees from burnt-out plantations had to use their "ingenuity" to feed their families, forcing a change in southern women's view of themselves and the world.[35]

The plantation mistresses and farming wives were only one part of the southern female population, however. There was much more incentive among the female slaves than among their owners to become confidence women. The simple game of tipping cradles over to get time away from baby-sitting was common among slave girls. "I'd get tired and make like I was asleep and would ease the cradles over and throw the babies out," writes Martha Harrison in her narrative of her slave childhood. "When I'd get tired, I would ease that baby over and Mistress would slap me so hard; I didn't know a hand could hurt so bad, but I'd take the slap and get to go out to play. She would slap me hard and say, 'Git on out of here and stay till you wake up,' and that was just what I wanted, 'cause I'd play then."[36]

The games were more deadly serious when adult women resisted slavery. Paula Giddings, in her history of black women in America, discusses how the shift to the "paternalistic" mode of slavery in the 1830s changed slaves' outright resistance, such as poisoning and burning their masters, to a "more covert or internalized" resistance. Some of this resistance was straightforward: mothers

---

35. Scott, *The Southern Lady*, 106.
36. Gerda Lerner, *The Female Experience: An American Documentary*, 14.

teaching their daughters to refuse to be the master's concubine. But some was more in the realm of the confidence game. Perhaps most interesting is slave women's success in their attempts to keep from bearing children who were meant to increase the master's "livestock." Women "used contraceptives and abortives in an attempt to resist the system," but they used them deceptively, a desperate kind of con game. Giddings mentions one plantation owner who kept from four to six slave women for the purpose of "breeding" and was mystified that in twenty-five years they produced only two children. Even when he bought new slaves, "every pregnancy miscarried by the fourth month." Eventually the old slave woman who was supplying an abortive medicine was discovered.[37] This woman had to be a con artist of sorts to succeed in her game of deception for twenty-five years. In literature, Frances Ellen Watkins Harper gives other examples of black women resisting slavery by playing games on their owners in *Iola LeRoy*.

Certainly it is necessary to make a distinction between women who play a confidence game once or twice in order to escape harm and women whose whole identity is bound up in the game, as is the case for criminal confidence women and, at least for the duration of the war, for women who worked as soldiers and spies. Nevertheless, to ignore the tricks many women played as they escaped desperate situations would cause us to miss a strain of the confidence-woman myth that played an important part in the cultural imagination, especially in the intersection of African American and white cultures. These typically short-lived games were very different from the long-term deceptions played by the southern plantation lady because they were resistive to the dominant culture and therefore had a distinct role in building a sense of self. This is clear in fiction depicting escapes that involve the confidence arts. One real-life story that has come down to us in the form of a memoir is that of Ellen Craft's grand escape from Maryland to the North. Her disguise was a multiple one, involving simultaneously racial, class, and gender changes: she dressed as a white, middle-class male to cross the border to the North. Her story translated into literature in William Wells Brown's *Clotel*, and similar escapes show up in Stowe's *Uncle Tom's Cabin*, in which Cassy's escape is one complicated con game ending in Cassy's passing herself off as a middle-class white woman, and in Twain's *Puddn'head Wilson*, in which Roxanne dresses like a free black man in her getaway. Harriet Tubman was

37. Paula Giddings, *When and Where I Enter: The Impact of Black Women on Race and Sex in America*, 43, 46.

an escape artist supreme, although she used confidence tricks very rarely—most of her escape plans depended on straightforward courage and audacity.

Another force that encouraged a kind of deception mainly in the South was the possibility of "passing," a social escape from racial prejudice that was quite unlike the physical ordeals women like Ellen Craft put themselves through. A black woman who passed for white was more on the order of the everyday pretender, because she did not inherently question the rightness of racial prejudice. Few historical records deal with passing because part of its intent was to make the deception impenetrable. Therefore, the desire to do historical research is hampered in much the same way that research on the Underground Railroad is: the necessary documents would be destroyed, if anything was put down on paper at all. Some southern fiction gives details on methods of passing that worked, however. Kate Chopin, for instance, glances at the issue in her story "Désirée's Baby," in which the mother of Armond Aubigny obviously kept her black lineage a secret. Iola LeRoy's mother in Harper's *Iola LeRoy* likewise kept her secret from her children, and went so far as to perpetuate the racial divisions she herself was trying to avoid. Passing worked in the South in part because of the distinct stereotype that black women could not be "ladies" because they were in a different human category. On the other hand, passing was not relegated to the South, because many of the black women who decided to pass for white went with their white husbands to the North, where the prejudice against blacks was potent enough to make it worthwhile for black women to continue the deception there.

An analysis of the forces that impelled versions of the confidence arts in the South would not be complete without mentioning the border between the South and the North, which became an arena for confidence women during the Civil War. There are no statistics to show exactly how many women dressed like men in order to fight or how many women acted as spies, and therefore there are no statistics on the relative number from North and South. Richard Hall speculates that there were more Northern female soldiers. However, using the number of memoirs written by female soldiers and spies as a guide, it appears that more Southern women were willing to write about their tricks and disguises than Northern women. Belle Boyd, Rose O'Neal Greenhow, and Loreta Janeta Velazquez, each of whom wrote a memoir of her participation in the war, were all Southern women who were extremely patriotic to the secessionist cause; S. Emma Edmonds is the only Northerner whose memoirs I have found, although certainly several other Northern women dressed as men or spied for the Union.[38] The devices used by the Southern women differed from Edmonds's in an interesting way. Edmonds disguised herself "down," as a male or female black slave, as a beggar woman, as a naïve Kentucky boy. The Southern women disguised themselves "up"; they played the lady or, in Velazquez's case, the dashing gentleman officer. The Southern women charmed their way into the confidence of the enemy; the Northern woman got information by making herself invisible. Such generalizations, however, depend heavily on the published memoirs of the women involved, making the stories suspect as historical truth. One can say for certain only that there seems to have been more of an urge in the South to tell the stories of the "lady spy" than in the North.

Obviously, the South was a ripe field for certain types of confidence woman, as were the cities in the North. Other sections of America apparently did not see the confidence woman as frequently, perhaps because these regions were rural and gave other avenues for achievement, as on the frontier. The rural Northeast, for instance, had few confidence women. I have found no informal histories about con women there outside the cities. Likewise, fiction writers like Jewett, Freeman, Phelps, and Stowe describe women living in rural areas who are quaint and pious, or sometimes obstinate and strong-minded, many with a rebellious streak, resisting their limited gender roles, but they typically do not describe women who play confidence games.

There are everyday pretenders in the fiction, however. Most notable is Lillie Ellis in Stowe's *Pink and White Tyranny*. In fact, it is a phrase from that book that I have found most helpful in defining the confidence woman: Stowe uses the phrase "the story she told of herself" in reference to Lillie's lie about her age. John Seymour might very well not have married Lillie if he had known she was twenty-seven, not a girlish twenty, when he courted her. That novel is a close analysis of a very accomplished everyday pretender in the Northeast, but Lillie is really a woman misplaced, a New York belle lost in the small-town hinterland. In her other novels of New England, Stowe describes more mundane pretenders. In *The Pearl of Orr's Island,* for instance, Stowe remarks in an offhand way that "Mara had from nature a good endowment of that kind of innocent hypocrisy which is needed as a staple in the lives of women who bridge a thousand awful chasms with smiling, unconscious looks, and walk, singing and scattering flowers, over abysses of fear, while their hearts are dying within

---

38. Frazar Kirkland also tells the stories of both Southern and Northern women fighting as men in the Civil War in *The Pictorial Book of Anecdotes of the Rebellion.*

them."[39] Tina in *Oldtown Folks* is another example of everyday pretense, winning everybody's heart by being what everybody wants her to be. She is an actress and a mimic, two attributes of many confidence women, but she does not make full use of her confidence skills. Other writers of the Northeast infrequently developed characters of this sort, too. Harriet Prescott Spofford, for example, creates an everyday pretender in her story "Mrs. Claxton's Skeleton." Mrs. Claxton uses tears to get her way with an obstinate and unreasonable husband; she works around him by a combination of patient submission and unbending will. To outsiders, Mrs. Claxton's marriage appears idyllic, but it is actually a living hell. Mary Wilkins Freeman, who usually created female characters that are odd but strong and for the most part straightforward, also occasionally described some powerful everyday games. In "The Shoulders of Atlas," Miss Farrel keeps a youthful complexion by regular doses of arsenic; she dies for her insincerity. In "A Gala Dress," Emily and Elizabeth Babcock have only one black silk dress between them, but they manage, by various ruses, to make it appear that they have two, thus upholding their appearance of middle-class gentility, in a very homely game of pretense. In *Jane Field,* the game becomes more intense, as Jane tries to save her daughter's life by pretending to be her own dead sister, but even here the deception is by default, never planned with the kind of calculation one expects from a confidence woman. All these examples point up the difference between the small deceptions that some women create in their daily lives and the very intense, life-changing deceptions of the confidence woman.

Why the confidence woman does not appear in the rural Northeast, which had not broken down stereotypes as the frontier had, is another question. Perhaps the dearth of confidence women in the rural Northeast, both historically and in literature, is in part a result of the shortage of men caused by the absence of the many men who went on long sea voyages—often never to return—and others who abandoned their families to go West. Jewett and Freeman both describe what Nina Auerbach calls a "community of women," reducing the need for confidence games because one could gain status and a sense of achievement in other ways. Anna Prince in Jewett's *A Country Doctor,* for example, is able to reach her goal by persistence and intelligence, for her patients are for the most part other women and old men. It is interesting, however, that despite the paucity of confidence women as characters in the fiction of the Northeast,

39. Harriet Beecher Stowe, *The Pearl of Orr's Island: A Story of the Coast of Maine,* 229–30.

a surprising number of northeastern writers are themselves confidence women in that they draw readers into their texts by disguising them with characteristics of conventional literary genres. Many northeastern writers were the "literary domestics" described by Mary Kelley: women who ran house and home as dutiful wives or daughters but who wrote novels in their "spare time," always trivializing the seriousness of their work and sometimes writing under pseudonyms,[40] suggesting a con game in itself. Many wrote fiction that purports to be one thing—usually a sentimental romance—but in fact has a subversive subtext that plays a very unsentimental game on the reader. Phelps, Stowe, Stoddard, and Wharton are all writers of the Northeast who make their fiction into a confidence art.

When the Confidence Woman Arises

America is not unique in its having confidence women, but it is unusual in that such a large number of them were concentrated in so short a time. Although there are differences between the criminal confidence women of the growing cities and the Southern lady spy in the Civil War, for example, American confidence women had much in common, for they most often arose from the disparity between stereotypical expectations and the realities women had to face. To understand why the confidence woman became prevalent in the late nineteenth century, we need to look at the ways in which that disparity increased as the century went on.

When women's expectations coincide with their daily lives, there is not much pressure to play games or create fictions about themselves. If a woman believes in the ideal of submission, she will try to subdue her own desires; if an active woman believes she has a true opportunity to improve her lot within the system, she will pursue that opportunity. The two ends of this spectrum can be represented by, on the one end, the women of the early nineteenth century who wrote spiritual diaries and, on the other, women like Maimie Pinzer, an ex-prostitute in the first decade of the twentieth century. Anne Firor Scott, referring to the personal diaries of many women who lived in the South in the early nineteenth century, points out that "women whose families and friends thought them 'spotless' were themselves convinced that their souls were in danger." These women sincerely tried to make themselves pure in the eyes of their God and at the same time to fulfill the image of the southern gentlewoman, the "true woman." They did

40. See Mary Kelley, *Private Woman, Public Stage: Literary Domesticity in Nineteenth-Century America.*

not see any reason to pretend to be other than who they were expected to be. They believed in the ideal of the southern lady that they tried to live up to. Half a century later, Pinzer, a Jewish woman who wrote a series of letters to her benefactor and friend telling the intimate details of her life, gave up the life of a prostitute to become a legitimate entrepreneur and social reformer because, after 1910, her creative and business talents could find an outlet. She became the "new woman," no longer needing her games to survive.[41]

When women's expectations do not coincide with their daily lives, an incongruity results. Southern gentlewomen in this position from the Civil War to the turn of the century can be represented by Madge Preston, the southern lady who no longer believed in the ideal but who could see no way out of her unbearable situation and so presented one front to her family and friends and quite another in her personal diary; and new women in this position can be represented by Madeleine, the woman who quit her job as a saleswoman in a major department store to return to a more lucrative career as a prostitute. Madeleine responds to the tension between the ideal of the well-dressed, well-read lady and the reality of her family's disgraceful poverty by deciding to be a prostitute and later a con woman.[42]

The years between 1830 and 1900 were years of vast change not only for the nation but also for American women. Susan Conrad suggests that an important shift happened in the expectations of American women in the 1830s as a byproduct of romanticism. Part of the romantic credo was a tolerance for—even an active searching out of—the unique, the diverse. Women intellectuals felt a new and finally acceptable desire to look into women's past, to find female heroes.[43] At the same time that this psychological expansion was beginning, social strictures were tightening. It was in the 1830s, as factories began to take industry out of the home, that the separate spheres for women and men became a shaping force. The ideology that accompanied this movement to a wage economy was in direct contradiction to the romantic justification of diversity, for it gave to middle-class women a single, domestic role and attached strong moral and social value to it.

The 1830s also saw the beginning of the great waves of immigration. As cities grew and more and more immigrant women found themselves caught in an industrial trap, the opposition between the ideal of womanhood—described in religious

41. Scott, *The Southern Lady,* 12; Ruth Rosen and Sue Davidson, eds., *The Maimie Papers.*

42. Beauchamp, ed., *A Private War; Madeleine: An Autobiography.*

43. Conrad, *Perish the Thought,* 96–97.

tracts, taught in Sunday school, and restated in story after story in the ever more widely circulating ladies' magazines—and the reality of long hours and poor pay became very clear. Many immigrants' daughters wanted to separate themselves from the old ways, wanted to dress well and have some independence.[44] Some of them would be the ones who would consider becoming confidence women. But it would take a generation for the confidence woman to develop. Although Longstreet could write about his confidence men in 1835 and Hooper could create a Simon Suggs in the 1840s, confidence women were not a major element in American society until the 1860s. There are several reasons for this. One reason is that most of the histories of famous women, the publication of which was encouraged by romanticism, were not published until the 1850s. Some became quite popular, especially Elizabeth Oakes Smith's *Woman and Her Needs* (1851). Likewise, Elizabeth Ellet's *The Women of the American Revolution* (1848) went through four editions by 1850.[45] Such records of powerful, unusual women would influence women's thinking, making them aware of a potential not admitted by the stereotype of true womanhood. It is significant that Loreta Velazquez, according to her own statement, read tales of heroic women when she was young, especially stories about women who had dressed like men, since she would become famous herself as a cross-dressing soldier in the Civil War. It is also significant that she devoted many pages in her autobiographical narrative to the stories of such women. For a woman to dare to be a confidence artist, she had to have a sense of personal power. Accounts of strong women from the past who broke out of restraining stereotypes could only have strengthened that new self-image.

Other changes in the 1850s likewise gave women a new sense of possibility. In 1848 the Seneca Falls Women's Rights convention spearheaded by Elizabeth Cady Stanton and Lucretia Mott began an upsurge of feminist thought. There were succeeding conventions in the next decade, bringing the "woman question" into the spotlight. In 1848 married women gained the legal right to own property for the first time in New York. That legal advancement in itself marked a change in society's attitude toward women, but perhaps more important was the process by which women brought the new law about: petition gathering.[46] The organizational skills that women like Ernestine Rose, Elizabeth Cady Stanton, and Paulina

44. Elizabeth Ewen, *Immigrant Women in the Land of Dollars: Life and Culture on the Lower East Side, 1890–1925,* 106–7.
45. Conrad, *Perish the Thought,* 117, 123.
46. Miriam Schneir, ed., *Feminism: The Essential Historical Writings,* 72.

Wright Davis learned in the twelve years it took to get the law enacted helped them become the leaders of the growing feminist movement. After vigorous work by Stanton and others, the property law changed again in women's favor in 1860, allowing married women, among other things, the right to keep their own earnings. Such social changes caused an upheaval in the traditional view of women, creating openings for new views to take hold in the belief systems of both men and women. That one of those views spawned the growth of confidence women is a strong possibility.

The changes in women's status did not happen suddenly. The antislavery groups of the 1840s were one precursor to the women's movement. Sarah Grimké made the connection between the antislavery movement and the women's movement clear by making explicit analogies between slavery and the condition of women. In 1838 a group of ministers in Massachusetts berated her for leaving her appointed sphere to speak in public. She published her influential "Letters on the Equality of the Sexes and the Condition of Women" in answer. Grimké's boldness in retorting to the ministers and in speaking to mixed audiences at this time in the nineteenth century created a model of assertiveness for other young women. The powerful effect female speakers had on other women should not be underestimated. In such supposedly traditional, rural communities as Parsons and Columbus, Kansas, for example, speeches by Susan B. Anthony in 1876 caused enough change in the behavior of her auditors to elicit this remark from an unknown subscriber to the *Columbus Courier:* "After Susan B. Anthony lectured in our city last Spring, we noticed a marked change in the demeanor of the ladies of our city—and now since Susan is here again and given us another 'piece of her mind,' matters are assuming a serious aspect—things are not what they seem to be. We do not understand these gatherings among the fair sex. There is a conspiracy some where. Man, arouse yourself! or your liberties will be gone."[47]

Changes in the status of women were not limited to the middle class; less affluent women were affected by change as well. With the introduction in the early 1830s of the power loom and the model factory system in Lowell, Massachusetts, lower-class women were given a new economic role. Although middle-class daughters were the first workers at the Lowell textile plant during a time when the factory was remarkable for its moral and educational tone, by the 1840s, when factory owners used speed-ups and lower pay to increase profits,

47. *Columbus Courier,* January 13, 1876.

the majority of workers were women of the lower classes, and when, a decade later, working conditions became even worse because of cheap immigrant labor, working women came to see that the new order would not respond to their needs on its own. Already in 1834 women went on strike for higher wages in Lowell, and in 1844 they founded the Lowell Female Labor Reform Association. The association did not succeed in changing working conditions, but it did succeed in convincing the Massachusetts legislature to consider the question of women's problems at work; it was the first time in United States history that women were allowed to be witnesses before a legislative investigating committee.[48]

These social changes had a significant influence on some women's self-image. There has been much discussion since the 1970s about the effects of the current women's movement on female criminality, although generally the idea that a relationship exists must be used with a great deal of caution. But certainly women's crime has changed in recent decades. The words of one Los Angeles policeman in the 1970s help explain how changes in social attitude have altered the forms of women's crime today and how similar changes in the nineteenth century might have helped create the confidence woman. Speaking about the changes in the female criminals he has had to deal with, the policeman said, "You can see them grow in confidence. Like they opened a new door and realized all of a sudden that they can walk through it." A contemporary female criminal herself describes how the change came to her: "It was the radios that changed things for me: like I got a whole new look at what I was doing. . . . one day it hit me. Wow! . . . I was knocking myself out for a bunch of five-buck radios. I don't know what it was at the time, but like, I couldn't see myself taking anything other than that. Like I had a block or something. Then it was like a flash. . . . I can see it now . . . how dumb I was. I mean, if I was going to rip something off, why the hell didn't I take Cadillacs?"[49]

In the 1970s, female criminals, perhaps encouraged by the new view of women, began to see that they could move from petty crime to more serious sorts—they "opened a new door"; in a similar manner, nineteenth-century confidence women opened a door of possibility, fostered perhaps by the new "frontiers of the imagination," to use Susan Conrad's phrase, arising in midcentury. The realization that they could make things go their way if they used a little daring and ingenuity made all the difference.

48. Schneir, ed., *Feminism,* 49–50.
49. Freda Adler, *Sisters in Crime: The Rise of the New Female Criminal,* 15, 11.

Many historians have commented on how the Civil War in combination with other major changes in the late 1800s speeded the changes in women's condition by forcing women to be more independent as men went off to battle and by teaching them how to organize as they aided the war effort in various ways, from nursing to sewing uniforms to being camp followers. But the war had an even more direct effect on women who were ready to test their military powers. It was an open field for female spies and for women who desired to be soldiers and were daring enough to disguise themselves as men. The decade of the 1860s was the beginning for the wave of confidence women that helped shape America for the next thirty years.

It is possible to explain why confidence women came on the scene in large numbers after 1860; it is equally possible to explain why the numbers had diminished by World War I. As women gained more varied and lawful opportunities for expanding their lives in the 1870s and 1880s, the confidence woman began to give way to the "new woman." On the frontier and in the South, the Grange gave women equal footing with men during the 1870s, and the Populist party continued that tradition into the 1890s. Education for women opened up after the war, both in colleges for women and in the normal schools. Teaching became an option for single women, and later women could choose to be typists and sales clerks, a major difference from just a decade or two earlier, when such careers were not open to women, who were limited to work in the factories if anywhere outside the home.[50] For a short while at the end of the century, some women were even allowed to become medical doctors, although that did not last very long, and Louisa May Alcott could switch from writing stories about confidence women to writing stories about women artists. As more women became wage earners (14.7 percent of women over sixteen years of age in 1870; 20.6 percent in 1900), the "true womanhood" ideal lost power and a new generation of "new women" would read popular pamphlets in the 1920s about "how New York working girls live." Young women could be package wrappers at department stores, cigar-stand saleswomen, models, chorus girls, life insurance saleswomen, or advertising account executives. This relative abundance of options for women was quite a change from the seven typical jobs outside the home that women could choose from in 1840, according to Harriet H. Robinson, writing in 1883 for the Massachusetts Bureau of Labor

50. See Mary P. Ryan, *Womanhood in America: From Colonial Times to the Present.* For the following data on wages, see Schneir, ed., *Feminism,* 254.

Statistics. She mentions as examples jobs as domestic help, going door to door to do sewing or weaving, and some teaching.[51]

During the years of change, when cities like Chicago were growing rapidly, creating opportunity for prostitutes and female criminals, when women were actively questioning their subordinate roles although there was yet little real change, when the war was giving women a chance to use their confidence skills in the name of patriotism, the confidence woman flourished. She was both a product of the times and a precursor of a new generation of women, who would be ready to confront the twentieth century with less need for games.

51. See Betty Van Deventer, *How New York Working Girls Live;* for seven typical jobs, see Harriet H. Robinson, "Fourteenth Annual Report of Massachusetts Bureau of Statistics of Labor, 1883," 55.

3

Types of Confidence Women in History

I f confidence women are to become vivid in our imaginations, we must be able to clearly see all the varied forms they took in the nineteenth century. These forms fall into three overlapping categories: criminals, adventuresses, and soldiers or spies. The criminals include swindlers, badger artists, panel-house workers, credit defrauders, and bank robbery decoys; the adventuresses, just this side of criminality, include clairvoyants, fortune-tellers, quack doctors, gold diggers, and fortune hunters. Both criminals and adventuresses are out for profit, directly or indirectly. Soldiers and spies are out for fame and glory, all in the name of a good cause. In addition to these three types of confidence women are two other categories of women closely akin to them, but with important differences: escape artists and everyday pretenders. Escape artists include women who escape from slavery or other danger; everyday pretenders include women who "pass" as members of an alternate group or class and women who use other kinds of subterfuge in their daily lives, sometimes manipulating their husbands or fathers or creating a social facade so that no one can see the truth about their less-than-ideal lives.

The historical records that would fill out the picture of these women are not easy to find because most such women have not yet been studied seriously. It is only in sensationalist and informal histories that they appear with any regularity, making it almost impossible to verify the data given. As one reads the accounts of the various confidence women's exploits, one gets the distinct impression that they are in large part fictionalized, made characters in a history that is more story than anything else. Still, behind the exaggerated rhetoric of the popular historians, who enjoy pointing to confidence women as amazing freaks, lies a reasonably clear picture of what some confidence women were like at the end of the last century. For even though stories proliferate around these women, there is a core of truth: these women did exist, and many were either sentenced to jail for fraud and robbery or given military commendations for their bravery.

What is in question is exactly how these women understood their own actions and what their motivations were. To come to a perspective on that, it is especially interesting to compare accounts of the women in the different sources, including the autobiographies that some of the women wrote. When May Churchill tells of her own exploits, her tone is amusing but matter-of-fact; she is unquestionably serious about her profession. When she writes about Sophie Lyons, on the other hand, she, like the informal historians, makes Lyons seem larger than life. Similarly, when Sophie Lyons writes about Carrie Morse, she makes her sound miraculous. These women were likely to exaggerate their own actions, but they went even further when exaggerating their peers'. It is as if when one begins to tell stories about confidence women, even in autobiography, one is given license to spin yarns. In the autobiographies, it is what comes between the stories that is intriguing psychologically, for the women step back and evaluate their lives from a subjective point of view, revealing much more than the informal histories do.

Still, for my purposes as a literary historian, the legends are as important as any reality, because our fictions have power to shape our lives. Jane Tompkins in *Sensational Designs* explains the "cultural work" that popular literature did in the nineteenth century, "teach[ing] readers what kinds of behavior to emulate or shun . . . provid[ing] a basis for remaking the social and political order in which events take place."[1] The confidence-woman stories taught that women could be self-directed, courageous, humorously daring—in direct opposition to the Christian, self-sacrificing, mother-centered model taught by much domestic fiction. Such stories were part of a new literature for a new time, as women made the transition into the twentieth century. That the confidence women were such unusual types made the stories more palatable: a criminal woman would never consciously be considered a role model, although her assertive attitude and her joie de vivre could do their work subliminally; soldiers or spies would be almost impossible to emulate, although their daring and inventiveness could suggest alternative roles and new ways of thinking for women.

1. Jane Tompkins, *Sensational Designs: The Cultural Work of American Fiction, 1790–1860*, xvii.

It would be an ambitious project to sort out the fiction from the fact in the stories about confidence women in order to analyze just how much is fiction-making and how much is a true recital of how some women had already changed—a project I have attempted only minimally here. My focus instead has been on recovering the stories that have been and are being told about the confidence woman and on analyzing what the stories mean within the American culture of their times. When possible I have preferred to rely on the memoirs, letters, or diaries of the confidence women themselves to understand the sorts of deception the women say they used and what their motivations were, although the number of such sources is small, and even these sources are not "factual." Detective reports and sociological studies written during the period are the next most reliable sources, because they are sometimes eyewitness accounts and they always show the biases and assumptions of the confidence women's contemporaries. In many cases, however, the information I have on confidence women of the nineteenth century comes from books written only recently, the accounts undocumented and hyperbolic. To do a full historical study, one would have to go back to the newspapers of the time and track down letters and court records. Until that is done, we are left with the stories as they are given. The dearth of formal historical scholarship on the confidence woman suggests that we are not ready to confront her intellectually, although we have allowed her into our popular imagination.

The Criminal Confidence Woman

The confidence woman who must be dealt with first is the criminal one, for she has been the most dangerous to established cultural expectations about women, both in the nineteenth century and now. Women in the nineteenth century were expected to fit one of two extremes: the "true woman" ideal of domesticity, piety, submissiveness, and purity, or the opposite—the temptress, the brutal murderess. Women as victims and women as shrews were culturally accepted, as were the frivolous belles. Late in the nineteenth century, as more women began to enter the professions and take political power, the range of images widened to include women as workers and as businesspeople; even feminists and political radicals began to fit into the cultural expectations, whether welcomed or not. All these images of women found a place in the American understanding of womanhood, but there was no place for the criminal confidence woman. She was too logical, too daring, too self-regarding, too independent, too selfish, too sordid, too calculating, too extravagantly greedy, too able to identify herself without reference to a man to fit in anywhere. It is the criminal confidence woman we are most astonished to discover, for she is the type of confidence woman we have heard the least about. For a culture to see a particular type of woman, it must be ready to admit that she could exist; there must be some paradigm for the woman to fit into so that she can be labeled and understood. In the nineteenth century there was no such commonly accepted paradigm for the criminal confidence woman; her criminal actions broke the commonly held expectations about females and female crime so boldly that she could ply her trade without being readily recognized. It is evident that one of the reasons for the criminal confidence woman's success was precisely that she was, in this sense, invisible.

G. T. W. Patrick, a leading American turn-of-the-century psychiatrist whose ideas are representative of the psychological theories about women common in the last decades of the nineteenth century, made explicit the relationship between women and crime that was generally accepted at the time. He wrote an article for a general audience in 1895, printed in *Popular Science Monthly,* entitled "The Psychology of Women." The prevailing psychology is rather complex because women were commonly acknowledged on the one hand to be deceptive and excellent liars, but on the other hand to be incapable of premeditated crime. Patrick wrote that woman's "greatest moral defect is her untruthfulness," that "deception and ruse in woman, far more than in man, have become a habit of thought and speech," and that she "excels in tact, and extricates herself from a difficulty with astonishing adroitness." One would think that with this view of women it would be common sense to expect women to be con artists, and to a certain degree that was the expectation. However, the conning expected of women was of a trivial, domestic sort, limited to spur-of-the-moment manipulations, as Patrick says, out of "habit."[2]

To contrast the accepted psychology of women's criminality with an actual female criminal's behavior, consider Cassie Chadwick, an excellent example of a criminal confidence woman who used the expectations about women even as she broke them. Chadwick, née Elizabeth Bigley, emigrated to the United States from Canada when she was a teenager. She practiced her confidence arts early

2. Patrick, "The Psychology of Women," 8, 7.

on by flaunting a calling card that read "Miss Bigley—Heiress to $15,000" at a few elite dress shops, thereby coming into her first wardrobe on the strength of extravagant promissory notes she generously signed.[3] Certainly, Chadwick's "untruthfulness" in this situation was not out of habit. She had to have the cards made up specifically for the purpose of gulling the store owners, reasoning that their avarice would get the better of their prudence. She banked on the supposition that the store owners would not expect a teenage girl to have such forethought and audacity. And she was right.

The store owners were simply acting upon the beliefs of the time. It would not have been the expectation for women to be criminal confidence artists, because despite their "tact" and "adroitness" women are, according to Patrick and the common psychological theory he articulated, "markedly deficient" in "slow logical reasoning," making them incapable of formulating an intricate criminal scheme. Furthermore, "woman's sympathy and love, her physical weakness and tired nature, her domestic and quiet habits, ill adapt her to the criminal life." That is not to say that the psychology did not allow for "murder by poisoning, domestic theft, and infanticide," all considered typical female crimes. For Patrick states that women are like children, unable to control their emotions and desires; they have a "naturally infantile constitution" and are products of "arrested development." Self-control is essential to carrying out a confidence scheme; women were considered by their very nature incapable of doing so. The female crimes recognized by nineteenth-century psychology are crimes that were totally uncontrolled, horrible murders and mutilation: "When women do become criminals their crimes are often marked by greater heinousness, cruelty, and depravity" than men's because criminal women are so much like unreasonable children. As Patrick succinctly put it, "When women become bad they become hopelessly bad."[4]

Given such a theory of female psychology and female criminality, it is easy to see how criminal confidence women could go unrecognized. A confidence game is not "heinous," and, instead of being done on the spur of the moment, it is rigorously thought out. According to Patrick and the psychology he outlined, therefore, confidence women could not exist. This all played into the hands of confidence women, of course, because they based their whole art on manipulating

3. See Jay Robert Nash, *Bloodletters and Badmen: A Narrative Encyclopedia of American Criminals from the Pilgrims to the Present*, 119–20.
4. Patrick, "Psychology of Women," 6–9.

their victims' confidence in their innocence. For instance, the psychology said that a woman's "irritable nerves" made her incapable of disguising her emotions, that her face would always show what she was thinking. Obviously, the confidence woman would make great use of this misconception, letting her face show the emotions most conducive to her plan, all the while pretending to be unable to control her expressions. Criminal confidence women broke the expectations about women and women's crime by premeditating their actions with very logical reasoning, by being neither "tired" nor "quiet," by perpetrating crimes against property rather than persons. Furthermore, they made use of the very expectations they disrupted by disguising their actions behind the stereotypes.

The disruption between psychological theory and the confidence woman legend appears readily in an examination of Cassie Chadwick's further career. From her modest beginning, Chadwick developed the heiress ruse into a full-fledged confidence scam, finally representing herself as the illegitimate daughter of Andrew Carnegie. How Chadwick conned bankers from New York to Ohio into lending her millions of dollars is the story of how nineteenth-century confidence women played the game.

Chadwick was no longer beautiful when she portrayed herself as the future heiress to $400 million, but she was modestly genteel. She knew how to dress to suggest taste and innocence at once. The scheme began one day in New York in 1894, when she "ran into" a lawyer who was an old acquaintance from Ohio, and ended ten years later, when Chadwick's hoax was finally uncovered. In the intervening years, she played on the presumption of some of the shrewdest bankers of the time that no woman would dare to take on the great Andrew Carnegie himself. She also played on the bankers' greed and poor ethics. If they would lend her money—as much money as her lavish tastes required—she would pay them back with exorbitant interest. For she had convinced them that she would inherit the Carnegie empire when Andrew Carnegie died.

In the 1890s, one could not approach an Andrew Carnegie and ask him if he had a bastard child. Besides, the evidence was all there. Had not a reputable lawyer driven with Chadwick to Carnegie's very door, her "father's house," she said? And had not Chadwick gone inside and stayed for twenty-five minutes (talking to the housekeeper) and then waved to perhaps Carnegie himself (in fact, the butler) as she walked away? Finally, had not that lawyer seen a promissory note for $2 million slip out of her hand, and was not that note signed in Carnegie's own writing? The lawyer took that note and another $7 million in supposed promissory notes to a respected bank and deposited them in a safe-deposit box without the cashier inspecting them for possible forgery. Chadwick had achieved the appearance of great future wealth. She then "naïvely" agreed to loans with illegally high interest rates, which that bank and several others in New York and Ohio pushed on her.

Throughout this charade, Chadwick had to have absolute control of her face, her emotions, her actions. Her feigned naïveté and semblance of gentility were never questioned by the men she came in contact with, from the shrewdest banker to the lowliest cashier. Her unassuming manner covering a bold audacity, her intricate preplanning—down to writing herself false promissory notes and determining how best to convince the lawyer that she was who she said she was—and her consistent and persistent role-playing exceeded the expectations about women commonly held by her society. As a result, Chadwick was relatively invisible even though she spent her money extravagantly, spending as much as $100,000 for one party alone.

It was not until Chadwick, several years and several million dollars later, requested a loan of a mere $190,000 from a Boston bank that her scheme was uncovered. Upon doing a routine check, the bank discovered the vast debt Chadwick had incurred and called in an earlier loan. Chadwick's extravagance made her incapable of repaying, setting off a chain reaction among her other creditors. Andrew Carnegie himself finally heard about the hoax and publicly disavowed Chadwick and the promissory notes.

The story of Cassie Chadwick and her million-dollar fraud appears to be a story worth retelling. We hear often enough about "The Great Train Robbery," for instance, because of its daring. But I have found reference to Cassie Chadwick in only three sources, two written by the same man, and newspaper accounts are the only documentation of the story's facts. Chadwick is not mentioned in standard reference books: encyclopedias, women's who's whos, books about female crime. She appears only, so far as I have been able to find, in the sensationalist histories of Jay Robert Nash, a recent compiler of stories about eccentrics of one type or another, and John S. Crosbie. Apparently, no nineteenth-century novels were written about Chadwick—although an account of her "doings" was written in 1905, culled from newspaper stories—and criminals like her do not come under analysis in discussions of female criminality.[5] This silence is intriguing. Cassie Chadwick is intriguing. Did she come out of nowhere? Presumably she existed,

5. See John S. Crosbie, *The Incredible Mrs. Chadwick: The Most Notorious Woman of Her Age,* another informal account that is based on newspaper stories and on the compilation

but did she actually do what the accounts say she did? This is one point at which the distinction between legend and fact would be very illuminating in a discussion of the variety of women's actual lives in the late nineteenth century. However, for the purpose of understanding the confidence-woman figure as a power in the cultural imagination, the mere fact of the legend is enough. If the "cultural work" is to nudge a society into a changed view of women's roles and possibilities, then the stories told about Cassie Chadwick do that work without verification of their absolute validity.

Even though I have not found serious historical discussion of Chadwick's life, it is clear that if she did as she is said to have done she was not alone. There were many criminal confidence women at work in the late 1800s, as the various detective reports of people like Allen Pinkerton and Thomas Byrnes show. These detectives describe in first-person accounts people they have met or have heard about in their own time, making their reports very interesting in terms of their effects on nineteenth-century culture. Of course, the rhetoric they used was influenced by the sensationalist language of the penny papers, which had been a major force in America for almost half a century by the time these men wrote. But beneath the rhetoric, we catch glimpses of what some confidence women actually did.

Most of the crimes Byrnes ascribes to women in his encyclopedia of crime depended on shopkeepers or strangers on the street trusting these female criminals. In a typical description, Byrnes emphasizes the criminal's appearance: he describes Louise Jordan, pickpocket and shoplifter, as "lady-like in manner and appearance"; she "wears good clothes."[6] Byrnes has a good-humored respect for these women. He often says that a particular female criminal is "a clever woman," often enough "one of the most clever women in America." He also usually adds that she is "well worth knowing."

Although most of the women Byrnes included in his book were pickpockets or shoplifters, he did tell of a few who engaged in blackmail. He included Sophie Levy—Sophie Lyons's maiden name—who lured wealthy merchants to her luxurious hotel room, then somehow divested them of their clothing and demanded payment if they did not wish to be "exposed"—a variation of the badger game. One man wrote Lyons a check for $10,000 to save his reputation.

---

of such stories made in 1905 (*The History and Story of the Doings of the Famous Cassie L. Chadwick the So-Called "Queen of Finance,"* by Laning Company).

　　6. Byrnes, *1886 Professional Criminals,* 208.

According to Byrnes, Lyons had a female accomplice who would immediately go to the bank and cash the check before the victim could stop payment. In this particular case the check bounced, but the man did not press charges. Jay Robert Nash devotes several pages in one of his collections of stories about criminal women to Sophie Lyons, including a description of the incident Byrnes describes, using her married name there. But the check in this story was for $5,000. Allan Pinkerton, too, in his memoir *Thirty Years a Detective,* claims that "Sophie Lewis" asked for the $10,000 check, but received only $5,000 and found it worthless when she got to the bank.[7] As I mentioned before, Pinkerton seems to have mingled stories about several different confidence women into his one generic "Sophie," invariably writing that the scams failed and ultimately turning his Sophie into an opium-eating, lascivious murderess, which is not at all the case with the Sophie Levy/Lyons we find in Byrnes. According to the publishers of Sophie Lyons's autobiography and according to Nash, Lyons in fact went on to become a vastly successful real estate agent.[8]

The slipperiness of names and numbers in the informal histories and detective accounts points up the difficulty of determining exactly who did what. It appears that the stories about Sophie Levy/Lyons and Sophie Lewis are based mainly on the life of one woman. Because it is Sophie Lyons, née Levy, wife of Ned Lyons, a well-known criminal of the late nineteenth century, who writes an autobiography, I will presume that she is the woman Pinkerton is referring to. Even as one tries to sort out the historical facts about confidence women, one realizes how much of that history has been fictionalized, part of the reason that I focus on the confidence-woman myth. However, Sophie Lyons is not all myth. She did, for instance, spend time in Sing Sing in 1871 and 1872. The fact that the story of her life is not clear symbolizes the need for formal historical research on her life as well as on the lives of the other confidence women I will discuss.

Another confidence woman, whom Byrnes styles a "confidence queen" and "an excellent talker," was Bertha Heyman, of Milwaukee, Wisconsin. Heyman's scam was similar to Chadwick's. She pretended to be worth $8 million and in one case talked $455 out of three brokers who gladly agreed to take care of her "securities," actually a worthless stack of papers that they, like the bank cashier in Chadwick's case, had neglected to inspect. Byrnes enthusiastically reports, "This remarkable woman used to lodge at the leading hotels, and was

7. Ibid., 206; Nash, *Look for the Woman,* 259; Pinkerton, *Thirty Years a Detective,* 236–55.
8. Nash, *Look for the Woman,* 260.

always attended by a maid or man servant . . . [in] elegant quarters . . . [;] when plotting her schemes she would glibly talk about her dear friends, always men well known for their wealth and social position. She possesses a wonderful knowledge of human nature, and can deceive those who consider themselves particularly shrewd in business matters."[9]

Annie Reilly, also described in Byrnes, played on another assumption about women: that they have a natural maternal instinct. Her victims were the women who hired her as nurse for their children. She gained the confidence of her employers by cuddling and exclaiming over their children. Within a day, or at most two, of gaining access to their homes, she would make off with the family jewels.[10] All these women show the kind of forethought that the popular psychological theory said was impossible for women, and none of them committed the kind of crimes that were expected.

The confidence woman's most important tools were her ability to speak and dress appropriately for specific occasions. These women created fictions through which to work their will, always giving the impression of utter sincerity. It is interesting to see how different this kind of talking and fiction-making is from the fast talk associated with the confidence man. Thomas Byrnes makes the difference clear. In the nineteenth century, innocence and naïveté were expected womanly characteristics and were projected from a woman's carriage, speech, and dress. Criminal confidence women would be careful to "dress up to their business," Byrnes explains. "I do not mean that they should indicate their business by their dress. No, no; just the opposite. They attire themselves so as to attract the least attention from the class of people among whom they wish to operate." Female pickpockets, according to Byrnes, are "humble in their attire, and seemingly unassuming in their demeanor," while male pickpockets are "entertaining conversationalists and easy in their manners" and generally more extravagant. If a confidence woman were to work in middle-class society, she would dress in a refined manner, to fit in with rather than stand out from the other women. Ellen Peck, a woman Byrnes says "rose to the front rank among confidence women," would gain people's trust by her "neat and quiet way of dressing and ladylike manner."[11] Unlike the confidence man, whose fast talk and self-assurance carried the game, the confidence woman in the nineteenth century usually modulated her speech and feigned ignorance to win her victim's

9. Byrnes, *1886 Professional Criminals,* 201.
10. Ibid., 205.
11. Ibid., 35, 55, 319.

trust. Like the cardsharp or pool hustler, she gave the impression of naïveté and mild confusion to lure her victim on.

There are, of course, exceptions to this general rule: for example, the unnamed woman in the section on women in Byrnes's *Darkness and Daylight,* who attracted rich men to her home to sell them phony financial tips. Bertha Heyman, in her luxurious hotel room, and Sophie Beck, with her splendid false-front company and worthless stock, likewise used the show of wealth and ostentation to draw people on. Even for women like these, whose self-assuredness was part of their lure, however, the impression of being a lady, soft-spoken and nonaggressive, was paramount. The roles confidence women had to enact were quite different from the roles open to the confidence man. The fact that they were able to play the roles at the same time they were subverting them is a mark of the confidence woman's criminal genius.

The criminal confidence woman broke not only the expectations concerning the types of crime a woman would commit but also the assumptions about the physical appearance of female criminals. The theory was that female criminals are always in some way physically deformed, which again made the generally attractive—if not beautiful—confidence women invisible to society. The study of female criminals began in the 1890s with the work of Caesar Lombroso and William Ferrero. Their book *The Female Offender* has become a classic in female criminology, and Lombroso is now called the father of the biological-positivist school. Lombroso scientifically "proves" that female criminals are throwbacks in the evolutionary scale: their skulls show severe anomalies, he argues, and their faces are decidedly masculine. Lombroso describes the differences between female criminals and their "normal" counterparts, comparing "cranial capacity," "facial angle," and other features, and finds criminal women distinctly inferior to noncriminals. Interestingly, he also finds differences among criminal women according to the type of crime they commit. Among the women's crimes that Lombroso included in his study are poisoning, homicide, infanticide, murder, wounding, prostitution, theft, arson, and complicity in rape—not confidence games.[12] Only in the last chapter, under the heading "Crime and Mental Illness," does Lombroso add swindling as a category, and he considers it there to be a serious crime.

However, criminal women are not as different from "normal" women as criminal men are from their normal peers, according to Lombroso, primarily because women in general have not evolved as far as men have (recall Henry Adams's

12. Caesar Lombroso and William Ferrero, *The Female Offender,* 14.

lyricism on this): an evolutionary throwback does not have as far to regress. Furthermore, women are seldom great criminals because of their inherent biological limitations; they are incapable of the genius men have evolved to. Still, serious crime committed by women seems much worse than that committed by men because, as Lombroso says, we expect women to be passive and eminently noncriminal, "the natural form of retrogression in women being prostitution and not crime." Lombroso makes the expectations concerning women in general and female criminals in particular quite clear: as a double exception, the criminal woman is consequently a monster.[13] Her normal sister is kept in the paths of virtue by many causes, such as maternity, piety, and weakness; when these counter influences fail and a woman commits a serious crime, we may conclude that her wickedness must have been enormous before it could triumph over so many obstacles.

Given this understanding of female criminality, with its monstrous wickedness and accompanying physical deformity, we can see how someone like the elegant Ellen Peck would go unrecognized as a criminal at all. But when confidence women were recognized for their criminal deeds, the men who wrote about them had a tendency to expatiate on their beauty. Nash, writing in the 1980s but apparently basing his assessment on earlier sources, calls May Churchill a "statuesque girl with flaming red hair and a pure white complexion"; "her beauty was such that she completely stupefied the elegantly attired males in her presence." Allan Pinkerton describes Sophie Lewis (Lyons) this way: "Sophie Lewis was a beautiful girl when I first met her. Her hair was of raven blackness and curled gracefully around her broad low white forehead, beneath which her lustrous eyes gleamed with a soft brightness that was bewitching. Her bright-red lips and pearly teeth gave an additional charm to a face that was unmistakably beautiful."[14] The Sophie Lewis/Lyons described here seems to come right out of a fairy tale: a Snow White who before the story's end turns into a witch. Perhaps it is the contrast between what the detectives were led to expect about criminal women and what they found that leads to the exaggerated admiration the men had for the appearance of the confidence women they met.

Ellen Peck used her elegant good looks to strong advantage. For years she lived well by her confidence scams, often being under indictment but seldom brought to trial. In 1878 she pulled off her biggest con, according to Byrnes,

13. Ibid., 32–33, 152.
14. Nash, *Look for the Woman,* 80–81; Pinkerton, *Thirty Years a Detective,* 236.

convincing a soap manufacturer to give her $19,000 by pretending to be a female detective hired to investigate theft by his employees. She told the man that the $19,000 was to buy information about the employees' financial condition so that the manufacturer could get restitution. The information was false, of course, and the soap manufacturer tried to bring Peck to trial. Meanwhile, Peck was swindling the other swindlers—a "crooked diamond dealer," a seller of patent medicines, a buyer of inside stock information. Byrnes wrote, "She delighted in outwitting professional criminals, and invariably succeeded in her tricks."[15]

Confidence women like Ellen Peck understood how to use social and psychological stereotypes to their own advantage. "Womanliness," which a woman conveyed with looks of innocence, weakness, emotionality, and an evident desire to please, became a potent disguise for confidence women of all sorts. Even if the "feminine arts" practiced by many women were conceded to be artificial, acted out by well-trained women according to society's specifications, they were considered to be of limited scope, merely to make women more attractive, and further evidence of womanly weakness. The psychology admitted that women might deceive and manipulate in this manner, but the possible criminality of their motivation and their action was denied. The reluctance to consider any women to be criminal confidence artists, or criminal artists of disguise, is the direct result of an understanding of what a disguise implies: that there is a real woman under the artificial womanliness who will have to be reckoned with. Because it was threatening to the sexual hierarchy to conceive that some women were not as sincere, humble, and powerless as society wished them to be, and because many of these women themselves often preferred to keep the disguise intact so they could hide behind it and use it as they would, standard history books and much nineteenth-century literature avoided discussing the confidence woman. Only now, as feminist historians look to little-used sources to describe a different American history from the one we have traditionally been taught, and only now, as feminist literary scholars bring long-unread women's books back into print, does evidence of the nineteenth-century confidence woman appear.

As the analysis of criminal confidence women makes clear, the disguise of "womanliness," with the impotence and inconsequence that it implies, is the disguise most often assumed by criminal women who want their victims to discount them. By pretending to please, they make their victims self-confident enough to let down their guard so that the swindle can proceed. Evidence of the

15. Byrnes, *1886 Professional Criminals,* 317.

purposeful use of the womanly disguise can be found in the case of Mary Hansen, who played her game using the stereotype of the hysterical woman overcome by her emotionality, rather than the stereotype of the naïve and passive "lady."

Mary Hansen in some of her swindles in the late 1880s used a variation on the inheritance trick. She would tell her mark that she needed to pick up her inheritance at a certain time in a distant city or else it would be forfeited. She, her story would go, did not have the necessary train fare and needed money to pay for an official seal, the total amounting sometimes to as much as $2,500. In her supposed desperation to "borrow" the train fare and other monies, she would begin "crying and shouting, clapping her hands and running around the saloon and saying that she was ruined if she did not get the money at once." Her hysterical outburst was so disturbing and her offer to give the mortgage on her house or some other security so convincing, that the money was invariably handed over. Mary Hansen's version of "womanliness" earned her a small fortune.[16]

The Poillon sisters used the womanly disguise in reverse, being as unwomanly as they could when the right time came. Charlotte and Katherine Poillon made a significant amount of money by becoming engaged to older men via love letters and then suing them for breach of promise when the men broke the engagements. The two women were eloquent in their love letters, but when their suitors met them, the men lost interest, not just because the women were extremely heavy, but also because they were more or less purposely "unwomanly": Charlotte dressed like a man, which was bad enough in itself for a suitor who has been caught into certain "romantic" assumptions because of the letters, but she also was proud of her boxing skills, using them to fight evictions and once to earn a little side money exhibiting her abilities for the public. In 1903 the sisters took in $17,500 for one breach of promise suit, and in 1915, they brought in $23,338 for another. Nash puts it this way: "Trapping lonely, wealthy men into promising marriage and then threatening to expose their cadlike actions after they had backed away from their earthly pleasures was a Poillon specialty, demur blackmail of a sort which profited the sisters handsomely for decades." Nash does not specifically state why the men decided to back out of marriage, but the other details he gives in the entry seem reason enough.[17]

16. Ibid., 314–16.

17. Nash, *Bloodletters and Badmen,* 446–47. Nash is the best contemporary source of information on historical confidence women. However, he does not give direct documentation for any given entry in his encyclopedias; instead, he lists all books, articles,

This story shows the exuberance with which even present-day informal historians write: the boxing episode, although presumably true, is obviously added for the relish it gives. It also points up the problem with trying to talk about nineteenth-century confidence women based on sources that do not give direct documentation and whose purpose is as much sensationalism as it is history. Any one story could well be pure fabrication, passed on through time. But the stories en masse suggest two things: first, that some criminal women were involved in fraudulent schemes—enough so that a distinct species of legend grew up around them; and second, that because of the similarity of the techniques described in these stories, one can theorize about women's confidence arts as a whole, even if those arts are mainly conceived in the cultural imagination.

Criminality itself had captured America's fancy long before 1900, as David Reynolds shows in his study of antebellum crime literature. Some important European writers of the early twentieth century, too, such as André Gide, Bertolt Brecht, and Albert Camus, were intrigued by the idea of criminality, sometimes considering criminals antiheroes. The criminal can be looked at in a positive light, as someone who resists the system and dares to make his own decisions. In America, an outstanding criminal like Al Capone could become a cult figure, winning an admiration that is part of the American psyche. Some Humphrey Bogart movies are a popular form of the criminal-as-hero fantasy. In the nineteenth century, Billy the Kid caught the American imagination, as did Belle Starr. Although we seldom hear of them now, in the late 1800s some confidence women, also, were cult heroes, making headlines regularly. Thomas Byrnes uses glowing praise for the women he catalogues as professional criminals, calling them "the cleverest of pickpockets," and the like. William Dewey, chief of the New York police in the 1880s, dubbed Sophie Lyons "The Queen of Crime," telling newsmen, "Sophie Lyons is one of the cleverest criminals that the country has ever produced."[18] Today we still hear of Belle Starr, a thief who used violence as her tactic, not the confidence arts, but we do not often hear of the women who lived by their wits. Such women could be considered antiheroes, for they resisted the stereotypes, negative and positive, that restricted women in their day, paralleling the feminist movement, but on the underside of society.

---

newspaper stories, and other documents he used at the end of the book, making verification of his stories difficult. In his most recent encyclopedia of crime, his tone is more scholarly than in his earlier work, and some documentation occurs at the end of each entry.

18. Nash, *Look for the Woman,* 258.

The criminal confidence women did not try to change the system that the feminists argued against; instead, they used it to their own advantage. Their resistance was apolitical, although May Churchill did drop some socialist language into her autobiography in hopes of excusing her choice of career. Yet it *was* resistance of an important kind, whatever its motivation. Mary Ryan, a feminist historian, explains in *Womanhood in America* that immigrant girls, captivated by the images of well-dressed young women they saw in women's magazines, would become extremely dissatisfied with their ten-hour-a-day jobs that earned them a meager three dollars a week and would often turn to prostitution as a lucrative alternative, despite its dangers. Ryan describes their set of choices as a trap: they were "caught between class exploitation and sexual discrimination." She tells, as an example, of one young woman who, in order to have the expensive clothing and fast life pictured in the popular media, "descended to the lowest chamber of woman's oppression, the brothel." Some young women would have been satisfied to get out of the factory even without the riches. Ryan says that for them the only escape, if any, was through marriage. However, there was another alternative some immigrant women chose, which Ryan mentions only as an alternative for men: they could become criminals. Ryan explicitly eliminates property crime as a "short cut to glamour" for women: "Immigrant boys, impatient to taste the fruits advertised in America's popular culture, took to thievery and flooded the juvenile courts of industrial cities. Immigrant girls saw a short cut to glamour in prostitution."[19] However, as Byrnes's compilation of professional criminals and Pinkerton's professional reminiscences both show, some immigrant women tried thievery too.

May Churchill (Sharpe), who tells her story in her autobiography, *Chicago May: Her Story,* was an immigrant from Ireland. She ran away from home and came to America full of hope at thirteen, in 1889. "It did not take me long to get the hang of prices and wages. The first were too high, and the second too low," she says.[20] At first she tried living with relatives in Nebraska, but soon she eloped with a dashing young robber and began her life of crime. May Churchill was never a prostitute, yet she wore diamonds and always traveled first class. She resisted the oppressive economic system and sexual exploitation not with theory or through political action, but through crime. Her way would not lead to a changed society, but it did lead *her* out of the role of victim. I find it illuminating

19. Ryan, *Womanhood in America,* 218, 221, 228.
20. Sharpe, *Chicago May,* 25.

that Ryan failed to mention the criminal alternative that some women chose. The confidence woman has not been silenced only by men.

Sophie Lyons, "The Queen of Crime," is another confidence woman who could be seen as an antihero. She is an intriguing example of how the confidence woman used the stereotypes about women to her own advantage, of how invisible the confidence woman was in her own time—even, at one point, to her own husband, and of how successful she could be. She is also an example of a powerful woman who has been almost entirely deleted from history.

Lyons, a native-born American, began her career as a pickpocket, taught, according to Nash, by her mother. She married young, twice, her second husband a well-known burglar and bank robber. Her husband wanted her to fulfill the true womanhood ideal, give up her trade, and have babies. Lyons, however, enjoyed her profession too much to quit. She would wait until her husband left to do a job (according to Nash; Lyons herself at this juncture never admitted her husband's criminal activity), then steal away herself to pick pockets on the other side of the city, returning in time to act the dutiful wife.

On one of these escapades, Lyons was caught picking pockets at a fair. The detective who arrested her drew this admiring portrait of her actions at the jailhouse: "She could mold her face to every shade of emotion. She could make her eyes at will a fountain of tears. She treated us to a moving display of her art. She was by turns horror-stricken, proudly indignant, heartbroken, and convulsed with hysterics. Who could press a charge against such a blushing, trembling, sobbing young beauty piteously claiming that it was a dreadful mistake . . . ?"[21] Lyons apparently had the "womanly" masquerade down very well. She was released and immediately went back to the same fair where she had just been apprehended, dressed this time, however, as an old hag, and ended up leaving with a goodly amount of loot.

It is this sort of brazen manipulation and defiance of the system that makes the criminal confidence woman an antihero, for she dared to make her own choices in life. Lyons asserted her individual humanity in the face of a society that was very willing to reduce her to her appearance. Perhaps we do not hear about her because she overturns too rudely the old beliefs in women's passivity or the newer beliefs in women's superior moral nature. The fact that Sophie Lyons does not show up in the most recent biographical compilations of important women in history suggests that her particular brand of assertiveness and success is

21. Nash, *Look for the Woman*, 256.

unpalatable to almost everyone. Belle Starr, on the other hand, does appear, perhaps because her violence puts her in the "woman-as-monster" category.[22] Certainly, since a popular historian like Nash could find enough information to write multiple-page entries on both Churchill and Lyons, the documentation is available for more serious treatment.

Yet Lyons did have many admirable traits, one being her courage. She was once arrested for grand larceny and sent to Sing Sing state prison, where her husband was serving a long sentence. It has been speculated that she intentionally got herself arrested, for within weeks she had effected her husband's escape, and he returned the favor not long afterward. The scheme she devised again shows how criminal confidence women were able to manipulate female stereotypes. Soon after arriving at the prison, Lyons curried the favor of the head matron of the women's section, so the story goes, landing herself a job as the matron's personal maid and nanny in recompense for her tender care of the matron's dangerously ill child. In this position, Lyons was able to roam the prison at will and could even go as far as the market in town, dressed in a maid's outfit rather than the prison uniform. She always had the matron's children with her, making her look particularly harmless. In this way, she was able to smuggle in a change of clothes, a wig, and a lawyer's pass so that her husband could simply walk out of the prison. In this way, too, she was able to orchestrate her own escape by making an imprint of the front door key and slipping it to her husband when he came in disguise to visit her; she then made her escape when the time was right.[23]

Lyons broke the expectation about women's being incapable of planning a great crime when she became a bank robber in the 1880s. Usually no confidence skills were involved in the jobs; she simply signaled an accomplice when all the bank employees were watching a circus parade go by so that the accomplice could slip in and empty the tills unnoticed. The idea of following various circuses from one small town to another for the purpose of robbing banks was hers. In one of her bank-robbing schemes she did make use of her confidence skills, however. She would dress elegantly and drive up to a bank in a carriage. Her

---

22. Neither Sophie Lyons nor May Churchill appears in *Who Was Who in America*, published by Marquis Who's Who in Chicago, including lists compiled through 1989. Belle Starr, Jesse James, and Billy the Kid all appear on the list. *Notable American Women, 1607–1950* (Cambridge, Mass.: Belknap Press) likewise includes Belle Starr, but has no mention of Lyons or Churchill.

23. Nash, *Look for the Woman*, 257–58; Lyons, *Why Crime Does Not Pay*, 64–78.

accomplice would convince the bank clerk to go out to the carriage to talk to this most important potential client; Lyons would keep the clerk busy in a long conversation about her estate and the bank's stocks until her accomplice could finish his work inside the bank.[24]

These were not minor operations. Within a few years, Lyons was so successful that she owned "a villa on the Riviera, a townhouse in Manhattan, [and] a ranch in the West." She decided to become educated, having the ability neither to read nor to write, and set about learning literature, music, art, and languages with the help of tutors. With her new skill, she was able to enter high society, hobnobbing with the Vanderbilts and the Reyersons while she stole their jewels. Once she was caught in Paris picking a man's pocket, but her rich friends were so shocked at the very idea and she herself was so indignant that "the Prefect of Police apologized, kissing Sophie's hand and begging forgiveness as he led her to a carriage."[25]

Lyons's criminal career ended in the 1890s soon after she was double-crossed by Carrie Morse, her confederate in a phony bank scheme in New York. Morse took off with the money; Lyons barely escaped arrest, through the help of a friend. She was hurt to discover, she later wrote, that some women criminals did not hold to the "good faith" code that men did.[26] Lyons went straight at just over forty years old, perhaps because she had become too famous, Nash speculates; she then became a real estate agent, netting over a million dollars in this profession.[27] As a final move, she became a writer, producing a syndicated society column and booklets meant to reform criminals—perhaps her final con.

Sophie Lyons's story partakes of the Horatio Alger romance, although without the virtue one expects of Alger's heroes. The penniless street girl, illiterate until she is in her thirties, becomes the great Sophie Lyons, millionaire and lady by middle age. Yet hers is a name unknown to most of us. The romance of her life was important to the cultural imagination of her time, however, for her autobiography sold well. Lyons's and other confidence women's autobiographies leave us with an image of women who were assertive and coldly rational under their womanly guise, of women who found a way out of economic and sexual oppression in a unique manner that we at last should recognize.

24. Nash, *Look for the Woman,* 257, for both stories.
25. Ibid., 258–59.
26. Lyons, *Why Crime Does Not Pay,* 103. The Carrie Morse story is on pp. 89–103.
27. Nash, *Look for the Woman,* 260.

Crime as Insanity: A Labeling Theory

There was no place in nineteenth-century theories about female criminality for the criminal confidence woman, but perhaps she was given a place somewhere else. In the late nineteenth century a woman who disrupted social expectations as rudely as the criminal confidence woman did would most likely have been labeled "mad" instead of criminal. Elaine Showalter discusses madness as the "female malady," noting that the number of women incarcerated as patients in the newly formed mental institutions of the nineteenth century far exceeded the number of men. Meanwhile, the number of females in prison was (and still is) far below the number of males.[28]

Showalter suggests that in Victorian England women who were "abnormal or disruptive" were considered mad by reason of what Victorians called "moral insanity." She points out that John Conolly, a leader in mid-nineteenth-century "humanized" psychiatry, recommended commitment for all "young women of ungovernable temper [who persist in] . . . defying all domestic control."[29] Extending the definition of insanity to include ungovernable girls is a form of social control: any female who refused to fulfill the "womanly assumptions" could be called insane and locked in an institution, and an awareness of this possibility undoubtedly affected women's behavior.

In the American West, also, there is at least one clear example of the use of the insanity label to control unusual women. Mary Sawyer, also known as Mollie Monroe, was declared insane by a probate court in Arizona in 1877, with no reason given. But historian Susan L. Johnson argues that it may have been because she dressed like a man, prospected for gold as an equal with men, swore, drank, and chewed tobacco. She became a legend, her strikingly nonconformist behavior made comprehensible to newspaper audiences by a sentimental motivation: that she came west because of a broken heart. Sawyer herself made no such claim, but on being caught after escaping one time out of many from the asylum where she was incarcerated for twenty years, she said, "If I'd a' only had my breeches and my gun I'd a' been all right."[30] There is no indication that Mary Sawyer was a

28. See Elaine Showalter, *The Female Malady: Women, Madness, and English Culture, 1830–1980.*

29. Ibid., 48.

30. Susan L. Johnson, "Sharing Bed and Board: Cohabitation and Cultural Difference in Central Arizona Mining Towns, 1863–1873," in Armitage and Jameson, eds., *The Women's West,* 84–85.

confidence woman, for apparently she did not use her male attire to disguise her sex, but the mechanism for misnaming a criminal confidence woman as insane would be the same as that used to incarcerate women like Mary Sawyer because of their unusual behavior.

In English mental institutions, male and female patients included "murderers, burglars, and thieves," for by the 1870s psychiatrists had come to believe that "crime is a disease like insanity and epilepsy," subject to cure by "moral management," a view reflected in Edward Bellamy's immensely popular Utopian romance, *Looking Backward, 2000–1887* (1888). The concept of "moral insanity," according to Showalter, "redefined madness, not as a loss of reason, but as deviance from socially accepted behavior." Obviously, a criminal confidence woman could easily be interpreted as insane under this new definition, especially since she often did not fit the description of the female criminal offered by the Darwinians: they believed, like Lombroso, that female criminals would be easily recognizable because of "their ugliness and gracelessness." Showalter suggests that " 'insanity' is simply the label society attaches to female assertion, ambition, self-interest, and outrage."[31]

Present-day labeling theory associated with criminology explains that what is called deviant will vary from society to society and that the labels given to certain actions tell us more about the society doing the labeling than about the actions or actors themselves. Eileen Leonard, making a feminist interpretation of male-centered labeling theory, argues that "because of the patronizing attitude toward women, they may have their deviant actions treated as 'sickness' rather than criminality." Viewing deviant behavior as "sickness" implies a lack of personal choice, making the deviant woman a victim of her disease rather than an active agent making a reasoned decision about how to live; thus, her criminality is rendered invisible, covered by the veil of sickness. Carol Smart in *Women, Crime, and Criminology: A Feminist Critique* agrees that women are more likely to be called "sick" than criminal. She points out the symbolism of the conversion of Holloway, a women's prison in the United Kingdom, into a psychiatric hospital. Smart notes that there is no way to prove how often the "sick" label is correctly applied, and calls for more serious study of the issue. She argues that "women 'fit' more easily [than men] into the model provided by the 'sick' analogy because of the cultural stereotypes pertaining to women," and she asks whether women being diagnosed as mentally ill more often than men "reflect[s] a situation in

31. Showalter, *The Female Malady*, 39, 40, 118, 29, 118, and 72.

which more women than men do actually suffer from mental disorders such as neurosis, or whether a system of differential diagnosis can be said to exist in which different standards or expectations of behaviour are applied to women." Smart sums up the feminist interpretation of this phenomenon by explaining that if for women crime means sickness, then, first, the crime is irrational and has no meaning for the woman; second, socioeconomics are at most a "trigger" of the action, not a cause, so that the crime becomes a personal action rather than a political statement; third, the sickness label denies intention; and fourth, calling female crime "sickness" prevents us from feeling the urgency of the need to redefine crime from a woman's point of view.[32]

Part of this problem in definition is that the current and past definitions of a healthy woman are not the same as the definitions of a healthy adult, making a woman's act of rebellion against an oppressive condition a sick response rather than a rational one. Current psychological definitions of healthy womanhood grow directly out of their precursors in the nineteenth century. Although the twentieth-century passion for statistics is new, the information a group of research psychologists obtained in the 1970s could easily be applied to attitudes a century earlier. Inge Broverman and colleagues gave out questionnaires in the early 1970s to seventy-nine psychiatric professionals, forty-six men and thirty-three women. Most of the respondents, both men and women, gave the same answers when asked to describe healthy males and healthy adults, but those same respondents, again both men and women, described the healthy female in quite a different way: the healthy female, they said, is submissive, easily influenced, not adventurous, not competitive or aggressive, easily hurt emotionally, conceited about her appearance, and not objective.[33] Given such a definition of mental health, now or a century ago, it is no wonder that the confidence woman would be considered sick.

The difficulty in determining whether a woman is mentally ill or criminal lies not in the criminal woman nor in her actions, Smart says, but in "who is in a position not only to define mental illness but to enforce that definition, and also [in] whether these diagnoses are influenced by the double-standard of mental

---

32. Eileen B. Leonard, *Women, Crime, and Society: A Critique of Theoretical Criminology,* 82; Carol Smart, *Women, Crime, and Criminology: A Feminist Critique,* 147, 148, 159, 147–48.

33. Cited in Edwin M. Schur, *Labeling Women Deviant: Gender, Stigma, and Social Control,* 208.

health which applies to men and women."[34] If that double standard is still in force today, then it surely played a part in the labeling of criminal women in the late nineteenth century.

Although there are few direct statements by criminal confidence women of the nineteenth century—other than the heavily edited autobiographies of Sophie Lyons and May Churchill Sharpe—regarding their motivations for crime or their reactions to their success, the statements of criminal confidence women in the 1980s might give us some insight into whether women's crime was indeed madness or some more rational response in the late 1800s. In interviews with almost fifty criminal women of the 1980s, Susan Nadler discovered that most of the women who chose crime did not do so from a need for money, although this data is skewed because Nadler purposely chose to interview women who had come from the middle class, with all the advantages and value assumptions that go along with that background, in an effort to understand why some women choose to be criminal when there is no obvious reason to make that choice.[35]

What she found was that women who choose crime often do so as a way to free themselves from what they see as a restrictive role. Her interviewees consistently reported the "liberating" effect of crime, which is ironic since all the women interviewed were in prison. Before becoming embezzlers, burglars, and con artists, these women had been model wives and mothers or hardworking, straight-A students in elite private colleges. These were women who were or would have been successful if they had stayed inside their assigned roles. But they were not satisfied there.

Jo Ann Giorgio, a middle-class Italian woman and once an outstanding history student at a private eastern college, became a confidence woman in her early twenties and worked con games for fifteen years, making an average of $3,000 per week. She became known as the Contessa, commonly recognized to be the best con woman on the East Coast. The Contessa says she played the games in part because they gave her a surge of pleasure: "It fascinates me to win, the power. . . . Well, it's like a rush, it's love. . . . it's . . . sex." Completing a successful scam gave her a sense of overwhelming power that she could get nowhere else: "You own that person. You know, you're getting over on society. . . . You're . . . better than they are." Amber Fairchild, a black confidence woman of the 1980s, explains

34. Smart, *Women, Crime, and Criminology,* 156.
35. See Susan Nadler, *Good Girls Gone Bad.*

that for her "the thrill of the crime was strong."[36] She too played her criminal confidence games for something more elusive than money. In interview after interview, the same message comes across. The women "went bad" in order to shape, however antisocially, their own lives.

The confidence women who wrote about their criminal careers in the nineteenth century denied that they enjoyed their crimes, yet the energy and almost loving detail with which they write about their schemes and their successes lead the reader to discount their protestations as mere form. Certainly the criminal confidence women were not insane, but perhaps since they did not fit the prevailing concept of what a female criminal would look like, not much has been written about them from the criminologist's point of view.

In current analyses of the female criminal, the focus is not on gender attributes, as it was in the nineteenth century, but on such sociological determinants as women's relative access to the tools of crime and their opportunities for criminal apprenticeship. In 1895, G. T. W. Patrick noted a disparity between the number of male criminals and female, a disparity that could have been caused by some of the same factors that cause a similar disparity today: that society is not as quick to report and admit female crimes as male and that for women "social control in the form of informal sanctions . . . is imposed more consistently and for more minor deviations." Today, and certainly in the nineteenth century, "females are more closely supervised and more strictly disciplined" than males are, making it physically more difficult for women to become criminals.[37] If restrictions on and supervision of women are relaxed, the number of female criminals increases.

It is significant that of the twenty women Byrnes cites as professional criminals, almost all were immigrants, mainly from Ireland and Germany, some from England, and one from France. The confidence women Nash describes, except for Sophie Lyons, likewise were immigrants. They were not affluent and often were married to male criminals. One can imagine that these women were not as closely watched as the middle-class women of the time who were indoctrinated with and who internalized the code of "true womanhood," careful to do nothing that would mar their reputations. Then again, women like Sophie Lyons and May Churchill, who were intermittently quite well off, still chose to be swindlers, suggesting that the cause for crime is complex and could well involve a desire

36. Ibid., 104, 105, 173.
37. Dale Harrentsian, "The Nature of Female Criminality," 413, 416.

for a broader, more active life than the nineteenth-century stereotypes allowed. As May Churchill allegedly explained when she rejected a life of security with her rich husband's family, "I want to risk myself."

In the 1800s, criminal confidence women understood what "true womanhood" meant, even though they could not or refused to live that ideal, and they used the assumptions about women's piety, purity, domesticity, and submissiveness to their own advantage. In the 1970s and 1980s, the assumptions were different: the Contessa carried a briefcase when she pulled her scams and talked convincingly of stock options and police corruption. If she preferred to play the game in which she naïvely asked someone to hold her money for her, she had to pretend to be a foreigner. Amber Fairchild said she commonly pretended to be just arrived from South Africa when she played that game, wearing a dashiki and speaking in a heavy South African accent.[38]

As these interviews make clear, the criminal confidence woman is highly rational, whether we like the uses to which she puts her rationality or not. To call her insane would entail the use of a very dangerous extension of the definition of madness. Characteristically, however, the confidence woman herself sometimes uses the insanity label to her own advantage. Showalter tells the story of Augustine, a fifteen-year-old inmate of Jean Martin Charcot's institution for hysterics in nineteenth-century France. Charcot is famous for the photographs he made of women suffering from different types of mania. Augustine, who showed all the attributes of a confidence woman, was a favorite subject of his. The girl apparently loved being photographed: "Among her gifts was her ability to time and divide her hysterical performances into scenes, acts, tableaux, and intermissions, to perform on cue and on schedule with the click of the camera." Eventually, Augustine turned violent (as any normal fifteen-year-old imprisoned in an asylum might) and tried to leave the Salpêtriere. As a result, she was thrown into a locked cell. "But Augustine was able to use in her own behalf the histrionic abilities that for a time had made her a star of the asylum," Showalter explains. "Disguising herself as a man, she managed to escape."[39]

Henry Maudsley, a contemporary of Conolly's and a critic of his "moral insanity" theory, was skeptical about the genuineness of hysterics in general. He believed that there were "nowhere more perfect examples of the subtlest deceit, the most ingenious lying, the most diabolic cunning, in the service of

38. Nadler, *Good Girls Gone Bad,* 168.
39. Showalter, *The Female Malady,* 154 (both quotations).

vicious impulses."[40] Maudsley was referring specifically to hysterical invalids who indulged their desire for a petty tyranny over their husbands and families, but his skepticism would have been well placed if he had been noting the uses to which criminal confidence women sometimes put the symptoms of hysteria.

Ellen Peck, for instance, whom Thomas Byrnes called a "dangerous confidence woman" because she was so successful at her trade, used the insanity plea to her own advantage as a way of evading trial for her scam as a detective for a soap manufacturer. Several times she was released from the necessity of going to trial by claiming she was too ill to appear, and when she was finally given an ultimatum to appear in court, she suddenly went "insane" and was sent to an asylum. The soap manufacturer she had swindled gave in and dropped the criminal charges, opting for a civil suit instead. Peck quickly "found her wits again." Her husband ended up suing the soap manufacturer for $100,000 to make up for all the trouble that had been caused.[41]

Edith "the Swami" Salomen likewise succeeded in escaping imprisonment for fraud by stabbing an orderly in the hospital where she had been put while awaiting trial and by running through the hospital corridors shouting. She was adjudged insane and sent to an asylum, where she married one of her doctors, who immediately signed papers for her release. Once out of the hospital, Salomen returned to her confidence trade.[42] In addition to feigning mental illness, some confidence women used false physical illness to evade punishment. Herbert Asbury, in his study of early Chicago, tells a story about Kitty Adams, a strong-arm woman, who used the sickness ruse in a different way to get out of jail. Her confederate asked for a reprieve for Adams, saying she had a physical sickness: tuberculosis. Adams forthwith "punctured her gums with a toothpick and coughed and spat blood at such a rate that the sympathetic members of the Board were convinced she wouldn't live a week."[43] Once released from prison, Adams immediately picked up where she had left off when she was arrested. Sophie Lyons pretended to be sick when she first went to Sing Sing in order to get a less arduous job than most of the female prisoners had. She was given a position in the prison hospital, a circumstance that led to her being on hand to nurse the matron's ill child and from there to her escape.

40. Ibid., 134.
41. Byrnes, *1886 Professional Criminals,* 318.
42. Nash, *Look for the Woman,* 337.
43. Asbury, *Gem of the Prairie,* 123.

Labeling women insane rather than criminal is one method of denying criminality in women, and by extension of denying the existence of the confidence
woman. Other sorts of labels accomplish a similar denial. The concept of "female" crime is in itself a label that disguises the confidence woman under a
more stereotypical category and thereby minimizes her action. One example
of such minimization is the attitude toward shoplifting. This crime has been
defined as gender-related because women who shoplift are presumably extending their domestic roles rather than branching out into a nonfeminine sort of
crime. According to Carol Smart, most criminologists consider shoplifting "role-
expressive." This is in line with the way female deviance is understood now
and has been in the past, an understanding that "is based predominantly upon
biological or psychological drives and urges which are deemed to be peculiar
to the female constitution or psyche." Smart explains that female criminology
through the 1960s was similar to Lombroso's in the 1890s, postulating the "non-
cognitive, physiological basis of criminal actions by women." Promoting such
a theory is a form of social control, Smart says, for if women are criminal due
to some physical or psychological aberration, then they are not rebels or part
of a counterculture making a rational response to social conditions. It is also
social control in that being labeled has great power in determining one's self-
image, according to Eileen Leonard, who discusses this issue in her examination
of contemporary labeling theory.[44] If a woman thinks of herself as a rebel or as
"Queen of the Shoplifters," she will behave differently than if she thinks of herself
as sick, or as simply carrying out her biologically determined feminine role.

Calling shoplifting "role-expressive" is another way of silencing the confidence woman, reducing her power in society. In reality, shoplifting—as distinct
from kleptomania, the designation properly given to the shoplifting perpetrated
by certain middle-class women of the nineteenth century as an extension of the
era's consumerism, as Elaine S. Abelson explains—is very far from domestic in
the hands of women of the underclass and confidence women of all classes.[45]
Take for example the career of Mary Hodges in Chicago between 1861 and 1871.
Herbert Asbury in his study of the Chicago criminal world in the late nineteenth
century tells of how she was celebrated as the shoplifter and pickpocket "who
drove a cart into the shopping district several times a week and drove it away

44. Smart, *Women, Crime, and Criminology,* 10, 11, 27; Leonard, *Women, Crime, and
Society,* 66.
45. See Abelson, *When Ladies Go A-Thieving.*

loaded with plunder." Or take the career of Mollie Holbrook, who in 1865 organized a band of shoplifters and pickpockets. Such women—whether historically present or present only in legend—were not expressing any domestic role in their trade; rather, they were being aggressive thieves.[46]

One of the confidence arts that a shoplifter has to have is the ability to maintain an innocent expression even while the crime is being perpetrated. Byrnes explains that nonprofessional, middle-class, occasional shoplifters are easy to spot because of their guilty and furtive demeanor, their "frightened glance . . . sneaking attitude." The professional shoplifter, however, is a confidence woman, "ladylike," a "person of fair apparel" who has to know how to distract shopkeepers with her talk and how to slip merchandise into specially prepared pockets or purses. Kate Armstrong, one shoplifter Byrnes described, broke the stereotype of the emotional woman in the way she handled herself when on a job: "Her operations have been greatly aided by her respectable appearance and her perfect self-control."[47] If a shoplifter is caught in the act, she has to be able to talk her way out of arrest, most often by being sure that she never has more than one item in sight or easily found on her person at a time, having handed the other items to an accomplice or hidden them well, and by feigning indignation or flustered surprise that she had "forgotten" to pay for the one item in her hand. Being able to steal while maintaining an air of innocence takes, among other things, forethought. One has to enter the store prepared. Mary Boston in the 1890s had her daughter walk along with her under her voluminous skirt. The mother would knock an item onto the floor; the daughter would snatch it up and deposit it in one of the many hidden pockets sewn to her mother's underclothes.[48]

To label shoplifting "sex-related" and "role-expressive" is to trivialize the criminal boldness and intelligence professional shoplifters must have. The shoplifter is a confidence woman who makes a statement about sexual stereotyping by her very existence. She is a resister—albeit apolitical and not very far-thinking—not a conformist. Her actions also make an economic statement in a time when women were expected to dress well but for honest work were paid barely enough to survive. We misunderstand professional shoplifting, a form of the confidence game, when we reduce it to kleptomania, a stereotype about women and the home.

46. Asbury, *Gem of the Prairie,* 63, 99.
47. Byrnes, *1886 Professional Criminals,* 30–32, 209.
48. Asbury, *Gem of the Prairie,* 216.

The whole idea of calling women confidence artists seems to go against the grain of American society, yet the idea that women use deception and the lie is constantly reiterated. In 1950, in his classic study of female crime, Otto Pollak tried to explain the significant difference between the number of male criminals and the number of female ones by saying that female crime is "hidden."[49] This would have been the perfect opportunity for a criminologist to study the confidence woman, but Pollak saw the term *hidden* in a different light. He was referring to women's "constitutional" deceitfulness, and he analyzed it as a product of women's ability to pretend to have an orgasm, theorizing that it is in this act that all women practice lying. The "masked nature of female criminality" takes the form of child abuse, or of women's instigating men to do the dirty work. He speculated that women are just as criminal as men, but that they conceal their actions by committing crimes at home, so the statistics do not show the truth. Like Patrick and Lombroso, Pollak believed that when women go beyond petty crime done in the open they turn extremely violent, even more so than men, and do their best to hide their violence where no one will see it. Interpretations of female crime like Pollak's again label women's actions as either petty or violent. For Pollak, criminal women are not sick but malevolent, and whether their crime is trivial or horrible, criminal women are in effect the average woman taken to an extreme, not rebels, not unique individuals taking control of their own lives as they go against their society. The actions of the women remain constant; it is the unperceptive labeling that reduces an aggressive crime to something trivial.

Apparently female criminology has not advanced much in the last three-quarters of a century, although in the last two decades feminist criminologists have begun to initiate change. However, there remains a problem even with the new, feminist interpretations. The problem becomes clear in the extremely negative reaction that female criminologists have had to Freda Adler's book *Sisters in Crime,* in which she postulates that the women's movement of the 1970s has led to the increase in women's crime because women have begun to see that they can succeed as criminals in a way they hadn't dreamed of before. The criticism has stressed how Adler misinterprets statistics that show an astronomical increase in the percentage of female crime in the 1970s and 1980s without regard for the fact that the base for figuring the percentage change— the total number of female criminals at some date in the past, against which the new numbers are compared—was so small that only a few additional female

49. See Otto Pollak, *The Criminality of Women.*

criminals could make the percentages skyrocket, whereas even a small increase in the percentage of male crime, having a so much larger base of comparison, far outweighs the seemingly huge increase in female crime, numerically. If there are 100 female criminals, a 10 percent increase is 110. If there are 1,000 male criminals, a 5 percent increase is 1,050: the percent increase is less, but the numerical increase is 5 times greater. Adler's critics also take issue with her glorification of the new female violence, pointing out that most female crime is still nonviolent crime—property crime, especially larceny, or prostitution.

The problem I see in this debate is the vociferous rejection of Adler's thesis: that women's liberation also means a kind of liberation for female criminals. There still seems to be a desire to deny the possibility of serious criminality in women, as if there is something constitutionally different about women that makes them incapable of "real" crime. I take the increase in criminality in the 1970s and 1980s, however slight, to be a sign that some women are beginning to choose the life they will, to "risk" themselves, to strike out for autonomous self-definition in this antisocial way. It is unclear whether the women question the value system of the socioeconomic order that shapes their desire for gain or whether they imagine the destructiveness their actions can produce in others' lives, but the daring, the imagination, and the assertive attitude toward life are nevertheless worthy of study. In the nineteenth century, the "wonderfully multiplied" shoplifters that Byrnes mentions (even though we must remember that Byrnes identifies only twenty female criminals, compared to two hundred males) are additional evidence of a similar liberating trend. In the nineteenth century, the criminal confidence woman's assertiveness, her refusal to accept her role passively, would be even more significant.

A further kind of labeling also appears to have made it hard for us to recognize the criminal confidence woman: too often women who play a confidence game that happens to involve a sexual element are considered to be prostitutes instead of confidence women. Carol Smart has noted that when female juvenile delin-quents commit crimes, their crimes are "sexualized": larceny, a crime, becomes "incorrigibility," a personality disorder, for girls if there is a sex offense in any way involved. For instance, if a girl steals a car and then has sex, the sexual action takes precedence. She is called "incorrigible." The term does not change when boys commit the same crimes along with sexual offenses. If a boy steals a car and then has sex, he is a car thief. In a similar fashion, the confidence game becomes "sexualized," earns the label "prostitution," when the con woman uses sexual bait as part of her scheme, whether the sex act is completed or not.

Prostitution is considered by criminologists to be "role-expressive," a "field of deviance 'appropriate' to a woman's role," and therefore to be expected.[50] When a confidence game like the badger game or the panel house is mislabeled—reduced to an "appropriate deviance"—the true nature of the confidence woman is lost.

Allan Pinkerton tells the story of a confidence woman—although he does not give her that name—that shows how complicated the issue of sex becomes in some female crime. The woman, Helen Graham, accused a man, Mr. Ingalls, of "attacking her virtue." Ingalls stated that he had done no such thing, and that two men, apparently her accomplices, had demanded $500 to make things right. When he refused, she threw red pepper in his eyes and he had her arrested. Pinkerton explains that at the trial, "while Mr. Ingalls was relating his story, the fair prisoner was visibly affected, her face flushed and the tears welled up in her eyes, which a moment ago, were flashing with indignation. All of this was not lost upon the spectators who imagined that these emotions were the outgrowth of outraged honor and womanly feeling." But the judge had some information on Helen Graham, also known as Mary Freeland, that showed she had been involved in similar escapades in the past. "The mask was torn from the fair face, and she stood revealed as a beautiful fiend, whose seductive wiles had been the ruin of many who had been led by the witching spell of her charms into the abyss of moral destruction." This twofold description shows a split-second reversal from one stereotype to another: first the woman is an image of moral superiority, her virtuous emotions driven by moral outrage and personal humiliation; then the woman is unmasked as the temptress, the witch, the "fiend." There is no middle ground; if she is not an angel, she must be a devil. There is no place in this scheme for her to be what she really was—a small-time swindler.

Part of the reason for the extreme reaction is the sexual element in the extortion. Freeland had indeed used her sexual charms to lead the man on, in a typical form of the badger game. Freeland herself gave a sexual tone to the crime. However, Pinkerton's language in describing her "unmasking" is not the language one would expect in the discovery of a con artist; instead, it very closely resembles the standard nineteenth-century rhetoric used to condemn prostitution: she had led the man into "ruin," the "abyss of moral destruction." Pinkerton uses his most scathing tones as he recounts Mary Freeland's past, filled with cast-off lovers and blackmail schemes: "She was a sort of moral free-booter, no grade of society being too high and no degradation too low, for the operation of her

---

50. Smart, *Women, Crime, and Criminology*, 18, 13.

hellish designs."[51] Extorting $500 is not a "hellish design." Freeland's purpose was not to plunge the man into sin and "degradation" but to divest him of his money. Freeland used sexual stereotypes to play her larcenous game. Pinkerton reacted to the stereotypes rather than to the attempted extortion. To him and to the judge who would sentence her, she was not a small-time criminal, but a depraved sexual temptress, frighteningly attractive, a "beautiful fiend."

It is commonly agreed that prostitution is the stereotypically female crime, so much so that in many definitions prostitution is sex-specific, being said to be a woman's selling her body. Carol Smart shows how, like shoplifting, prostitution is considered "role-expressive," under the presumption that women normally "bargain" with sex to get married, which society considers an appropriate action. Bargaining for money instead of marriage becomes a crime but is an obvious corollary to the "appropriate" behavior. Although men are presumed to commit crimes for money as an expression of their tendency to be concerned with making a living as the breadwinner, women are presumed to commit crimes as an expression of their tendency to be concerned with "securing a mate or living vicariously through their men" as mere aiders and abettors. Thus, the only crime that has traditionally been thought "appropriate" to women, Smart says, "besides shoplifting, is sexual deviance."[52] Because these are the only two areas of crime that criminologists and members of law enforcement have considered appropriate for women, authorities even today often try to pigeonhole women's crimes into one of the two categories, unless the woman is seen as a pawn of the man involved or unless she has stepped over the line into murder. Once again the interpretation of women's actions devalues them. Such interpretations appear immediately absurd when applied to the actions of real women. Could May Churchill, for instance, who had to defend herself against being called a prostitute, be described as "securing a mate" or "living vicariously" when she brought a man to her "creep joint" for the sole purpose of distracting him long enough to allow a confederate to steal his wallet?

Whether prostitution is a form of the victimization of women or a form of women's free choice is not at issue here. The point I want to make is that prostitution itself, the exchange of sex for money, is not a confidence game,

51. Pinkerton, *Thirty Years a Detective,* 196, 200, 204. Pinkerton's lurid language is akin to the language of those "immoral reformers" that David S. Reynolds describes in *Beneath the American Renaissance.* The detective appears to delight in the titillation of the scene even as he pleads righteous indignation.

52. Smart, *Women, Crime, and Criminology,* 12–13.

while confidence games using prostitution as a front, like the badger game, are not prostitution. Therefore, to label con games associated with sex "prostitution" is a way to deny the existence of the confidence game, and therefore of the confidence woman. According to Lombroso's list of female crimes, such criminal activities as blackmailing, shoplifting, picking pockets, the panel-house game, and the badger game did not exist. Prostitution was the main nonviolent crime. It is easy to see how confidence women in the nineteenth century who used sexual appearances as part of their confidence game would be mislabeled. When sex—whether it includes intercourse or not—is a diversion for larceny, the sex is not the main crime. It acts as a cover for the real purpose. The woman is not a prostitute but a swindler.

One difference between prostitution and confidence schemes is obvious: prostitutes do not disguise their occupation. Mary Murphy, in a study of prostitution in the West, comments that common prostitutes do not try to deceive anyone; in fact, they must "advertise" their profession because they are in such dire competition with their peers.[53] One can see prostitution as a business, however insalubrious: from the small one-person business in which a woman, after paying her rent, sits in the window of her crib or stands at the door to bargain directly with her customer, to the lavish houses in which perhaps as many as forty women work, their elegant dresses and the fine furnishings all part of the business decor. The Everleigh sisters in Chicago in 1900 were straightforward businesswomen who built what some considered the most luxurious house of prostitution in the world. They were educated women with a handsome inheritance that they invested in a rational and businesslike way. Men would come from all over the country for a night of pleasure in a house that had $650 gold-plated spittoons, a gold-plated bathtub, and the services of prostitutes who were ladies in dress and decorum, bedecked with splendid jewels. The Everleighs hired the finest chef, often charging $50 a plate for dinner, and kept only the finest wine. The women stayed in business for twelve years, retiring with $1 million in cash and hundreds of thousands of dollars in jewelry, fine art, and furniture. Herbert Asbury remarks, "For them the wages of sin were economic security and a comfortable old age."[54]

The Everleigh sisters did not have to use confidence arts to be successful. They had plenty of success with their straightforward service, although it is

53. See Murphy, "Private Lives of Public Women," in Armitage and Jameson, eds., *The Women's West.*
54. Asbury, *Gem of the Prairie,* 247–54.

probable that everyday pretenses of constant gaiety and unabashed flattery of the male ego were involved. But to pretend that the Everleigh sisters and their employees "lived vicariously" or worked for any reason other than money is an effort to fit women who break the female stereotypes into some governable pattern. Asbury notes that if the women who worked for the Everleigh enterprise at $100 a week had left their employ and taken jobs that were legal, they would have been working in a factory or a department store for from $6 to $10 weekly. To be a prostitute with the Everleighs was a straightforward and rational choice, given the restrictions of the society at the time; it was also a rebellious choice, given the same restrictions.

My purpose, however, is not to deal with the definition of prostitution as a crime. Rather it is to argue against the confusion of confidence games with prostitution. A confidence game by its nature involves disguise, manipulation, and trickery. Prostitution usually does not, although whenever a prostitute pretends she loves her customer and is thrilled with his attentions, she becomes an everyday pretender. Madeleine, the pseudonym of a nineteenth-century prostitute who published her autobiography in 1919, talks about how different she was from the prostitutes who worked in the same house with her in Kansas City. The other prostitutes routinely made up stories for their clients about their childhoods and about how they came into prostitution, stories pathetic enough to suit the customers' desire to pity them. Likewise, the other prostitutes would pretend to drink liquor in order to sell more and would pretend to enjoy the customers' caresses; in fact, they would often avow love. Madeleine was considered a liability to the house because she refused to participate in any of these ruses (although she would at other houses later). Note the difference between this kind of conning, which is a sort of flattery meant to keep a customer coming back, and the kind of game a criminal confidence woman plays. The criminal confidence woman disguises who she is and what she wants; the prostitute merely disguises how she feels and tells lies about her past. When Madeleine left the bordello, her "landlady" cautioned her: "When other women speak of us you must assume an attitude of scorn, not only to protect yourself from suspicion, but that you may also feel it for yourself and have no temptation to return."[55]

Cassie Chadwick provides a good example of the distinction between the two types of criminal. She was a prostitute in a bordello after finishing a jail sentence

---

55. *Madeleine: An Autobiography,* 88. Other details in this paragraph are from pages 69 and 71.

for panhandling, but this was long before she conceived the Carnegie scam. At the bordello she met and conned a Leroy Chadwick into believing that her job at the house was to teach etiquette only. He believed her and ended up marrying her.[56] Hers was the manipulation of a confidence woman, and when the game worked, Cassie's days as a prostitute were over. According to the Contessa, prostitutes in the second half of the twentieth century are considered mere hustlers—"they're the lowest"—not even close to the prestige of a confidence artist.[57]

Some confidence women do use prostitution, or something similar to it, as one of their ruses. By criminologists' emphasizing the prostitution over the confidence scam, women's crime is harnessed by the stereotype. An example of a confidence scam that confuses the distinction between prostitution and swindling is a job Madeleine once did for a "Madame C" in Chicago. She pretended, at the madam's request, to be an innocent girl, lost in the big city, tricked by the madam into coming to the room of one of the madam's patrons, a millionaire. He would pay the girl and the madam for the pleasure of the seduction. "After he had accomplished the ruin of the girl he would compensate her with a sum of money, which sum depended upon her refinement, her education, her good looks, and whatever he estimated her loss to be; his price for a high-school girl was naturally greater than his price for a servant girl." Madeleine brought a high price because she was quite well read and always behaved in a ladylike manner. She discovered that the more she fought him off, the better he liked it, so that in the end she earned quite a bit of money. For the madam, supplying spurious virgins became a regular enterprise. "She had become so expert that men not only 'stood for it,' but they appeared to like it, since she again and again worked the same scheme on the same man."[58] Once, the millionaire discovered that the innocent girl he was with was not what she said she was, but he blamed the girl, not the madam, thinking that the madam had been tricked too.

Obviously, in this very profitable business of hers, the madam was involved not only in prostitution but also in a confidence game. The madam's joy in her own ability is the joy of the confidence woman, too: Madeleine remarks that "it is to be doubted, indeed, if her money could have procured for her one-half the pleasure she derived from her methods of obtaining it. After she had tricked some man out of a sum of money, and he had left the house with every expression of good

56. Nash, *Bloodletters and Badmen,* 119.
57. Nadler, *Good Girls Gone Bad,* 97.
58. *Madeleine: An Autobiography,* 108–9, 109.

will, Madame was in her element. She expanded and glowed with enthusiasm about her victim whom she considered a 'good sport' in submitting, with such good grace, to being duped."[59]

Prostitutes also needed a certain amount of confidence skill to pretend to be drinking in order to get the customer to buy more wine, since liquor sales accounted for most of the profit in a house of prostitution. The woman would empty her glass into a spittoon when the man was not looking or dance out of the room to dump the glass out—unless, of course, the "liquor" in her glass was simply colored water in the first place. But sometimes the game required more skill. Once Madeleine and her friend Olga sold a drunken man the same bottle of liquor several times.[60] This maneuver is an old confidence scam and should be recognized as such.

Madeleine describes a more complicated confidence game she played at one assignation house. Men who came to such houses presumed they were paying for sex with "respectable" women: not common prostitutes, but housewives or working women who sold their bodies only occasionally and by stealth. But the truth was that Madeleine and the other women like her had rooms in the house, and it was necessary for them to take steps to make it look as if they had come to the house for just that one time. They would put on a coat and walk around outside for a while "in order to acquire an outdoor glow." However, the game went much further than that. "To the men we met we were anything that the occasion might require. We were married women, widows, girls from good homes, working-girls, business girls, professional women, or whatever else the men in question had ordered." She and another woman did their work well. "Since we were both intelligent girls of modest demeanor, who let the men do most of the talking, we encountered no difficulty in playing the different roles we assumed."[61] Like the confidence women Byrnes describes, Madeleine used "womanliness" as a disguise, her silence being her version of "fast talk."

Most of the women who came to the assignation house, Madeleine says, were "the real articles of which we were the spurious representatives." Those other women were not confidence women; Madeleine was. Again the difference between prostitution and the confidence game is clear. Of course, these other

59. Ibid., 114.
60. Ibid., 69, 141.
61. Ibid., 188–89.

women then went home, wearing what Madeleine calls "the Mantle of Respectability," a small confidence art, perhaps, unless it is better called hypocrisy.[62]

When Madeleine became a madam herself, she discovered that she had to use a certain amount of trickery to keep obstreperous customers and the police at bay. Mary Murphy describes a similar kind of game-playing among the madams of the West. For the most part, Murphy says, the madams, unlike confidence women who played on the womanly ideal, in an indirect way *filled* the ideal, for "they kept a house; they played the role of mother to their 'girls'; they wielded influence and used their sexuality behind the scenes, rarely making overt use of what power they may have had." Actually filling the ideal of the true woman to some degree, rather than merely pretending to, the madam did not pretend to be *other* than a madam. But at times she was forced to play a game in order to obtain protection from the police and the courts, using her "skill and charm to play upon men's vanities" as a way to avoid arrest or fines. She also used her "subtle game" to manage unruly clients.[63] In this case, however, the prostitute is using a confidence art, quite different from a confidence woman using prostitution.

The panel workers and strong-arm women are examples of confidence women using prostitution as a disguise for additional crimes. Both of these types lure men to a house or an alley with the promise of selling sex—which they sometimes did—but with the primary intention of robbing the men, sometimes using violence. Such women are certainly not engaging in a "role-expressive" activity. Asbury remarks on the astonishing number of strong-arm gangs after the Civil War and on the success their members had, much of which was due to men's being ashamed to admit they had been taken by women. Such reticence on the part of the victims and the corollary reticence of the women themselves can explain the sparsity of information on criminal confidence women of this type.

A final example of how something like prostitution was part of some complicated confidence scams is May Churchill's career as "Queen of the Badgers." The badger game was one of the most common criminal confidence games women played in the nineteenth century. It relied on illicit sex, or at least the promise of it, and on the consequent social disapproval; therefore it was easily mistaken for

---

62. Ibid., 189, 190.

63. Murphy, "Private Lives of Public Women," in Armitage and Jameson, eds., *The Women's West*, 196, 201.

simple prostitution. But an examination of "Chicago May's" practice can make the distinction clear.

Churchill, who gave up her marriage to a rich man for the thrill of the confidence arts in the 1890s, was beautiful, according to the *New York Times:* she had "eyes that were large and brilliant and teeth wonderfully white. Her features were baby-like in their soft roundness, and she made a picture of sweet innocence." Churchill used her appearance well, first to attract a man, then to distract him: "She would begin by inviting a wealthy admirer to a smartly decorated apartment used only for business purposes. May would make passionate love to the gentleman . . . while plying her lover with drugged champagne. When the caller passed out, May would take his valuables and wallet, throw his clothes out the window, and depart." Her male confederate would be at the victim's side when he awoke, saying that May's husband had taken her away and was enraged enough to sue—unless he could be bought off. Churchill's trade was quite profitable. She worked in New York and Chicago, modernizing the game by introducing cameras installed behind false walls, a refinement of the game that some say she invented, although she credited her lawyer with the idea. Once the United States became too "hot" for her to remain here, she went to Europe, where she blackmailed lawyers and the sons of the nobility.[64] It is apparent that the badger game could pay well and that, although it sometimes used sex and a form of prostitution, it was a property crime first, not a sexual one.

The criminal confidence woman has in large part been lost to our cultural imagination. She has been labeled insane or sick, stereotyped as a prostitute or a shoplifter, or disregarded altogether. I would like to see more serious study of these nineteenth-century women, who Byrnes said "wonderfully multiplied" in the 1870s and about whom Asbury and Nash have found so much to write. Losing them altogether would be a significant loss for the American woman's heritage.

The Noncriminal Confidence Woman

The Adventuresses

Whereas the criminal confidence woman has become dim in our national memory, the adventuress of the nineteenth century is still distinct. Because she stayed

64. Nash, *Look for the Woman,* 81, 82, 83.

within the law most of the time, the adventuress does not call up the specter of the female criminal; she seems less dangerous because she makes a gesture toward following the rules. Thomas Byrnes uses the term *adventuress* to describe those women who operated in the gray area between outright crime and conventional behavior. Models for artists, women who acquired gloves and trinkets from various men, women who provided only one meal a day for themselves and found men to buy the other two were all adventuresses in the nineteenth century. Betty Van Deventer would rank adventuresses as the less proficient sort of gold digger. Theodore Dreiser's sister, who provided the model for his character Carrie Meeber in *Sister Carrie,* is one adventuress who is familiar to most American literary scholars. The older woman who would repeatedly set up a boardinghouse and run it on borrowed money until she went bankrupt, then move to a different part of town to start over was an adventuress, too. One of the most imaginative of the adventuresses Byrnes describes is the woman who "engineered beggars." She would find as many scruffy children as she could, add some artistic touches to enhance their impoverished look, then line them up and down the streets leading from wherever the current high-society ball was being held. Tipsy party-goers often gave alms freely; the "engineer" would, of course, get a good percentage of the take. This woman came as close to being a criminal as she could without stepping over the line. Byrnes notes that such women were on the increase in the 1880s.[65]

Another form of adventuress is the spiritualist: table rapper, fortune-teller, medium, automatic writer. The Fox sisters, Margaretta, Catherine, and Leah, were the most famous of the mediums and supposedly began the nineteenth-century upsurge of spiritualism in 1848. They made much money from seances and large-scale performances in which the dead allegedly communicated with members of the audience. Margaretta and Catherine both admitted they were frauds in 1888, although they recanted later. Their famous "rappings" were apparently made by cracking the joints of their toes against wood. Madame Blavatsky, the founder of modern-day Theosophy, was believed by many to be a fraud, and Leonora Piper was another spiritualist whose fraudulent claim to be a medium for a dead French cavalry officer was at last found out.[66]

---

65. Byrnes, *1886 Professional Criminals,* 372–74.
66. See Paul Kurtz, *The Transcendental Temptation: A Critique of Religion and the Paranormal,* for a discussion of spiritualism in late-nineteenth-century America, especially p. 343, for information on the Fox sisters.

In 1947, Violet McNeal wrote an autobiography—*Four White Horses and a Brass Band*—in which she details her experience as a fraudulent medicine woman. Beginning in 1904, at the age of sixteen, she became enamored of and later married a man twice her age who brought her into the trade slowly, by having her "read minds"—that is, memorize an alphabet code so that she could make it seem that she was reading the mind of someone who had whispered a secret to her partner. The two went from Chicago to Oklahoma City to Denver to Vancouver to St. Louis to Kansas City; McNeal thus is one of the few confidence women I have found who concentrated on the Midwest. As her husband/confederate fell more and more under the sway of opium, McNeal took over the trade, becoming, she says, the first medicine woman since "Madame DuBois" (about whom she says no more). McNeal dressed in oriental clothing to make her concoctions seem more magical. One especially good seller was a pill for potency, which she would describe in explicit detail. Eventually, McNeal was earning enough to buy diamonds and fine clothes, although her husband (actually, Will McNeal was a polygamist, so the marriage was a fraud, too) lost most of the money gambling. Finally, McNeal struck off on her own with another woman as her aide. They used an alligator for what she calls "ballyhoo": to get the crowd to come over. McNeal would pretend to hypnotize the alligator by turning it on its back so that it could not turn over until she nudged it. She worked in the years before World War I in a scam that did not have much to do with her gender, an interesting turnabout from the kinds of games women were more likely to play in the nineteenth century.

Most women like Violet McNeal are not well known. Others made the headlines and have continued to pique our imaginations. Two such well-known adventuresses are the Claflin sisters, Tennessee and Victoria (Woodhull). Our awareness of these women, however, focuses more on their political theories about feminism and free love than on their less salubrious activities. But Victoria Woodhull is a perfect example of how less than strictly upright behavior can pave the way for effective, vigorous rebellion later on, since she moved from a shady youth to an outspoken adulthood, becoming a force in the fight for women's rights. Both women considered themselves to be clairvoyants from the time they were children. Tennessee had the more famous career as a clairvoyant and magnetic healer because their father made her alleged gift into a business, whereas Victoria was married off young, also for money. It was commonly acknowledged that Buck Claflin was a confidence man himself, keeping his family on the road as town after town became too dangerous for him to live in. One of Tennessee's more profitable fraudulent operations was the "cancer infirmary" her father and she, as his minion, ran in Almira, Ohio. Tennessee pretended to be a doctor administering miracle cures. One of her patients died of breast cancer after submitting to various painful "treatments" Tennessee had prescribed, resulting in a warrant for her arrest. The charge was manslaughter, the warrant made out after a committee of doctors went to the infirmary and saw the pitiable condition of the patients there. The Claflins had already fled town. In this case, Tennessee crossed the line into criminality by mistake, blurring the categories as so many adventuresses did. Tennessee was a well-known quack doctor, much in the mode of Violet McNeal, having her name on an elixir that was advertised as a cure for almost every ailment imaginable. Roxanna Claflin, her mother, helped in that enterprise; there are stories about Tennessee and her mother concocting the brew.[67]

Victoria did not sell her "gift" as crudely as Tennessee did, but then, she was not under the tutelage of her father. Rather, Victoria set out her sign, wherever she was, as a fortune-teller. Twice she made tours through the South, earning a small fortune in the doing. Once she went under an alias—Mrs. Harvey—until she and her paramour were discovered by their respective spouses. Just how fraudulent Victoria Woodhull's clairvoyance was is debatable. She claimed to believe in her trances and visions, although when she and Tennessee called up spirits, including Shakespeare and Rembrandt, at clients' request during their seances, conscious trickery was clearly involved.

The most famous of Woodhull's adventurings was her assistance to Cornelius Vanderbilt, the financial mogul: she began a lucrative career on Wall Street using money she had earned by giving Vanderbilt financial tips from the great beyond. Woodhull is a good example of a confidence woman as prototype of the modern feminist because of her grand designs, her great vigor and intelligence, and her later transformation into a vocal member of the feminist movement. Woodhull had had a vision as a girl that she would be not only rich and famous but also a world leader. The first two she became; the last she made a bid for by running for the presidency even before women had the vote. In her own time, Woodhull was feared by many, for her ideas and her personality overturned too many expectations about womanhood. It is significant that even in the twentieth century, biographies of Woodhull play down her association with fortune-telling, giving her tours a sentence or two. The emphasis has been on her political and feminist characteristics, with very little information on her confidence games, as if that side of her has to be denied if we are to respect her other attributes.

67. Johanna Johnston, *Mrs. Satan: The Incredible Saga of Victoria C. Woodhull.*

Adventuresses were an energetic element in women's history, deserving of more serious study than they have received so far.

The Soldiers and Spies

Some of the most outstanding confidence women of the nineteenth century were those who participated in the Civil War as soldiers and spies. They had the élan of many of the adventuresses, but were not motivated by a desire for money or improved social status. Perhaps it is because the soldiers and spies had a reputable cause for which they used their confidence skills that they, alone among the confidence women before the turn of the century, wrote their own stories, telling in detail about their disguises and ploys.

Because the rhetoric of confidence women writing about their own experiences is quite different from the rhetoric that a sensationalist historian uses, I devote an entire chapter to the image of the confidence woman we derive from autobiographies written by both criminal and noncriminal confidence women, some of the most detailed of which were written by spies and soldiers. The important point is that, despite their popularity in their own day, female spies and soldiers have largely been eradicated from our cultural memory, although many books for children carry short biographies of some of them. Since these stories have been relegated to juvenile literature, it is no surprise that our culture has discounted them. Just recently, however, a serious historian, Richard Hall, has looked closely at the stories of some of the women who fought in the Civil War in his book *Patriots in Disguise* (1993). This is a sign that, now that women's studies has created a place for itself in the academy, the lives of women formerly discounted have begun to be recovered.

Like the criminal confidence woman, the soldier and spy boldly broke stereotypes, sometimes stepping into male territory so completely that people firmly believed they were men. Female Civil War soldiers and spies—including women such as Belle Boyd, Rose O'Neal Greenhow, S. Emma Edmonds, and Loreta Velazquez—represent some of the strongest personalities in American history. Their actions had important effects on the course of the war, and their books brought a highly unusual image of American womanhood before the reading public, although it was an image that people could separate from their stereotypes about women and accept as exceptions to the rule mainly because the war condition was unique. However, the activity of many of the soldiers and spies did not end with the war, for these were women who went looking for excitement.

In some cases their careers after the war went in directions that were still far from conventional. Belle Boyd, for instance, went on to become an actress. Loreta Velazquez, according to her own account, did some smuggling and counterfeiting, then traveled with one husband to South America on a confidence scheme and with another husband, when that one died, to the Far West to dig for gold. But the motivations of and confidence arts used by the female soldiers and spies are much too complex to deal with here. Instead, before looking at these women closely in the next chapter, I would like to consider some women who border on being confidence women in order to set the boundaries of the term.

The Escape Artists and Everyday Pretenders: Contrasting Forms

Some women in the nineteenth century used confidence arts to one degree or another without becoming full-fledged confidence artists or adventuresses. Several women, whom I style "escape artists," had a moment in which they used disguise and deception, often with the same kind of flair common to confidence women and female spies, to evade some physical or emotional harm. The difference is that these women played their game once, for a particular goal, then put the disguise aside and returned to a normal (and often better) life. The similarity is that many of the techniques the women used are those of the professional confidence women and spies. In history, the most common escape was an escape from slavery, but the fiction of the time describes escapes from jails, bandits, and cruel fathers or husbands. In reading fiction written in the late nineteenth century, one is more likely to run into these escape artists than full-fledged confidence women.

One popular escape artist, who toured the country as living proof of her astonishing performance, was Ellen Craft, a slave whose skin color was almost white. In *Running a Thousand Miles for Freedom,* her husband gives a description of the journey he and she made from Macon, Georgia, to Philadelphia in 1848.[68] In the escape, Ellen Craft not only dressed as a man, she dressed as a middle-class white man, so her disguise crossed gender, race, and class lines. This story was so popular that William Wells Brown used it as the basis for his novel, *Clotel.*

Criminal confidence women, adventuresses, soldiers and spies, and escape artists were all very unusual types of women. They were rebels against a system

---

68. See William Craft, *Running a Thousand Miles for Freedom; or, The Escape of William and Ellen Craft from Slavery.*

that denied them freedom and growth. There is certainly an important difference between, on the one hand, the criminals and adventuresses who took their rebellion beyond the pale of legality, fueled by greed as much as by a desire for self-assertion, and on the other hand the soldiers and spies whose motivation was much more altruistic—they deceived for The Cause, whether it was for the Union or the Confederacy. Different again were the escape artists, who did not think of themselves as professionals in the art of deceit, as the other women did. Their rebellion was limited to effecting a change in their life circumstances, the deceit temporary and under duress. If some of these women went on to fight for an idea they believed in, to become revolutionists, like Harriet Tubman, that was a separate action, usually a straightforward one.

Harriet Tubman is a good example of an escape artist who used confidence arts infrequently. She typically did not use disguise in her rescues of slaves. Rather, she used fortitude and audacity—driving slaves out of the danger zone in a wagon, in plain daylight, struggling through the swamps and keeping up the morale of the group by threatening to shoot anyone who thought about turning back. However, there is one instance recorded in which she did use disguise and her ability to act. Earl Conrad, in his biography of Tubman, refers to a letter by Colonel Thomas Higginson, who "never ceased to marvel over her facility as an actress." Apparently, Tubman would often pretend to be an old woman, harmless and therefore essentially invisible. One time, she decided she needed to go into a small town where "one of her former masters" lived. Conrad quotes a newspaper article saying that "her only disguise was a bodily assumption of age," but she also carried, as cover, some live chickens. "As she turned a corner," the article reports, "she saw coming toward her none other than her old master. . . . she loosed the cord that held the fowls and amid the laughter of the bystanders, gave chase to them as they flew squawking over a nearby fence."[69]

Criminal confidence women and escape artists such as Harriet Tubman were obviously very different from one another. One thing these women had in common, however, was the courage to take charge of their own lives, even at great risk.

Recently, historians have begun to discuss another kind of woman of that time period who deceived her community on a regular basis, a kind of woman

69. Earl Conrad, *Harriet Tubman,* 70. Conrad quotes Colonel Thomas Wentworth Higginson's *Cheerful Yesterdays,* 8, and takes his description of the incident from an article by Frank C. Drake in the *New York Herald,* September 22, 1907.

who is less threatening to the female stereotypes our culture has long believed in. I call such women "everyday pretenders"; they are women who used disguise and deception in their daily lives in order to maintain the appearance of gentility or peaceful domestic life. The recently published diaries and letters of Madge Preston, a woman who kept a diary during the years 1862 to 1867 and simultaneously wrote copious letters to her daughter, give us one example of an everyday pretender. An examination of the two sets of documents side by side, which Virginia Beauchamp has done, reveals Preston to have been living a life of deception, at least during this five-year period, for in her letters she masks the self and the life that she shows in her private diaries, and she does it for a purpose: to pretend to her daughter and to the world that she and her marriage fit the womanly ideal.

In reality, Madge Preston was waging what Beauchamp calls her "private war" against her abusive husband. In her diary, Preston records her husband "striking [her] to the floor almost senseless." He hits her with his cane and beats her in the face so repeatedly that she must go to a doctor to find a remedy for the headaches and earaches that result. The doctor explains to her that she is not suffering from a cold, the ailment she pretends to consider the cause of her problems, but from a "violent concussion." By February 1865, after almost three years of abuse, Preston finally admits to herself that her husband is "insane" and "dangerous." In her diary at least, Madge Preston is eventually honest with herself. But for her daughter, and for the friends and teachers who will read the letters she writes, Preston describes her home life as idyllic, her husband as caring and overworked. At Easter in 1865 she tells her daughter "I never deceive you in anything" even as she explains that she is "not well enough" to go from home. The reality, as evidenced by her diary, is that Preston has in fact not recuperated from an earlier, quite savage beating. Beauchamp points out another illustrative example of Madge Preston's conscious duplicity. For one spring day, there is a gross contradiction between Preston's diary entry and the letter she wrote to her daughter that evening. In the diary it is clear that on a walk that day her husband does something with her niece that causes "evident agitation and embarrassment" for all parties concerned. Preston suspects that her husband and her niece are sexually involved, and apparently they do not try very hard to hide the liaison. But in her letter to her daughter, she describes the same walk as a romantic springtime outing; it is all peach trees in bloom.[70]

70. Beauchamp, ed., *A Private War,* 171, 177, 159, 176, 105–6.

Madge Preston created a fiction about her own life, expressly for her audience: she herself did not consider her marriage ideal, but she went to great lengths to give that impression to others. Still, I do not consider her a confidence woman. Criminal confidence women, adventuresses, and soldiers and spies all had a professional attitude toward their deceptions. They often threw off their disguises once the game was played to relish the reactions of those they had gulled. They enjoyed talking about their deceit and formed their self-definitions around their talents for masquerade. In this way, confidence women were like actresses, except that their audiences were not in on the fact that a drama was taking place. This attitude is very different from the attitude of Madge Preston, who did not revel in her deceit; in fact, one has to find it for oneself by contrasting her diary with her letters. The story she told about herself had no further purpose than to allow her to maintain her social position. She wanted people to believe that she was a happy wife, that her marriage was ideal. In this way she avoided the stigma of being labeled a failure, a woman with a "bad" marriage. Preston was an everyday pretender because she recognized that her marriage had in fact failed, but she worked hard to create the illusion that all was well. She represents those women in the nineteenth century who tried to uphold their public facade despite private woes, who seemed not to struggle with their condition, but whose public equanimity masked a private agitation. How many such women there were can only be guessed. Only when more private diaries are found and read can the prevalence of women like Madge Preston be reasonably estimated. The search for such women has begun, as Beauchamp's excellent study shows. The search for the confidence woman, however, still needs to leave the realm of the informal, sensationalist historian and the compiler of biographies for juvenile readers and enter this realm of serious discussion.

Such discussion could turn in several directions. Looking at the everyday deceptions of some women, for instance, the question arises whether "passing" constitutes a confidence game. Then passing itself bifurcates into color and gender issues. Passing can be defined as the ability to convince others that one is a member of a socially acceptable group despite one's actual alliance with an unacceptable (or less acceptable) one: a black woman passes for white if her skin, hair, and facial features are similar enough to white women's; a lesbian woman passes for straight; a woman passes for a man. Passing thus leads inevitably to a discussion of the relationship of the confidence arts to transvestism, a topic that leads into another complex of issues.

I will here take a quick look at each form of passing in turn, and then I will expand in Chapter 3 on the important connections to the confidence women who used passing in their games. In the first case, black people passing for white, passing is almost wholly dependent on nature—and the willingness to leave one's family and friends if the deception can work no other way. It can be as simple as not mentioning one's heritage or as complex as learning a whole new culture. Racial passing is complicated by the definitions of race. In the South in the nineteenth century, one was considered black if one had any black ancestry at all. The incentive to pass for white was strong in antebellum America because of the increasingly stringent proslavery laws. After the war, retribution against blacks continued to make passing an appealing alternative.

There is little data on black Americans passing for white, but much speculation. In his history of Negroes in America, written in the 1960s, Lerone Bennett states that hundreds of thousands of mulattoes passed for white, but there has not been much proof forthcoming. Even with the current interest in black women's personal narratives and fiction, little evidence for passing has been found. In nineteenth-century America, however, there would have been strong reasons for people of mixed ancestry to pass, for, according to Winthrop Jordan in his study of American attitudes toward blacks, the division between white and black was absolute; there was no hierarchy of mulattoes as in the English colonies in the Caribbean.[71]

The rewards for passing the color line were therefore very great in America, both in the antebellum South, where being black meant slavery or the extreme danger of it, and in the North, where being black meant social ostracism and little employment. If one succeeded in passing, then, there was no going back without severe loss, making it quite understandable that when a woman passed the color line she was silent about it, leaving us no historical record. However, despite the significant rewards for passing, certain conditions in America worked against it. For example, society's lack of mobility after the Civil War precluded many opportunities for passing that would otherwise have existed. After the war, black people had very little chance to move, being for the most part isolated in small towns or on farms in the South. By the turn of the century, when blacks began to move to the North and into the cities, passing was less and less countenanced by the black community because of a rising consciousness of and pride in racial heritage. Finally, as miscegenation decreased after the war because of the growing virulence of race hatred, there were increasingly fewer people

71. Lerone Bennett Jr., *Before the Mayflower: A History of the Negro in America, 1619–1964;* Winthrop D. Jordan, *White over Black: American Attitudes toward the Negro, 1550–1812,* 174.

of mixed race with skin light enough to make passing a temptation, as James Kinney points out in his recent study of miscegenation in America.[72] Still, some passing most certainly did occur. Those women who did pass would perforce be everyday pretenders, living a life of disguise and deception, but upholding the color line by not revealing the truth.

One famous case of passing that is pretty well documented is the case of Lucy Parsons, wife of Albert Parsons, the famous anarchist who was once nominated to run for president of the United States on the Socialist Labor Party ticket and who was ultimately hanged for his alleged part in the Haymarket bombing. According to Paul Avrich, who included a short biography of Lucy Parsons in his book *The Haymarket Tragedy,* when people asked Lucy what her background was, because she was rather dark-skinned, she said she was the child of John Waller, a Native American, and Marie Del Gather, a Mexican woman.[73] However, Lucy Parsons's biographer Carolyn Ashbaugh has found convincing evidence that Parsons was in fact born a slave on the plantation owned by James and Philip Gathings in Hill County, Texas. When Lucy and Albert married in 1872, Lucy apparently evaded the Texas laws banning miscegenation by creating fictional parents. Lucy Parsons kept up the pretense of being a Mexican-Indian woman all her life. After her husband's execution in the late 1880s, she became famous in her own right as an editor of various anarchist journals, as a public speaker, and as the editor of her husband's papers. She lived a life of deception in the racial disguise she created, but her motivation was more activist than most everyday pretenders, since her purpose was to join the system in order to change it. Perhaps, for her, passing was akin to soldiering and spying because it helped a cause. The difference is that the disguise lasted a lifetime. Ellen Craft, on the other hand, participated in a kind of "passing" that was momentary, lasting no more than a few days. Her motivation was escape, and her complex and innovative disguise was quite different from the social disguise Lucy Parsons and most women who passed had to create, for their motivation was long-term social acceptance, while hers was escape to a place where her real race was accepted.

In the case of lesbian women passing for straight, the deception was relatively easy, since in nineteenth-century America sex between women—at least of the middle class—was considered impossible. According to Lillian Faderman, good

---

72. James Kinney, *Amalgamation! Race, Sex, and Rhetoric in the Nineteenth-Century American Novel,* 22–25.
73. Paul Avrich, *The Haymarket Tragedy,* 11–12.

middle-class women in the nineteenth century were considered to have no sex drive, so even if they were caught in bed together in an embrace they were seen merely as loving friends, possibly seen so even by themselves. As the century moved toward its close, "new women" often had the chance to live together because they had become financially independent of men, but the relationship was seen as "pure" since women were naturally of a higher moral stature than men. Also, since the Civil War, the scarcity of men made two women living together seem like common sense. As long as there was no cross-dressing, sex was considered impossible: instead, such love was seen as "ennobling," according to Becky Butler. So many women were involved in this kind of long-term monogamous love relationship (as Faderman describes it) that the alliance was called a "Boston marriage" and was accepted by the community as such, the sexual issue not arising unless one of the women was an actress (and therefore likely to be debauched), looked masculine, or seemed insane. It was only in the 1920s that lesbian passing would begin in earnest because by that time European attitudes toward female sexuality had taken hold in America. Love between women in America after World War I became a "deformity" and a "disease" that at that point made passing necessary.[74]

Among the everyday pretenders, the women who passed for men would seem to come the closest to being confidence women, but transvestism in itself does not create a confidence game. It, like the other two forms of passing, is in the realm of everyday pretending. In escapes less dramatic than Ellen Craft's but demanding a similar rebelliousness, some women dressed like men so they could move freely in a society that allowed many more options for men than for women. For instance, female soldiers, by pretending to be men, escaped the secondary roles of nurse or camp follower to play a primary role in combat. However, such women did not subvert the male/female relationship by their actions—they simply "traded roles," to use Julie Wheelwright's words. Wheelwright concludes that these women found personal freedom during the time that they were in disguise but at the price of "wholesale adoption of what are seen as male values." Jonathan Ned Katz, in his documentary history of gays and lesbians in America, argues on the other hand that women who passed for men were sometimes revolutionists of a sort: "A basic feminine protest is a recurring theme in all

74. Lillian Faderman, *Surpassing the Love of Men: Romantic Friendship and Love between Women from the Renaissance to the Present*, 147–56, 178–89, 254–98; Becky Butler, ed., *Ceremonies of the Heart: Celebrating Lesbian Unions*, 21, 24.

these lives, appearing sometimes as a conscious, explicit feminism, other times as an inchoate, individual frustration, an only partly verbalized discontent, a yearning to break through the narrow bounds of the traditional female role— sometimes as a most pragmatic female survival tactic." Yet he sees, too, that however personally self-affirming transvestism could be for women, "their act of 'passing' implicitly confirmed this social definition"—that only men could have personal power. In addition, some of the women whose lives Katz documents suffered guilt and self-questioning for their actions. He says of their deception that "this inauthenticity might mean a life of fantasy, mental confusion and loss of reality possibly leading to madness." Such emotional distress was interpreted in 1886, by Richard Von Kraft-Ebing, a sexologist, as proof that women who tried to enter male pursuits were diseased psychologically—and by extension that women who dressed like men were even more ill, an example of the kind of labeling that undermines the assertiveness of women's actions.[75] It is clear that women who tried to create stable identities with their disguise were not confidence women, for the essence of a confidence game is that the artist is in full control, never "confused" about what the reality is. It is in part for this reason that a confidence woman's use of passing as a deceptive technique was more subversive than long-term passing of the kind Katz is speaking about. The confidence woman's ability to stand outside of her own masquerade gives her action a different meaning; the fact that she intentionally performed a typical man's actions while still fully aware of her femininity undermined the stability of the expected womanly role.

As a way to understand that difference, we might look at the story of Murray Hall, a woman who took on the guise of a man as a way of life. Hall could be considered an everyday pretender because she continued the disguise for twenty-five years, until her death from breast cancer. A political power in Tammany Hall and well received socially, Hall could drink whiskey and smoke cigars with the best of them, having "the apparent relish and gusto of the real man-about-town." Hall tried very hard not to step outside her new gender role: affidavits from many different people attested to how completely they had believed that Hall was a man. Hall had, over the twenty-five-year period, two wives and an adopted daughter. Although the wives presumably knew of Hall's deception, the adopted

---

75. Wheelwright, *Amazons and Military Maids,* 12, 70, 153. Katz, *Gay American History,* 209, 210.

daughter says she never questioned her father's masculinity.[76] Murray Hall's transformation was so complete, it is as if she on some level believed herself to be a man. Confidence women, however, take on the male guise for a short period of time and for a specific purpose; they trick others but never try to trick themselves.

The whole issue of transvestism becomes very sticky because women's motivations for wearing men's clothing were so very diverse. For some women, the clothing could have been a form of eroticism, as Marjorie Garber suggests in *Vested Interests,* although presumably in the nineteenth century such eroticism would have been less recognized than in the twentieth, when female sexuality has been more openly admitted. More often, the clothing was a way to escape social strictures of one type or another, which can tend more or less toward the confidence arts.

For instance, there were some lesbian couples who used disguise to fit into society without having to pretend about the true nature of their relationships; one member of the couple would choose to pretend to be a man rather than pretending to be merely friends with her partner. Such women's use of men's clothes could border on a confidence game. In America, one of the most famous couples of this sort was Annie Hindle, a male impersonator and actress, and Annie Ryan. The two were married in 1886 in Grand Rapids, Michigan, and lived peacefully in the community as husband and wife. According to a *Chicago Herald* article that appeared at the time of Ryan's death, Hindle was renowned for the "wonderful accuracy of her mimicry" in England, where she began her career as a male impersonator, and in America, where in 1867 she became New York's first true impersonator of her kind. Apparently Hindle married Ryan under the name Charles Hindle, wearing male attire for the wedding, but thereafter dressed like a woman, even though the couple "live[d] together openly as man and wife."[77] This contradiction may be in part explained by Annie Hindle's occupation. Having been a male impersonator puts Hindle in a different category from everyday women who donned men's clothing; it suggests that Hindle—and the community—

76. Katz, *Gay American History,* 232–38, gives long excerpts from several days of copy from various newspapers, including the *New York Times* and the *New York Tribune,* beginning January 19, 1901, and ending March 20, 1901.

77. Erna Olafson Hellerstein, Leslie Parker Hume, and Karen M. Offen, *Victorian Women: A Documentary Account of Women's Lives in Nineteenth-Century England, France, and the United States,* 185, 188–89.

thought of her disguise more as a game. It is interesting that the two were allowed to live together without legal repercussions, unusual for a case in which two women are "legally" married and one member of the couple sometimes wears men's clothes. According to Faderman, it is the wearing of male attire that raises the question of lesbianism and that elicits a strong reaction from the community; but, also according to Faderman, actresses and other socially suspect women who transgressed in this way did not raise the ire of the community the way a middle-class woman behaving this way did, although in the nineteenth century the community would have been more ready to presume that the liaison was sexual if an actress were involved.[78]

A final example of the complexity of the motivations behind transvestism is the case of Jean Bonnett. For a short time in the 1870s Bonnett pretended to be male so that she could become the leader of a group of young male thieves. She is not in the same category as the criminal confidence woman because she did not use her disguise to trick people out of their money; rather, she used it to participate in what the *San Francisco Call* termed the "spirit of heroism" associated with young brigands.[79] Jean Bonnett is like Belle Starr in that way, being an out-and-out thief, not a confidence artist, by trade; but she is unlike Belle Starr in that Starr did not disguise herself as a man, although she often enough wore men's clothing—another twist to the complexity of transvestism.[80] Jean Bonnett allegedly captained her band of boys for only a short while, but for that period of time she was a species of escape artist, living out her ambitions as only a young man, supposedly, could.

Obviously, defining the confidence woman in the nineteenth century is a rather complex enterprise. Perhaps it would be appropriate to think of the types of confidence woman in two different ways: 1) on a continuum, or perhaps a couple of different continuums, from the most professional to the most amateur, and 2) interlocked as subsets within the overall concept of confidence woman, for the soldiers and spies have much in common with the criminal confidence women, yet their motivations and goals make them very different; likewise, the escape artists

78. Faderman, *Surpassing the Love of Men,* 57, 157, 160–61, 167, 172–73, 187, 190. Faderman makes this point: "What was most threatening to both Europe and America from the sixteenth to the eighteenth centuries was not lesbian sex by itself, but male impersonation and all that was implied in rejection of the feminine status" (59).

79. Quoted in Hellerstein et al., *Victorian Women,* 185–86.

80. See Nash, *Bloodletters and Badmen,* 528, for the story of Belle Starr.

have traits in common with the adventuresses and the spies, yet they definitely make a separate group. The single continuum also does not take into account that the criminal confidence women and the spies are equally professional. One might almost think of two parallel lines: on one, criminal confidence woman to adventuress to someone who is not a confidence woman but has similar traits, the everyday gold digger; on the other, soldiers and spies to escape artists to, again, a woman who is not a confidence woman yet deceives regularly, the everyday pretender.

The overall idea of the confidence woman is relatively clear, however. The confidence woman is a woman in disguise, manipulating her environment and the people in it, telling a story about herself that plays on the prejudices of her listeners.

4

Autobiographies of Confidence Women

It is perhaps surprising that women who told stories about themselves in order to deceive their listeners also wrote books that purport to tell the "true story" after their careers were finished. Yet that was sometimes the case. In the nineteenth century, women who had been soldiers and spies in the Civil War felt free to record their deceptions for an admiring and curious public; no autobiographies by the other kinds of confidence women have been found until those written after 1900. The stories these soldiers and spies wrote were as much propaganda for a cause, Confederate or Union, as they were personal justification and autobiography. I will examine the memoirs of four such women—Belle Boyd, S. Emma Edmonds, Rose Greenhow, and Loreta Janeta Velazquez—concentrating on their ruses and how they presented themselves in their memoirs. Just how far their stories are "true" is debatable, but the important point is that the stories tell us something about how women dared to imagine themselves in the nineteenth century when they had a "Great Cause" permitting them to do so.

In the twentieth century, confidence women no longer needed a cause to give them the leeway to write their autobiographies. Admittedly, there are not many such memoirs, but two outstanding ones are those by criminal confidence women Sophie Lyons and "Chicago May" Churchill (Sharpe). The rhetoric of Chicago May, who wrote her memoir in 1928, is blunt, humorous, irreverent—at the other end of the spectrum from the tone that, for example, S. Emma Edmonds used in the 1860s. The two women are also at opposite ends of the spectrum of morality, yet the two are much alike in what they were willing to risk and in the richness of their stories. Perhaps these autobiographies are just another con, with the reader caught in the deception almost willingly. In any case, watching confidence women create an image of themselves on the page is a fascinating experience that allows us a glimpse into the minds of some of the most intriguing women of our past.

In order to understand the fictions that confidence women have created in their autobiographies, we have to keep in mind the limitations of published autobiography. Publishers can dictate certain styles and themes, and the expectations of the general public must be met. For women in the nineteenth and early twentieth centuries, the limitations were greater than for men, because the roles that were acceptable for women were very much more restricted than those acceptable for men. Those critics like Sidonie Smith who have studied women's autobiography explain that women in the past who told the stories of their lives essentially had to follow certain plotlines—the love plot, for instance.[1] Whereas men could tell stories of independence, how they broke away from their social groups, women had to tell stories of connection. However, Smith shows how women found "fissures in the figuration of 'woman'" that allowed them to write, to experiment with a self-expression not pre-designed for them. For confidence women, the pre-design was more complicated, but because these women had already broken the restrictive role expectations in their very public lives, the fissures could be greater and more numerous.

Confidence women in the nineteenth century wrote not only in the autobiographical tradition but also in the didactic tradition of what David Reynolds calls the "immoral reformers." In sensationalist literature, there are lurid details and a tone of exaggeration; but if the purpose is purportedly reform, as it was for the immoral reformers, this vigorous language is mixed with righteous platitudes. Most of the confidence-women autobiographers I examine take on the tone of the sensationalist literature made popular in the penny presses, which is in contrast to most female autobiography from the past, which tended to be mystical or concerned with womanly topics such as marriage and children. Sophie Lyons is the only one I examine who discusses children in any sentimental way, following the immoral reform tradition. However, Lyons never succeeds in achieving a convincing tone where her children are concerned. The autobiographies I look at also break the "dominant tradition of American women's autobiography" that

---

1. Sidonie Smith, "Resisting the Gaze of Embodiment: Women's Autobiography in the Nineteenth Century," 78. See Smith's *A Poetics of Women's Autobiography: Marginality and the Fictions of Self-Representation* for a provocative interpretation of women's autobiography.

Margo Culley has found, a tradition "root[ed] in Puritan beliefs about the self and the Puritan practice of conversion narratives."[2] Chicago May comes the closest to describing a "conversion": her introduction to crime and her growing professionalism.

Although there is no way to discover what these women really felt about their lives, about the violence surrounding the criminal confidence woman, for instance, and the apparent lack of emotional connection, the language they use implies that they reveled in independence and were in some cases as willing to commit violence as those around them were. In almost all the autobiographies, once the women begin describing what they have done, their tone is joyful and proud, or, if rueful, humorously so, the energy being in the tradition of the sensationalist press, so a certain amount of the vigorous tone probably comes from the writers' desire to fit into a publisher's required form. Certainly these autobiographies bear scrutiny by anyone who wishes to describe American women's autobiographical tradition.[3] The confidence women in effect began a new tradition, which in its own way is as daring as many of their physical exploits.

The Nineteenth Century: Soldiers and Spies Speak

Two of the most interesting forms the confidence woman took in the nineteenth century were of soldier or spy, for the venturesome imagination and the daring associated with both soldiering and spying are in direct opposition to some of our most strongly held assumptions about nineteenth-century women. The women who were spies and soldiers during the Civil War were an odd mixture of altruism and self-aggrandizement. We can hear the soldiers' and spies' voices most clearly in their published memoirs, written during or soon after the war, books which were extremely popular at the time but which disappeared from American bookshelves before the turn of the century. The stories of women like S. Emma Edmonds, whose memoir of her wartime experience was "an instant best seller," selling about 175,000 copies, caught the imaginations of their

2. See Reynolds, *Beneath the American Renaissance;* Margo Culley, "What a Piece of Work Is 'Woman'! An Introduction," 10.

3. It would be especially interesting if someone were to find the personal letters of these women to compare with what they have written. In particular, S. Emma Edmonds admitted to covering up some of the truth in her memoir and said she intended to write a revelation of what really happened, but that document has not been found. See the notes to Hall's *Patriots in Disguise,* 212.

contemporaries, exerting an influence on the women who read their work and on popular novelists who incorporated women of disguise into their own tales.[4]

Seeing women of adventure appear in stories was not entirely new for the American reading public. In antebellum America, many stories of women pioneering and pirating were told in the popular press, as David Reynolds shows.[5] After the war, too, such stories abounded. If one looks at a couple of editions of the *Police Gazette,* for instance, one finds that nineteenth-century readers from the 1870s to the end of the century could have come upon stories of women as actresses, circus gymnasts, bicycle riders, hot-air balloonists, wrestlers, "trouser wearers," and fashionable drinkers. The *Gazette* talks about women who whipped their lawyers and women who rioted when factory owners tried to reduce their wages, showing that some women by the end of the century had come into the news for their outspoken and relatively outrageous actions.[6] The kinds of female criminals the *Gazette* describes are not confidence women but prostitutes and murderesses—usually avenging unfaithfulness. In one story the newspaper tells of six stagecoach bandits who turned out to be women in male disguises, but upon discovery the women cried and said their Daddy made them do it. Stories about unusual women were not new, but such women's telling their own stories was possibly a result of the Civil War and the other major changes occurring at the time.

4. Hall, *Patriots in Disguise,* 83. One result of this popularity was the publication of books such as *The Pictorial Book of Anecdotes of the Rebellion* (1889), by Frazar Kirkland. It gives the stories, in exaggerated language, of many women who joined the Rebel and Union armies dressed like men.

5. Reynolds, in *Beneath the American Renaissance,* finds seven types of women in popular literature: the moral exemplar, the adventure feminist, the woman victim, the working woman, the feminist criminal, the sensual woman, and the feminist exemplar. In his study of literature before 1860 he did not find any confidence women; the female criminals he found were murderesses. The adventure feminists were women who dressed like men for ease of movement or as a way of life, not as a disguise. In my analysis, they are a kind of everyday pretender.

6. Gene Smith and Jayne Barry Smith, *Police Gazette* (1972). The editors of this compilation pick up the *Gazette* (also known as the *National Police Gazette*) from the time Richard Kyle Fox took over as owner and publisher, in 1876 (the first entry is from 1878). Before Fox the *Gazette* (begun in 1846) "was heavy and dull," according to Gene Smith's introduction, even though it dealt with "highwaymen and suchlike malefactors." Fox, however, delights in describing and creating etchings of half-dressed women and tells of the exploits of actresses in great detail, but neither he nor his anonymous writers tell the stories of confidence women. For a full description of the paper, see Smith and Smith, 13–19.

Perhaps it was in the nature of the confidence woman to want to tell of her adventures and clever tricks as a soldier or spy in this new kind of autobiography. In discussing these soldiers and spies, however, I do not wish to imply that all women who spied or fought for the Union or the Confederacy were confidence women. If a woman's spying involved obtaining information with a minimum of deception and sending that information on in some straightforward manner, the woman was not a confidence artist. If a woman wore men's clothes in order to enlist, as so many women did, with the intention of simply passing for male, she did not play a confidence game, although she would fall into the category of the everyday pretender. But if the spying involved intricate disguises, a careful manipulation of people's expectations, and a joy in the tricks one pulled, and if the men's clothing was donned as much for sport as for patriotism, impelling the woman to exaggerate her male impersonation and test its limits, then we have a confidence game. The emphasis is on the word *game*. In the autobiographies of many of these spies and soldiers there is no doubt that the women had fun with their deceptions and enjoyed telling in detail about the tricks that they had played.

To make clear why certain soldiers and spies can be considered confidence women, we might look at the admiring description editor C. J. Worthington gives of Loreta Janeta Velazquez, one of the most interesting and prolific of these autobiographers. His editor's preface to the 1876 edition of the Velazquez narrative, *The Woman in Battle,* gives a description of Loreta Velazquez and simultaneously offers a usable definition of a confidence woman: "Those who have seen her in male attire say that her skill in disguising herself was very great, and that she readily passed for a man. At the same time she is anything but masculine, either in appearance, manners, or address. She is a shrewd, enterprising, and energetic business woman, and in society is a brilliant and most entertaining conversationalist, abounding in a fund of racy anecdotes, and endowed with a mimetic power that enables her to relate her anecdotes in the most telling manner."[7]

The key qualities of a confidence woman are skill with disguises, verbal fluency, shrewdness, energy, and mimetic abilities. Whether the disguise be

7. C. J. Worthington, ed., preface to Loreta Janeta Velazquez, *The Woman in Battle: A Narrative of the Exploits, Adventures, and Travels of Madame Loreta Janeta Velazquez,* 12–13. For a full discussion of the verity of Velazquez's memoir and Worthington's possible role in helping to write it, see Hall, *Patriots in Disguise,* 207–11.

as crudely physical as wearing men's clothing or as shrewdly psychological as pretending to be naïve when one is not, most confidence women will be recognizable by their similarity to Velazquez. Another trait that is common to confidence women, as exhibited clearly in all these memoirs, is their self-satisfaction. Velazquez, for instance, says of herself, "A woman like myself, who had a talent for assuming disguises, and who, like me, was possessed of courage, resolution, and energy, backed up by a ready wit, a plausible address, and attractive manners, had it in her power to perform many services of the most vital importance, which it would be impossible for a man to even attempt." Likewise, Belle Boyd in her memoir, *Belle Boyd in Camp and Prison,* often describes the cheering or curious crowds that made her a celebrity: "In Tennessee I was serenaded by a band, and the people congregated in vast numbers to get a glimpse of the 'rebel spy.'" Rose Greenhow, too, applauds herself several times in her memoir, *My Imprisonment,* especially for her cool facade: "Although agonizing anxieties filled my soul, I was apparently careless and sarcastic."[8] These women do not hesitate to picture themselves as "resolute," "cool," and well loved by crowds. It is a form of their self-invention, almost as if they were writing about a fictional heroine. Having this air of being both a first-person and a third-person narrative makes the autobiographies elusive. The women are telling stories as much about the abstract woman—the woman of talent, "the rebel spy"—as they are telling the truth about themselves. As if they were engaged in another confidence scheme, the women are consciously creating an image of themselves for the reader to view. Unlike other confidence games, however, the reader here is aware of what the writer is doing, and so comes to glimpse the woman behind the disguise. But always the disguise comes first; there is the sense that the autobiographer is willing to change what actually happened to improve the story.

This willingness to do a quick-change for the success of the story marks the autobiographies of confidence women as unusual in a century when autobiographers presumed a central "I," an "irreducible core" that the writer revealed by tearing away masks. Sidonie Smith notes that this unitary self was actually a male self—and, in most cases, white—using women as the embodiment of the Other that helped define the man, so women autobiographers in general had that expectation to fight. In the autobiographies I examine here, the women head in the opposite direction: they put masks on instead of taking them off, and the

8. Velazquez, *The Woman in Battle,* 129; Boyd, *Belle Boyd in Camp and Prison,* 213; Greenhow, *My Imprisonment and the First Year of the Abolition Rule at Washington,* 37.

central "I" never appears. The women seem more interested in telling stories about themselves, making themselves into legends, than they are in baring their souls. Confidence women produced a type of autobiography that seems highly experimental and perhaps specific to them—they *created* a self by telling story after story, detailing disguise after disguise. Who were the real women behind the masks? The autobiographies never tell. A bizarre situation that is emblematic of this idea is the one Velazquez says she found herself in at the end of her career: she was acting as a double agent, pretending to work for the Union—under an assumed name, of course. Her job? To find that master of disguise, that most confoundedly successful Confederate spy, Loreta Velazquez. She took on the job of searching for herself with zeal and tells us that she almost caught herself, too.[9]

One major issue to be dealt with in examining these memoirs is the reliability of their purported authorships. I am attempting to look at the women behind the writing, but if the autobiographies were written by authors other than those stated by the publishers, everything comes into question. It is only in the last few years that there is any solid indication of the historical accuracy of these memoirs. In *Patriots in Disguise* (1993), Richard Hall tackles the question of validity head on, seeking to corroborate statements made by both Emma Edmonds and Loreta Velazquez by searching through war records and the private diaries of the soldiers in the regiments the women claim to have fought in. His conclusions about Edmonds's autobiography, *Nurse and Spy in the Union Army*, are unequivocal: "Although *Nurse and Spy* is a mixture of fact and fiction, it primarily is based on a hard core of fact and is essentially a true story."[10] The details Edmonds gives about the war and the people she knew in it are accurate, then; the fiction occurs in what Hall calls Edmonds's "cover story." In the memoir, she says that she worked as a female nurse, in female clothing, and donned men's clothing only when she performed as a soldier. He has found that this was not true: she dressed in male clothing from long *before* she entered the war, to escape marriage to a man her father had chosen, and she continued under her male identity, as nurse and soldier, during the war. Also, in the memoir she leaves out her male name and other identifying remarks because she in fact deserted the army (fighting increasingly severe bouts of malaria, she was afraid of detection as a woman) and was worried about repercussions from that. In the memoir, of course, she says

9. Smith, "Resisting the Gaze of Embodiment," 78, 80; Velazquez, *The Woman in Battle,* 429–30.
10. Hall, *Patriots in Disguise,* 206–7.

she left openly and honorably. Hall also finds some individual episodes hard to believe, but his overall judgment is that we can for the most part believe what Edmonds says she did.

The verdict on Velazquez is not as clear-cut. Her narrative, *The Woman in Battle,* has been disbelieved ever since it was written, about a decade after the war, mainly because of the influence of General Jubal Early, who had a prejudice against the idea that a southern lady could act in so unmannerly a way. According to Hall, Early claimed to have received a letter from Velazquez that showed by its poor grammar and spelling that she could not have written the book. However, Hall has done an excellent job of searching the records of the battles Velazquez says she was at and has found many of her descriptions to be highly accurate, down to obscure details about unremarkable incidents and about the weather on certain nights in question. "Almost invariably," Hall asserts, "Velazquez correctly reported the names, unit designations, official positions, and other details of the numerous people she mentions in her memoirs." Regarding those incidents that appear to be incorrect or untrue, based on the records, Hall argues that a memoir written so many years after the war would necessarily contain some mistakes, although this is only a *"partially* legitimate excuse" (Hall's emphasis). Some adventures, says Hall, especially those Velazquez says she took part in in Venezuela and on Wall Street after the war, are incontrovertible proof that she was where she claimed to be because she gives details that did not become common knowledge until nearly a century later. Other stories appear to be untrue, the records contradicting her claims rather than supporting them. All in all, Hall comes to this conclusion: the description of the Venezuelan exploit "demonstrates that significant portions of her memoirs are essentially true, and that instead of feeling compelled to an 'either-or' conclusion as to the authenticity of her overall story, we need to examine the various elements of it and determine what the evidence is, pro and con."[11] As to Velazquez's supposedly poor writing skills, Hall suggests that Worthington might have done some heavy editing but that the story itself is by Velazquez.

With all these caveats in mind, then, we can turn to the autobiographies of some soldiers and spies to see what kinds of images they created. There are three main kinds of disguise which the soldiers and spies used and which need to be discussed separately. The confidence game a woman played when she dressed

11. Ibid., 210–11, 208, 208, 210. See pp. 207–11 for a full discussion of the book's credibility.

like a male soldier was quite different from the kind of game she played as a spy, therefore necessitating different kinds of disguise, and the spy disguise itself took two directions: the charming and harmless I'm-just-a-lady disguise and the disguise of invisibility. Loreta Janeta Velazquez used all three disguises in her various careers as soldier and spy. Her autobiography is quite explicit about the kinds of deception she practiced in the war.

The disguise that was easiest to penetrate and therefore riskiest was that of a male soldier. The women who decided to be soldiers desired glory in a relatively traditional way—though usually traditional for men only. They wanted to be heroes; their desire was bent, as Velazquez put it, "on achieving fame, and of accomplishing even more than the great heroines of history had been able to do." Such a bold statement of purpose would have been rather alarming to Edmonds, who prefaces her narrative *Nurse and Spy* with a disclaimer: "Should any of her readers object to some of her disguises, it may be sufficient to remind them it was from the purest motives and most praiseworthy patriotism." She goes even further, using "womanly" language to describe her career: it is "blessed, self-sacrificing work," her disguises "the surest protection from insult and inconvenience," and she reminds the reader of "the moral character of the work."[12] Unlike Velazquez, who does not screen her pride behind any justification, Edmonds constantly intrudes the Christian note, as if she had played the part of a missionary on the battlefield. And in truth she *did* perform some very heroic, self-sacrificing acts as a male nurse, saving many lives and easing much pain.

But some of the two women's exploits were less like those of Christian missionaries and more like those of war-hardened soldiers. They did not blanch at carrying corpses off the field or making some corpses themselves. Velazquez was especially proud of her skill in battle and considered it a point of honor to fight as bravely as the best when she fought by the side of her fiancé. Not until the day before their marriage did her husband-to-be know that his friend Harry T. Buford, who had fought so gallantly at the Battle of Shiloh, was in reality the woman he thought he had left behind, the woman he meant to marry. In her memoirs, Velazquez remarks that she had no "womanish" fears for herself or her fiancé on the battlefield, "although," she admits later, "on reflecting over

12. Velazquez, *The Woman in Battle,* 62; S. Emma Edmonds, *Nurse and Spy in the Union Army,* 6.

the matter afterwards, it struck me that some slight emotion of that kind would perhaps have been proper under the circumstances."[13]

Edmonds was just as cool when she was in male disguise. In one particular battle, she fought in a fierce skirmish at the front, then stayed behind to help carry the dead off the field. Looking for a friend who had asked her to send his ring to his girlfriend, she finally discovered him in a multiple grave. Without hesitation, she jumped in and tried unsuccessfully to get the ring off the dead man's finger.[14]

One lie that Edmonds consistently tells is that she wore women's apparel when she carried out the duties of a nurse. People have often expressed wonder that Edmonds could don her disguise with so little effort. In the memoir she apparently switches from the attire and duties of a nurse to those of a soldier so often that she sometimes neglects to mention that the switch has been made. The reader must presume that no one recognized the nurse in soldier's clothing, or the soldier in nurse's uniform, for she makes no mention of any such difficulties. The truth is, apparently, that Edmonds entered the war disguised as a male and never took the disguise off, except to tell certain friends (who write in their personal diaries about their surprise). Velazquez, however, goes into great detail about her male clothing: how she convinced a tailor to make a sort of harness to go under her coat to ensure that she would not be recognized as a woman, how she glued a fine moustache to her lip and once thought she had lost it in her soup, how she practiced for hours before a mirror, imitating the "gait of a man, and admiring the figure I made in masculine raiment."[15] Dressing like a man was a game for her, not a survival tactic, although the game sometimes extended to having to behave like a man in view of people who openly suspected her of being a woman.

In *Vested Interests: Cross-Dressing and Cultural Anxiety*, Marjorie Garber deals with the power of the image of the transvestite and how it involves theatricality

13. Velazquez, *The Woman in Battle*, 208. This is one story that is most certainly a fabrication: the man Velazquez calls her fiancé simply was not there at the time. See Hall, *Patriots in Disguise*, 209. But my focus is on the legend Velazquez creates. For a similar story, see the anecdote about Annie Lillybridge and Lieutenant W— in Kirkland, *The Pictorial Book of Anecdotes of the Rebellion*, 621.

14. Edmonds, *Nurse and Spy*, 129.

15. For Edmonds's friends' comments in their personal diaries, see Richard Hall's *Patriots in Disguise;* Velazquez, *The Woman in Battle*, 57–58, 68, 42.

and an aspect of the carnival. The typical reaction of people to women who cross-dress is to normalize it somehow, thinking that the woman had to do it for her profession or did it for her soldier-husband, did it out of love. They try to offset "the extraordinary power of the transvestite as an aesthetic and psychological agent of destabilization, desire, and fantasy." Velazquez capitalizes on the destabilization; she enacts her own fantasy—that she can cross the borders of gender with impunity. For men, cross-dressing heightens their sense of their own maleness, Garber contends, because despite how they dress they do not lose their signifying body part, so that cross-dressing becomes ultimately an act of reassurance that they are indeed and always will be men and not women.[16] According to Garber, for women the result of cross-dressing appears to be something else, a reassurance that they too could be men. On the one hand, this "reinscribes the male" as the gender of power, as Garber would say, but on the other hand it creates a crisis in the gender category itself. The urge to normalize what the women have done by giving reasons for their behavior is a reaction to that crisis.

Velazquez makes such normalization impossible. Her "profession" is in itself socially unthinkable. A woman could be an actress, even if that profession was rather disreputable, and still be accepted in her society. A woman could not be a soldier. In fact, dressing like a male soldier was a crime, punishable by imprisonment. Yet Velazquez delights in giving details of her prowess in putting on the male guise; she heightens the theatricality of it, suggesting that gender is a pretense, a social construct, not an inherent quality. For example, she practiced not only walking like a man but succeeding in a man's culture. She tells us that her first husband took her to some saloons and gambling dens before she entered the war in order to shock her out of her idea, but she bought drinks all around and smoked cigars with relish. By her account, even close friends did not recognize her. Soon after, her first (soon to be killed) husband left for his post in the West, thinking that she would stay quietly at home; but Velazquez talked a friend into helping her act more like a man. He too took her to male hangouts, including a barber shop. At the saloons she refused to drink, as he had suggested, for she needed all her wits about her. But she was a favorite even so, for she told the men she was fresh out of West Point, which made her the protégé of older soldiers on leave. At all times she was careful not to betray the fact that she was a woman: "I . . . took pains to strut about in as mannish a manner as I could, and to imitate

16. Garber, *Vested Interests,* 71. See her chapter 5 for a discussion of male subjectivity.

a man's actions and gestures while washing my face and hands and arranging my hair."[17] Thus, being "mannish" becomes a game, one that women too can play.

In the late twentieth century, we pride ourselves on being able to see through subterfuge, and wonder how women could have succeeded in their disguises so well. But we should bear two things in mind. First, it is possible to trick even sophisticated late-twentieth-century viewers if the disguise is complete—as the producers of the 1992 movie *The Crying Game* banked on. Second, in the nineteenth century, roles were much tighter than they are now, making people less likely to suspect a trick. As Jonathan Ned Katz explains in his documentary history of gay Americans, which includes information on women who passed for men, "These documents reveal with what absolute intellectual certainty and passionate emotional rigidity certain kinds of work, behavior, and costume were once considered either 'masculine' or 'feminine.' Certain occupations or activities which in present-day America have become sex-neutral were earlier felt to be 'male' or 'female' in the same essential sense in which a vagina is female, a penis male, with a correspondingly strong negative response to any questioning of this sex typing."[18] Gender categories were extremely rigid, making the cross-dressing of women like Velazquez very upsetting—perhaps part of the reason some people have so vehemently disparaged her credibility. Whether she figured on this upsetting effect or not, Velazquez spends a great deal of time detailing her transformation into a man, giving amusing episodes all through her narrative.

But the issue of cross-dressing has wider ramifications than as a study of nineteenth-century gullibility. It in itself indicates a period of social crisis and represents the movement for change. Garber investigates in *Vested Interests* the meanings behind cross-dressing in various cultures and at various times and concludes that the transvestite becomes a kind of third sex, disrupting the binary opposition between subject and object, the "One" and the "Other." "This interruption, this disruptive act of putting in question, is . . . precisely the place, and the role, of the transvestite." The existence of cross-dressers indicates a "category crisis," suggesting that the old oppositions—"black/white, Jew/Christian, noble/bourgeois, master/servant, master/slave"—are not absolute. Cross-dressing is not a cause, then, but a sign of crisis in a culture; it will "focus cultural anxiety." When a transvestite crosses the boundaries of gender—

17. Velazquez, *The Woman in Battle,* 54–56, 74. More details about Velazquez's practicing a man's behavior are on p. 68.
18. Katz, *Gay American History,* 210.

and perhaps of class—the result is "both terrifying and seductive precisely because s/he incarnates and emblematizes the disruptive element that intervenes,
signaling not just another category crisis, but—much more disquietingly—a
crisis of 'category' itself."[19]

The years leading up to, during, and following the Civil War were years of
intense anxiety, as many categories in the United States were in flux. The end of
the slave system broke down one clear form of racial opposition, and the influx
of immigrants continually put into question who the American "we" included.
The *Police Gazette* was filled with articles meant to assert that "Coolies" and
"Sheenies" and "Coons" were not part of the "we." Gender differences were
of course also being overturned, as the "new woman" came on the scene. This
time of great "cultural anxiety" would, in Garber's view, presumably be a time
when cross-dressing would become common, as certainly seems to have been
the case. I discuss just a few women who wore men's clothing in order to fight in
the war, but, according to Hall in *Patriots in Disguise*, a myriad of other women
did the same. Frazar Kirkland's *Pictorial Book of Anecdotes of the Rebellion* (1889)
includes many more stories of both Southern and Northern women fighting
as men in the Civil War. Cross-dressing of another sort occurred just before
the war: in the 1840s, when white men cross-dressed in minstrel shows as
caricatures of black men and black women.[20] The crossing of category boundaries
was not a conscious effort to create change in the society; rather, it indicates
that change was already occurring. That women like Velazquez and Edmonds
could write their memoirs and achieve popular success shows the extent of the
gender anxiety that the traditional American culture was feeling. Antonia Fraser
explains the paradox of this avid public interest despite the simultaneous public
disapprobation in *The Warrior Queens*, a study of military women through the
ages, usually women who dressed like men. She speculates that "part of this
frisson—of fear or admiration—is undoubtedly due to the fact that woman as a
whole has been seen as a pacifying influence throughout history, this pacifying
role being perceived as hers by nature and hers in duty."[21] This mixture of fear and
admiration helps explain the dual response to the confidence woman in general.

The disruption of categories is wonderfully symbolized by a very unusual
example of cross-dressing that occurred in 1848: Ellen Craft, a slave woman,

19. Garber, *Vested Interests*, 13, 16, 32.
20. See Eric Lott, *Love and Theft: Blackface Minstrelsy and the American Working Class.*
21. See Fraser, *The Warrior Queens.*

crossed three boundaries at once by disguising herself as a middle-class white gentleman in order to escape her enslavement in Georgia. In one stroke, Craft exhibited the crises in the "black/white, . . . master/slave," and middle-class/lower-class categories. Her disguise lasted only a few days, but the repercussions were enormous. In the North, abolitionists used the escape as ammunition against slavery, forcing Ellen Craft and her husband, William, to give lectures. The Crafts ultimately had to make another escape—from the Northern liberals, to Europe.

Craft's tripartite disguise is symbolic of the threefold upheaval America was experiencing in the 1840s: unrest among women, among the lower classes, and among slaves—not that the Crafts thought about the wider meaning their escape could have. They made a personal decision, that it was necessary for them to leave Georgia. William Craft, according to his memoir of the episode, *Running a Thousand Miles for Freedom,* claims that the idea of the disguise was his; he presumably felt he had to downplay the audacity of the idea in his nonfiction narrative of the escape. He assures us, "My wife had no ambition whatever to assume this disguise, and would not have done so had it been possible to have obtained our liberty by more simple means." He explains that he believed that the best way to escape would be to walk away in broad daylight, rather than run through the swamps as so many others had done. The key to this escape was Ellen's skin color; having a half-white mother and a white father (her owner), Ellen could pass for white very easily. The plan was for Ellen to pretend that she was a white, middle-class gentleman traveling with her manservant.[22]

Although the idea was supposedly William's, Ellen engineered the rest: being a tailor by trade, she made a suit of clothes fit for a gentleman, bound her face in a poultice so that her smooth, beardless skin would not be noticed, rigged up a sling to make her right arm appear injured because she did not know how to write, and donned tinted glasses. With this disguise, she avoided talking much by claiming illness and had a good excuse not to sign her name if asked to do so.[23]

The journey from Georgia to Philadelphia lasted eight days. William convinced their master to give them Christmas passes for a few days, so they knew their time was limited. Ironically, neither of them could read the passes that would be their tickets to freedom. William says that Ellen fell weeping into his arms at the last moment, but at last called up all her fortitude. And she would need it

22. Craft, *Running a Thousand Miles,* 35, 29; Dorothy Sterling, *Black Foremothers: Three Lives,* 5–19.
23. Craft, *Running a Thousand Miles,* 34–35.

immediately, because the first part of the journey, at this point by train, entailed her sitting next to a friend of her master's. She pretended to be deaf so that he wouldn't recognize her, answering "Yes" very politely, only when he yelled. From the train, they boarded the first steamer, Ellen feigning rheumatism so that she could retire to her cabin. But she could not avoid the captain's table. There the conversation centered on the folly of her taking a slave north, because he would just run. Ellen held her own, even when someone offered her a good price for her husband.[24]

Illness is a good disguise in itself, as several criminal confidence women understood. On shore again, Ellen "hobbled" at the hotel and William ordered the poultices warmed. But the next day, the gentleman's illness and incapacitated arm did not stop the captain of the second steamer from demanding that he sign a paper before boarding to prove that he and his slave were who they said they were. Ellen tried to talk her way out of it, knowing that her illiteracy would be a clear sign that she was not a gentleman at all, but the captain would not give in. At last, a drunken military man Ellen had spoken to on the first steamer said he would vouch for the two and the captain signed for her—William Johnson. From the steamer, the two again boarded a train: Ellen in first class, William in the baggage car. Ellen was striking enough as a gentleman to cause two young women to flirt with her, according to the memoir, and she had to hold back her indignation when a "Christian" lady talked volubly about the righteousness of slavery.[25]

The final crisis of the escape occurred in Baltimore, the last and strictest port they had to manage before Philadelphia. William wrote, "Queen Elizabeth could not have been more terror-stricken, on being forced to land at the traitors' gate leading to the Tower, than we were on entering that office." The officer there was "eagle-eyed" and demanded that proof be shown that the gentleman was indeed the rightful owner of his servant. He spoke "in a voice and manner that almost chilled our blood." But Ellen refused to be cowed and argued back in a voice equally stern, "I bought the tickets in Charleston to pass us through to Philadelphia, and therefore you have no right to detain us here." The other people waiting in the office sympathized with the gentleman and, ultimately, wore the officer down.[26]

24. Ibid., 29–32, 41–50.
25. Ibid., 51–60.
26. Ibid., 70–73.

Ironically, when the Crafts went on stage to tell of their adventures, at the coercion of the abolitionists, Ellen did not speak, this silencing as symbolic as her escape had been. She stood to one side as her husband told the tale, and it was her husband who wrote the memoir. The "imperious voice" she used when she was in disguise became silent when she took back her labels—black, indigent ex-slave, and woman.[27]

The confidence women who dressed like men typically did not analyze the cultural effects of their actions. They had very personal reasons for doing what they did. Julie Wheelwright contends that Emma Edmonds "saw the assumption of a male role as an escape from a feminine identity that ensnared and even enslaved her." For Velazquez, the personal motivation was more fierce than such a need to escape from traditional feminine roles: "Ridicule, as well as danger," she states, "was what I resolved to brave when putting on male attire, and I really dreaded it less than I did my own heart-burnings in the event of my not winning the desperate game I was playing."[28] She risked her reputation and her fortune, spending, according to her story, $80,000 to recruit a battalion of men she could drill and lead into battle, in hopes of becoming one of the great heroines of history.

What is most surprising about Edmonds's and Velazquez's disguises is how well they worked on the battlefield. Neither memoir goes into details of everyday hygiene, presumably a Victorian reticence, but since Edmonds's disguise as Franklin Thompson lasted over a year, the women must have devised some workable system. Today a woman could not disguise herself like a male soldier for long; a woman would not get past the physical examination all new soldiers must undergo. But in the nineteenth century, physical exams occurred only when there was an injury, and often not even then. Unless a woman told someone her sex of her own accord or was recognized, she had a fair chance of going undetected, as long as she was a good mimic and stayed vigilant. Richard Hall tells the stories of some women who were detected not by the way they looked but by the way they acted: they put on their stockings wrong, or caught apples like a woman, or wrung out the dishrag the wrong way. Some women went undetected until the moment they had babies, in the field. Hall says there are many records of women in soldiers' dress to be found in letters and diaries, usually just brief mentions

27. Sterling, *Black Foremothers*.
28. Wheelwright, *Amazons and Military Maids*, 30–31; Velazquez, *The Woman in Battle*, 131.

of discovery at death or wounding.[29] In what Hall considers an apocryphal story, Edmonds mentions that she once came upon another woman disguised as a male soldier when she was herself dressed as a nurse, helping the wounded and dying on the field. This woman revealed her sex to her and asked Edmonds to bury her separately so that her secret could be kept to the end.[30] Although Hall says that it would be highly coincidental for Edmonds to have actually had such a meeting, this account agrees with the statements of several other women who dressed like soldiers in France and Spain and South America, that they were not recognized unless they wanted to be. Even in a hospital, because hygienic practices were so lax, a woman could maintain her male identity unless her wound were extremely serious or located in the hip or chest.

The kinds of scrutiny women underwent in the military also depended in part on the role they played in the war. Wheelwright suggests that women's "ability . . . to embark on a military career and to successfully disguise themselves within an all-male regiment [was] inevitably influenced by their class and social position."[31] Perhaps Velazquez was able to maintain her disguise for two years because she entered as an officer with her own battalion of men and full regalia. Her affluence and her upper-class tone usually kept questioners at bay, although there were formal charges filed against her for being a woman more than once. The famous case of "Dr. James Barry," a full inspector-general of British army hospitals in the nineteenth century, is an example of how thoroughly the male disguise could work, especially if the role one played were of high enough rank. Not until her death at age seventy-one was Dr. Barry revealed to be a woman, much to the shock of her military peers.[32] Mark Twain was enough taken by Dr. Barry's story to write a short chapter on her at the end of *Following the Equator.* He keeps her disguise a secret, as part of the joke, describing how fierce and skillful she was: "Among other adventures of his was a duel of a desperate

---

29. Hall, *Patriots in Disguise,* 156–57.

30. Edmonds, *Nurse and Spy,* 271. Edmonds's claim that she buried a female soldier is not unique. A story in Kirkland's *Pictorial Book of Anecdotes of the Rebellion,* "Frank, the Pretty Female Bugler of the Eighth Michigan," tells us that Frank "assisted in burying three female soldiers at different times, whose sex was unknown to any but herself" (p. 622). In regards to women's hospitalization without recognition of their gender, another story in Kirkland's book, about Annie Lillybridge, claims that she was in a hospital for several months, suffering from a wound to the arm, without her sex being discovered (p. 621).

31. Wheelwright, *Amazons and Military Maids,* 41.

32. Thompson, *The Mysteries of Sex,* 115–22.

sort, fought with swords, at the Castle. He killed his man." Such violence was offset by Barry's "mastership of his profession . . . his love of it and his devotion to it." With his usual humorous pacing, Twain saves Dr. Barry's gender for the punch line.[33]

Another important reason that women could successfully disguise themselves as men in wartime was the strong presumption in the nineteenth century, a presumption still potent today, that women were incapable of meeting the rigors of war. To be a soldier meant living in mud and listening to decidedly uncouth language, both of which conditions should have shocked a woman. Both Edmonds and Velazquez apologize for being so brazen as to sit through and laugh at ribald stories, but excuse themselves for simply doing their patriotic duty. Also in the nineteenth century there was great delicacy about requiring anyone, male or female, to remove his or her clothes. It is remarkable how often Velazquez was brought to the military court on charges of cross-dressing (and several of these court trials are on record), because she failed to keep her uniform and brace in good order, she argues, and how often she was thrown in jail with her sex unproven simply because she refused to admit that she was not a man. Obviously, people suspected her true gender, but the mores of the time prohibited anyone from finding out her sex directly.

One memorable instance not only points up the power of stereotypes in the nineteenth century but also shows how much fun a con woman could have. Velazquez found that, as time went on, rumors of a male impersonator doing wondrous deeds would precede her and make her disguise precarious. In Richmond, Virginia, after she had been a soldier and a spy and a soldier again, she was arrested on "the charge of being a woman in disguise" (an interesting crime!). The court, however, could not prove that she was not a man, so she was confined to quarters as a possible Union spy instead. People came to see her out of curiosity and to see if they could find out the truth. Velazquez recounts one particular visit by two fashionable ladies, a mother and daughter. She heard them coming up the stairs and determined to use the "little masculine traits" she had picked up. "I relied greatly upon these," she says, "to aid me in maintaining my *incognito,* for they were eminently characteristic, and well calculated to throw a suspicious person off guard. So, when I heard these visitors coming, I stuck my feet up on the window-sill, and, just as they were opening the door, I turned my head, and spit." The reaction to this maneuver was everything Velazquez could have

33. Mark Twain, *Following the Equator: A Journey around the World,* 711.

hoped for. The daughter drew back when she saw Velazquez and whispered to her mother, " 'O, ma, that can't be a woman! See how he spits!' "[34] How far this story is true can be only partially determined. How far it goes in making Velazquez a legend is evident in the retelling.

In the twentieth century, the obvious solution to the problem of gender specification would be to look and find out. But when Velazquez suggests to an old woman who keeps bothering her that she check to make sure, a proposition indicated in her book only by " 'Suppose you—,' " the old woman is so enraged that she rushes to the mayor to complain "that that nasty little fellow had insulted her."[35] One can only conjecture what Velazquez actually said.

Dressing like a man in the nineteenth century apparently was great fun, allowing a woman to see and do things unimaginable in a dress. Velazquez states outright, "I plunged into adventures for the love of the thing."[36] Whereas Edmonds seems to have been very serious about her fighting—she spends a good portion of her book describing precisely the types and amounts of ammunition a company has and explaining complicated military maneuvers—Velazquez is much more of a trickster. Her descriptions of battles are cursory, limited to a short self-congratulation, but her descriptions of her amours as a soldier are quite detailed. It is rather amazing how many young women fell in love with Harry T. Buford, although it must be remembered that playing at courtship is part of the "female soldier" tradition, common to many nineteenth-century books about women who fought in American wars, whether written by the women themselves or not. Even Edmonds has such a love story to tell, in a written interview she gave after the war. It is equally amazing how joyfully Velazquez led these women on, sometimes to the very brink of marriage; her joyful telling of the stories is her own contribution to the tradition.[37] But then, Buford was a gallant young officer with a big moustache who knew just what sorts of compliments a girl liked. Velazquez takes great delight in exposing the little arts her paramours used, arts she herself would use when she turned female spy.

34. Velazquez, *The Woman in Battle*, 284, 285.
35. Ibid., 286.
36. Ibid., 154.
37. Usually the tone is one of reluctant admission, followed by clear statements that all was innocent. See Herman Mann, *The Female Review: Life of Deborah Sampson, the Female Soldier in the War of Revolution.* Julie Wheelwright sees the flirting as "a theatrical flaunting of [a woman's] attempt at total immersion in a forbidden world" (*Amazons and Military Maids*, 55).

Velazquez's career as a soldier had a fitting end, her telling of which is clearly an example of the layers of storytelling Velazquez gives us, since this story defies verification. She was wounded, she says, and healing in the same hospital her fiancé was in, although in a different ward. When she was strong enough, she often visited her fiancé's sickbed as his friend Harry Buford and got him to talk about his girlfriend, Loreta. The fiancé did not recognize Loreta in Buford, even on the day Loreta was going to visit him so they could get married. Velazquez mentions that she rather enjoyed seeing how flustered her fiancé was as he prepared for the visit, Buford helping him shave and comb his hair, supporting him and bolstering his courage. When Velazquez finally came in to reveal that Buford and Loreta were the same, she found it harder to put the disguise aside than it had been to don it. She made her fiancé take out his photograph of Loreta and hold it up next to her face, but he did not understand her. "Well, Captain," she said at last, "don't you think that the picture of your lady-love looks the least bit like your friend Harry Buford?" According to this story—one Hall has shown to be highly doubtful—they got married the next day, Velazquez deciding to wear a dress for the ceremony, "for fear of creating too much of a sensation, and, perhaps, of making the clergyman feel unpleasant should I appear before him, hanging on the Captain's arm, in my uniform."[38]

Such a sense of humor and such vitality in the picture Loreta Velazquez draws of herself remind me of several fictional characters in the sensational novels of the time, reinforcing the sense that Velazquez is creating a fiction of her own life. The ludic quality of Velazquez's writing is in itself important. According to Anna K. Nardo, who has studied the meaning of play in literature, play/fantasy/folly "creates a context in which actions both are and are not what they are, both are and are not serious," resulting in a "ludic disorder" out of which "may come the potential for social change." The "game" that the confidence woman plays, whether as soldier and spy or in her other forms, is paradoxical. It both "scramble[s] the order and level[s] the hierarchy—temporarily," in Nardo's words, and "help[s] preserve the social order" by acting as a release valve. The game ultimately is a personal one "whereby adults make themselves at home in a world no longer designed to gratify their desires."[39] Like cross-dressing, the game is a sign of cultural crisis, a way of dealing with it.

38. Velazquez, *The Woman in Battle*, 332, 335.
39. Anna K. Nardo, *The Ludic Self in Seventeenth-Century English Literature*, 21, 37, 36, 6.

Not all soldiering was a game. For some women, it was serious and straightforward. Linda De Pauw, in her study of women in the Revolutionary War, describes some female camp followers as unrecognized soldiers, who helped husbands and lovers load cannon and keep the cannon watered. Often enough a woman would take over the gun if the man were shot: Margaret Corbin and Mary Hays were two such women in the Revolutionary War, eventually coming to be represented by the symbolic "Molly Pitcher" with her pitcher of water. These women were soldiers, but were not confidence women because they did not play any game of deception. The situation changed between the Revolutionary War and the Civil War a century later, however. According to De Pauw, in the Revolutionary War "only a handful" of women that we know about dressed like men and received full pay as soldiers, Deborah Sampson being the most well known, whereas in the Civil War "several hundred women soldiers were discovered," usually after they had been fighting for years.[40] The increase was in part due to a growing population, but I believe it was also due to women's reactions to a restrictive female role, which was arguably more restrictive than it had been in the eighteenth century. The extent to which simply dressing like men in order to fight made these women confidence women is debatable. If there was no sense of a game, if the women essentially thought of themselves as men during the time the disguise lasted, then their disguise was a form of the everyday pretense.

Most of the stories I have found about women transvestites in the Civil War involve white women. In fact, most of the stories I have seen about women in any way involved in the war are about white women. One black woman, Susie King Taylor, wrote a memoir, but in it I found none of the soldiering—in male attire or otherwise—that De Pauw discusses. Taylor was a camp follower of one of the first black troops in the Civil War. Most camp followers were the girlfriends or wives of soldiers in the unit who saw traveling with the unit as a way to help the cause at the same time they stayed close to their loved ones. Taylor's lack of soldiering was probably due to the fact that the black troop was very seldom allowed into battle, having to fight prejudice more than it fought the enemy. But Taylor does mention one activity she and her female compatriots performed that involved stealth and daring: they would help Union soldiers escape from

40. Linda Grant De Pauw, *Founding Mothers: Women in America in the Revolutionary Era,* 191.

the Confederate prison camp in Savannah, Georgia, and would put food through holes in the prison fence to try to keep the Union prisoners from starving.[41]

In literature, it is this latter kind of soldiering that appears most often. Although it is not as flamboyant as Edmonds's or Velazquez's fighting in male disguise, it still involves some confidence arts. Frances E. W. Harper describes slave women conspiring against the Confederacy in *Iola LeRoy.* The women use a secret code called "market speech" in which the price or availability of butter, for instance, indicates the relative success of the Union forces. Slave laundresses communicate with Union soldiers by the way they hang their sheets on the line; house slaves like Jinny use their confidence arts as they disguise their feelings about the war when the mistress is in the room, pulling "a long face" when she bewails Confederate losses, but dancing and cutting "caper[s]" as soon as she is out of earshot. Aunt Linda similarly sets up a secret meeting of the slave men and women in the guise of a prayer meeting around Aunt Katie's "sick bed," another ruse.[42] All these acts of deception are for the purpose of furthering the Northern cause and aiding the escape of black men as contraband of war.

It would be interesting to determine whether Native American women ever dressed like men in time of war, or used other confidence arts. The Native American culture, as I mentioned earlier, does not usually foster these kinds of deceptions (although the legendary figure of Changing Woman and other female tricksters certainly need discussion), but that does not preclude such occurrences altogether. I examined only one autobiography—*Life among the Piutes,* by Sarah Winnemucca Hopkins—and therefore cannot make any generalizations, but I did note that Hopkins participated in one ruse involving transvestism during the Bannock War, which occurred in the late nineteenth century. The Bannocks warred against the whites because of an injustice done them: some white men "abused" a Bannock woman, and when her brother shot the men, the whites retaliated against the entire tribe, taking all its ponies and weapons. Hopkins and the Paiutes became enemies of the Bannocks because her tribe regularly dealt with the whites, Hopkins being the translator.

Hopkins rescued her people, held captive by the Bannocks, by stealing into the enemy camp dressed like a Bannock man. She instructed the captive women

41. Susie King Taylor, *Reminiscences of My Life in Camp with the 33rd U.S. Colored Troops, Late First South Carolina Volunteers: A Black Woman's Civil War Memories,* 142.
42. Frances E. W. Harper, *Iola LeRoy or Shadows Uplifted,* 11, 12.

to pretend to gather wood farther and farther into the forest until they could run away. She does not detail how she succeeded in getting the men, including her father, away from the Bannocks, but apparently her father was impressed enough to say that for her bravery she should be made chief.[43] Hopkins is more typically a diplomat, but under stress of war she used other talents.

Taking part in a war in any way often has a strong effect on the women involved. Mary Catherwood's "Marianson" shows a low-key kind of soldiering, but her story makes clear how even such subdued resistance could change a woman's self-image. The story takes place during the War of 1812. Marianson Bruelle braves the English in an effort to save a Canadian deserter, dissimulating her motives at the post until she can steal a boat, then rowing to the middle of Lake Mackinac and lying on the bottom of the boat so that it seems adrift, until she can safely take the boat to the deserter, whom she loves. These are relatively minor wartime deceptions, but Marianson's reaction to her soldierly role reveals the power of female stereotypes in the potency she feels when she breaks them: "Indifferent to the Indian who might be dogging her, she drew her strip of home-spun around her face and ran, moccasined and deft-footed, over the stones, warm, palpitating, and laughing, full of physical hardihood."[44] This euphoric sense of well-being is in sharp contrast to the frequent image of the nineteenth-century woman lying on her couch, an invalid of soul and body.

War is a unique condition, calling out qualities that would otherwise remain hidden, even denied. For women, war can be a justification, a rationale, for allowing themselves to face danger and to lead. It is also a time when many women in the nineteenth century tried on the male guise for a hint of the freedom and adventure they otherwise found hard to experience. Many of the women who wore men's clothing were not confidence women, although they perhaps had to use some confidence arts. When a confidence woman turned transvestite, she wore the disguise as an actress would, enjoying the reaction of her audience.

But putting on masculinity as a disguise was not the favored game of confidence women during the war; rather, most confidence women put on an artificial femininity instead. As Loreta Velazquez wrote of women, "From the mere fact that she is a woman, she can often do things that a man cannot." The feminine games women played fall into three main categories: using their charms,

---

43. Sarah Winnemucca Hopkins, *Life among the Piutes: Their Wrongs and Claims,* 158–60.

44. Catherwood, "Marianson," 14.

assuming a naïve innocence, and feigning weakness. Each of the games employs a stereotype about women so that the disguise is in part constructed by the people the game is played upon. The difference between merely fulfilling the stereotype and using it as a means to a separate purpose lies in the women's awareness of what they are doing and what its effect will be. Velazquez, as a female spy, makes her manipulations of the feminine stereotype explicit by saying, "While indulging in [a] recital of my troubles I wiped my eyes with my pocket handkerchief, tried my best to squeeze out a tear or two, and looked as sorrow-stricken as I possibly could."[45] Tears, according to the stereotype, are part of a woman's charms, the first of the three feminine games. Confidence women have an uncanny ability to bring them on at will, usually as a last resort.

But there are other charms, too. Belle Boyd used flowers, an indirect flattery, to get Yankee officers to do as she wished. In one notable instance, Boyd was able to flatter a young Federal lieutenant, by giving him a bouquet, into giving her a pass to travel between Winchester and Fort Royal, Virginia, supposedly to visit relatives. In reality, she was carrying some important military information in letters to a Confederate general. Later, when the battle that followed turned out to be a victory for the South, a Federal colonel said, "That bouquet did all the mischief: the donor of that gift is responsible for all this misfortune."[46]

Belle Boyd was just seventeen when the war began; by the time she had escaped to England with Federal detectives hot on her trail, she was no more than twenty. It is easy to see how a young, energetic woman could attract the attentions of the Federal officers stationed in her house or on nearby roads, especially if the man who wrote the introduction to her narrative is right in admiring "her great beauty, elegant manners, and personal attractions generally." Boyd explains that having enemy sentries quartered in her house helped her immensely: "It was in this way that I became acquainted with so many of them; an acquaintance 'the rebel spy' did not fail to turn to account on more than one occasion." Her wry nonchalance about the officers' attentions underscores how her manipulations tickled her sense of humor: "To one of these [officers], Captain K., I am indebted for some remarkable effusions, some withered flowers, and last, not least, for a great deal of very important information, which was carefully transmitted to my countrymen."[47]

45. Velazquez, *The Woman in Battle*, 130, 241.
46. Boyd, *Belle Boyd*, 111, 133.
47. Ibid., 18, 74, 102.

Velazquez describes in detail how she too worked a lieutenant she met on a train: " 'I will be very greatly pleased if you will go through with me. It has been a long time since I have met any agreeable gentlemen, and I particularly admire officers.' As I said this I gave him a killing glance, and then dropped my eyes as if half ashamed of having made such a bold advance to him. The bait took, however, as I expected it would." She then remarks, "It was mere play for me to impose upon him." The propensity of many women—not just confidence women—to use their charms to get what they want is shown by a remark Velazquez makes about the time she was impersonating a soldier and was on duty as a military train conductor. The men followed the rules, she says, but the women tried to use their wiles to get around her as they had her predecessor. "My own sex," she tells us, "relied on accomplishing, by means of their fascinations, what was impossible to the men."[48] Naturally, the women in this instance failed.

These "charms" did not work on two types of people, generally: other women and some of the more hard-boiled detectives and soldiers. Velazquez explains, "I have always found it more difficult to beguile women than men into telling me what I have wanted to know." Belle Boyd compares an ungentlemanly detective who guarded her as she was taken to prison in Washington to Poe's Raven, impossible to cajole. Often Boyd appealed to more refined officers to rescue her from brutish soldiers. In the "Old Capital," where she and Rose Greenhow were at different times imprisoned, a guard once broke her thumb by hitting her hand with a musket butt, and twice guards pushed a bayonet to her chest out of fear that she was about to play some trick on them. Each time she had the offending sentry removed by an admiring Union officer.[49]

The public loved the female spies, gathering in great crowds whenever Belle Boyd or Rose Greenhow was transported somewhere under guard. When Boyd was allowed to walk in the Old Capital square, so many people came to watch and to sympathize that she lost the privilege. Newspapers carried almost daily accounts of her health and of where she walked. As she says, she was the fashion. Similarly, Greenhow had so many visitors to her home when she was imprisoned there that people came to call it "Fort Greenhow." The newspapers in Washington played up her ladylike character and her great abilities, often exaggerating her actions.[50]

48. Velazquez, *The Woman in Battle,* 354, 365, 149.
49. Ibid., 364; Boyd, *Belle Boyd,* 164.
50. Boyd, *Belle Boyd,* 252–53, 254; Greenhow, *My Imprisonment,* 168, 205.

Boyd, Greenhow, and Velazquez also became legends among the male soldiers and spies. A General Porter said of Greenhow, "She will fool you out of your eyes—can talk with her fingers." And Greenhow indeed did know some tricks. Her expertise was in getting information past the most alert guards in a cipher of her own. In order to discover her method, detectives ransacked her desk and her library. One time she left a chemical fluid, supposedly invisible ink, where it could be found on her desk at home. "I purposely left a preparation very conspicuously placed in order to divert attention from my real means of communicating and they have swallowed the bait and fancy my friends are at their mercy." Yankee sentries likewise feared Belle Boyd, for they had been told she might sneak up and chloroform them or stab them.[51]

But the truth is that one of the most potent of a female spy's ruses is the very opposite of violence: it is a pretended innocence, the second of the three primary feminine games confidence women played during the war. Again and again, the three women who used feminine stereotypes as disguise eluded their pursuers by putting on an innocent air. To some extent, the presumption of innocence begins with the enemy; Boyd says, for instance, that a Union general told her much more than he should have, so sure was he that he would wipe out Stonewall Jackson's army in the upcoming campaign. "In short," she concludes, "he was completely off his guard, and forgot that a woman can sometimes listen and remember." Boyd once used the ruse of acting like an innocent young girl to transfer some important letters through Union lines. She gave the most important messages to her black servant, since slaves "were 'non-suspects' and had carte blanche from the Yankees to do what they pleased."[52] The less important ones she placed rather conspicuously in a basket. One can imagine how harmless Boyd and the other woman looked, out for a walk with baskets on their arms. Even after the pair was stopped and the unimportant letters found, the women were allowed to go on their way with the most valuable messages because the Union officer was distracted by his anger at the lieutenant who had given Boyd the pass.

Near the end of her wartime career, Boyd used the air of innocence to protect herself and a Southern officer at the same time. She was blockade-running on her way to England with dispatches. A Captain H. needed to escape from the ship when it was taken by the Yankees, who were looking specifically for Boyd,

51. Greenhow, *My Imprisonment,* 214, 216; Boyd, *Belle Boyd,* 228.
52. Boyd, *Belle Boyd,* 102.

so Boyd, using the alias "Mrs. Lewis," distracted the guard as Captain H. got away. She knew where he was going and even communicated with him as the days and the search went on, but always she pretended ignorance of him. No one pressed her. "I looked very serious," Boyd recalls, "though all the while I was laughing in my sleeve, saying to myself, 'Again I have got the better of the Yankees!' "[53]

Greenhow did not much use her charms to do her work, but she was an expert at innocence. Her famous cipher and the almost magical way she could get messages past the most vigilant of guards she only half reveals in her narrative, but the little she says is enough to let us imagine a confidence art made by women for women. "Under the eyes of the detective police," she tells us, "I had received and answered dispatches from my friends," including President Jefferson Davis. She did so by writing "effusions" in womanly language—with secret meanings: "Tell Aunt Sally that I have some old shoes *for the children,* and I wish her to send someone *down town* to take them and to let me know whether she has found any charitable person to help her to take care of them" (Greenhow's emphasis). The meaning is "I have some important information to send across the river, and wish a messenger immediately. Have you any means of getting reliable information?" The "Aunt Sally" who received the letter was a female accomplice who answered in kind. The detectives and guards who read her voluminous outgoing mail remarked astutely, "For a *'clever woman Mrs. Greenhow wrote the greatest pack of trash' that ever was read*" (Greenhow's emphasis). Greenhow laughs at one man who worried when she sent him a secret message because he was surrounded by detectives. "He had not learned that therein was his immunity to do seemingly impossible things."[54]

In a very cryptic way, Greenhow mentions another of her methods of communication. She somehow used balls of thread for doing "tapestry work" in various colors as a means of communicating. "I had made a vocabulary of colours, which, though not a prolific language, served my purpose."[55] The way Greenhow used the stereotypes about the triviality of women's talk and women's occupations to disguise her real purpose is a striking example of the power of women's language, a topic currently being studied by feminist linguists. There is a rather frightening resemblance between the world that allowed, through its own prejudices,

53. Ibid., 319–21.
54. Greenhow, *My Imprisonment,* 90, 92–93, 111.
55. Ibid., 92.

Greenhow to communicate with a community of women outside the male prison house and the nightmarish future world imagined by Suzette Haden Elgin in *Native Tongue,* in which women who are rebelling against an invidious separation of the sexes use a secret language, hidden under the "trivial" conversations of their sewing circle. For Greenhow, the acknowledged war was between people of both sexes who fought for divergent versions of what the American nation should be, but there was a second, covert war between the female spies and the male soldiers whom the spies sought to undermine. The presumption of triviality, of an ineffective innocence, became a powerful weapon for the women who played upon it.

In her usual flamboyant style, Loreta Velazquez used the ruse of innocence, too. When she became a female spy, she became a remarkable one, if her own account is true. Time and again she discovered that the best way to throw detectives off her track was to go directly up to them. As she theorized, "The fact is, that human nature is greatly given to confidence; so much so, that the most unconfiding and suspicious people are usually the easiest to extract any desired information from."[56] The most effective disguise was to appear to fulfill a person's expectations about you; the person's "confidence" is in his or her own stereotyping perceptions. Velazquez took her theory to its logical limit by becoming a double agent, so that when the Federal detectives were looking for the infamous Confederate spy, they overlooked her, although she was always right on the scene, because, after all, they "knew" she was one of their own.

In one amusing incident, which furthers the legend whether it is strictly true or not, she was carrying with her on a train a suitcase full of money for the rebels. A Federal detective, whose job was to find the female spy with the money, sat a few seats behind her. He had a picture to go by, but because he never accosted her, Velazquez decided she should pump him for information and induced him to sit by her, using an Irish brogue as part of her disguise. He ended up telling her all about herself, even showing her the picture, a wrong one, of course. "She is one of the smartest of the whole gang," he told her. When the train stopped, he carried her suitcase, the one with the rebel money in it, for her. Velazquez calls the incident "a capital good joke."[57]

The head of the Federal secret service once asked Velazquez to pretend to be a Confederate agent, and she did, rather enjoying the triple game, but her

56. Velazquez, *The Woman in Battle,* 363.
57. Ibid., 417.

favorite assignment was her last, when the Federals had her try to track herself down. Velazquez followed her own trail to New York, then took off for Europe, making her getaway. Spying was a game many women enjoyed playing, and one they obviously played well. Velazquez states that she enjoyed spying even more than fighting (which for her was saying a lot), because in combat one has little real control. In spying, however, "the plan of action was mine; its execution depended upon myself; mine alone was the peril; and should I succeed in accomplishing my first point, in gaining the Federal lines in safety, the prosecution of my enterprise would be a contest of wits between myself and those with whom I was brought in contact, and from whom I expected to gain the information I was after. For these reasons I found a keener enjoyment in the performance of spy duty than I did in doing the work of a soldier."[58] Edmonds avers that her spying made her ashamed, but her detailed and energetic descriptions of her exploits belie that attitude, or at least suggest that she enjoyed the spying despite her principles.

All these stories create the legend of the confidence woman as soldier and spy, the exaggeration being part of the game. It would be interesting to find out just how far the truth of these stories goes. Richard Hall in *Patriots in Disguise* discusses some of the credibility issues, but many remain unsolved, especially for Greenhow and Boyd. Whether or not the historical accuracy of these memoirs can be proven, however, the psychology of the confidence woman seems clear. The sense of control, of power, that Velazquez refers to above, was important to all the female spies and to confidence women in general. When the presumption in society was that women were weak and timid, some women needed to prove that they were exceptions.

The presumption of weakness itself became the basis of the third kind of confidence game female spies played when they donned the disguise of femininity. If women are weak and timid, they cannot be very dangerous, so one can tell them things with impunity: that was the reasoning that worked in Belle Boyd's favor and that ended up bringing the Confederates to a victory for which Stonewall Jackson himself thanked Boyd. The Confederates were coming into Fort Royal to fight the Yankees there. According to her memoirs, Boyd learned from an officer stationed in her house that the Yankees intended to retreat across the bridges and then blow them up, trapping the Confederate army until a bigger Yankee regiment would descend upon them. The officer was free in his conversation because he presumed the teenaged Boyd could do nothing with the information.

58. Ibid., 296.

They could hear the approaching Confederate forces, but none of the Southerners living in the house were willing to risk trying to reach them before the trap was set. So Belle Boyd went herself. She explains, "I had on a dark-blue dress, with a little fancy white apron over it; and this contrast of colors, being visible at a great distance, made me far more conspicuous than was just then agreeable."[59] But the very fact that she was conspicuous made her seem unimportant, and her "fancy white apron" was a symbol of innocence that allowed her to cover the ground she needed to, right under the eyes of the enemy, until the Yankees at last realized what she was doing.

Belle Boyd, the supposedly weak and timid young gentlewoman, ran from her house, after locking an impertinent reporter in his room, toward the nearing Confederate army; she ran through Union soldiers' bullets, a shell exploding once close by, the bullets so thick she later found several lodged in her skirts. As she ran, the Confederate soldiers cheered her on; "their shouts of approbation and triumph rang in my ears for many a day afterwards, and I still hear them not unfrequently in my dreams."[60] Boyd got the information to the Confederate commander in time: a special contingent of soldiers hurried to the bridges and saved them at the last moment.

The Yankee papers exaggerated what Boyd did, making it seem that she had led the battle. There was something fascinating about a woman who seemed to fit the feminine stereotype making such a daring run and helping bring victory to her men. The public purposely created its own *"frisson"* as a way to deal with this woman who defied all the expectations about a woman's duty. Her equally defiant response when she was held captive in the Old Capital and was asked to sign an oath of allegiance became a legend, too. She said, "I hope my tongue may cleave to the roof of my mouth . . . hope my arm may fall paralyzed" before she would bow to what she considered a tyranny. As she spoke, the other prisoners, like the soldiers, cheered. At last Boyd was made "Captain and honorary Aide-de-Camp to 'Stonewall' Jackson" in recognition of her service.[61] Her dream of power and respect came true.

The "feminine wiles" of charm, naïve innocence, and weakness that the three Southern spies used depended on assumptions about gentlewomen, or "ladies." Northerner Emma Edmonds, however, manipulated the assumptions about less

59. Boyd, *Belle Boyd,* 123.
60. Ibid., 126, 122–33.
61. Ibid., 182–83, 210.

"respectable" levels of society. She played a different game from the others, by eliminating "the feminine" rather than heightening it. She did not disguise herself as a charming young girl, but as a beggar woman or black water boy. Unlike Boyd and Greenhow, who were civilians, Edmonds apparently had an official commission from the secret service, and sometimes had to depend on help from her male peers to escape the enemy.

Whereas the Southern women made themselves very present to the men they duped, Edmonds preferred to make herself invisible. She did this by taking on the characteristics of people the enemy would discount because of their class, their race, or their ethnic background: her disguises were as beggar women, black slaves, and rustic boys. For instance, in one of her more famous escapades, she gained admittance to the enemy camp by disguising herself as a hag, an old Irish peddler, complete with cakes and brogue, playing as much on assumptions about class and nationality as on assumptions about women. On her way to the enemy lines, she got lost in the swamp and ended up at a nearly deserted house, where she found materials with which to enhance her disguise: mustard, red ink, pepper, and green glasses. With the imagination and skill of an actress, she "blistered" one side of her face and applied a "patch of court-plaster"; then she painted red around her eyes and tinted her face with ocher. The pepper made her eyes look festered, and she took care to bring a "pepper-handkerchief" with her to keep her dismal appearance intact.[62]

Once at the enemy lines, Edmonds did some "fast talking" in a sentimental vein to ingratiate herself with the sentries. Her language and manner strengthened the impression of weakness: "Och, indade," she reports herself saying, "I wish yez was all at home wid yer families, barrin them as have no families, an sure its we poor craythurs of wimmin that's heartbroken intirely, an fairly kilt wid this onnatheral war." Even as she proclaimed herself "fairly kilt" by the war, she was garnering information from the soldiers about a trap the rebel forces were setting for the Yankees. All the while, she reports, she was in pain from the blister and plaster on her face, and the continual application of the pepper had so "disfigured" her eyes that she no longer needed the green glasses.[63] The discrepancy between Edmonds's courage and ingenuity and the sense of inconsequential weakness

---

62. Edmonds, *Nurse and Spy,* 162–64.

63. Ibid., 165, 167. Although Edmonds herself was a Canadian, her mother was Irish, and, according to Hall, Edmonds learned her Irish brogue from an old Irishwoman. This is one episode that Edmonds said made her ashamed for her "mean" deception (Hall, *Patriots in Disguise,* 86), but the vivid detail belies that.

she was creating for the soldiers shows her understanding of psychology. For she used against the soldiers their own prejudices about the powerlessness of old, poor women, especially Irish ones (for prejudice against the Irish, the current immigrants, was rife at the time), just as Boyd had used the stereotype of the weak girl against the officer. Using a ploy of the criminal confidence woman, Edmonds played the role the soldiers were most likely to find harmless.

Edmonds disguised herself as an "invisible" female in other ways as well. In one of her forays as a spy, she tells us, she dressed like a female slave, and was sent to cook for the Confederate general. Because they were accustomed to ignoring such female slaves, the general and his staff talked freely at the dinner table in her presence, discussing their plans for the next day and giving data about reinforcements, exactly the information Edmonds had been sent to get. As an added benefit, she picked up some documents that she later discovered were orders for troop deployment.[64] Despite the fact that a spy was somehow getting information about Southern strategy, no one considered the black cook dangerous. "I visited the rebel generals three times at their own camp-fire, within a period of ten days . . . unsuspected and unmolested," Edmonds notes.

Such invisibility could take many forms. Although Belle Boyd's invisibility was always of the feminine, ladylike sort, she tells the story of a Miss D., "a lovely, fragile-looking girl of nineteen remarkable for the sweetness of her temper" who disguised herself as a "peasant-girl" in a "country market-cart" to get across the lines and give information to General Bonham for his battle at Bull Run. Miss D. was able to pass "through the whole of the Federal Army" because the soldiers did not "see" her.[65] Had she gone as the genteel Miss D., she would have had to use other arts to make her way.

Velazquez also sometimes played the game of invisibility in her spying for the Confederate cause, but in a more aggressive manner than Miss D. Like Edmonds, she would sometimes disguise herself "down" to a lower-class type, although never to the extent that Edmonds did. One of her disguises was as a poor widow, virulently anti-secessionist, trying to earn a little money by carrying dispatches for the Union to a Federal general. The information was actually misinformation, and Velazquez had had no contact with the Union authorities, since she was really on assignment for the South. She describes her game: "I had the most innocent air in the world about me, and pretended, half the time, that I was so stupid that I

64. Ibid., 263–64.
65. Boyd, *Belle Boyd,* 91–92.

could not understand what his interrogatories meant, and, instead of answering them, would go off into a long story about my troubles, and the hardships I had suffered, and the bad treatment I had received" from the Confederates.[66]

The game of innocence and the game of invisibility are obviously closely akin. The difference I am focusing on is that the type of innocence played by the young lady Belle Boyd, with her bouquets and baskets, is not the same as the innocence of a hag, a peasant girl, or a poor widow, because the stereotypes and prejudices the con woman must manipulate are not the same. Whereas "ladies" were discounted because of their supposed triviality and naïveté, women of what was considered an inferior race, class, or ethnic background were discounted because of their real powerlessness in American society as much as for their presumed stupidity.

Confidence women are aware of the very useful fact that the construct "woman" often makes real women invisible, and they use the power of dress and environment to create the kind of invisibility they choose. In the twentieth century, women like Velazquez and Edmonds are still at work. According to Michael Decker, considered in the criminal underworld to be one of the most successful assassins, women in the 1980s "comprise[d] about 60 percent of the world's top assassins." Decker explains that "women are excellent. Because nobody suspects women. A woman can get closer to a man than a man can get to a man. They can go to parties unnoticed, they can go anyplace unnoticed." He describes one female assassin who is currently top of the line: "She was very capable of taking a small amount of information and building it into a very elaborate presentation. For example, she could pose as anyone, to get information. With a tiny bit of research, she could walk in and present herself as someone who's done something for years and years."[67] The ability of confidence women to be invisible and to play a part at the same time has not changed from the nineteenth century to the twentieth, although the stereotypes that they use have. The description of the female assassin of the 1980s has an uncanny likeness to the female spies of the Civil War.

Some men are aware of the usefulness of the relative invisibility of women, too. John Larney, a pickpocket in New York City in the 1870s and 1880s, dressed like

---

66. Velazquez, *The Woman in Battle,* 359.

67. Quoted in James Mills, *The Underground Empire: Where Crime and Government Embrace,* 330.

a matchgirl to catch his victims off guard.[68] Tom Driscoll in Twain's *Pudd'nhead Wilson* dresses like a woman when he robs the houses of his fellow townspeople and disguises himself like a woman again to get away from the judge's house after the murder. In both cases, people perceive the woman, but do not "see" her. No one suspects the woman of robbery or murder, despite the fact that she is always on the scene.

Emma Edmonds seems to have made invisibility the mark of her profession, for she was able to apply the concept in several different ways. For instance, on her first sally into enemy territory—the South, for her—she disguised herself not as a woman but as a young black man. She got clothes from contrabands, sheared off her hair, colored her skin black, and wrangled a wig of real hair from a supply boat steward. "I commenced at once to remodel, transform and metamorphose for the occasion," she comments.[69] An excellent mimic, she spoke in a slave dialect. Because slaves, whether male or female, were simply overlooked, Edmonds could "lounge" among the enemy soldiers, once she was behind their lines, as they talked about reinforcements and their fear that Lee might not be able to hold out against McClellan, and she could listen to a male peddler who was a spy for the Confederates (a man she ultimately turned in) without ever raising the suspicion that she was a spy herself. By playing on the assumption of the soldiers that black water boys must by nature be harmless, Edmonds succeeded in noting down the exact armaments of the Confederate force and the number of soldiers the Yankees would have to face. Even though, as the slaves noticed, she gradually lost her dark skin color—her skin was probably dyed—she remained invisible to the white enemy.

In fact, Edmonds was so invisible that her own commanding officer did not recognize her when she reported back to him, according to her memoir. She says that she had to "chalk" her face and dress like a woman for him to see her. In fact, she claims that she in effect had to disguise herself as a white woman to be seen at all, even by her best friend. However, this story must be untrue, since Edmonds never *did* dress like a woman in the army and so would not have had to make such a transformation either way. Several questions are raised by this fact: Just

68. Byrnes, *1886 Professional Criminals.* Marjorie Garber likewise cites Thomas Middleton, the Elizabethan playwright, as saying that confidence men dressing like women in order to manipulate other men "was a common phenomenon in London streets" (*Vested Interests,* 30).

69. Edmonds, *Nurse and Spy,* 106.

how conscious was Edmonds of the gender game she was playing in her memoir? How conscious was she that her whole memoir was a confidence game? And how many layers of disguise does her deception create? A white woman pretends to be a white man, who pretends to be a black man, that pretense intensified in the memoir by pretending that she had dressed like a woman all along. When she dresses like a black woman, the layers of disguise are compounded even more. Like all confidence women, Edmonds understood that a person's clothing is his or her best disguise, a thought seconded by Velazquez: "Clothing, and particular cuts of clothing, have a great deal to do towards making us all, men or women, appear what we would like the world to take us for." Marjorie Garber makes the implications of this clear when she considers "the degree to which *all* women cross-dress as women when they produce themselves as artifacts."[70]

Over the years, Edmonds supposedly masqueraded as a rebel prisoner (and was conscripted into the rebel army in the process!), a dead soldier (even when dragged out from under her horse by her feet and her pockets rummaged, she did not give a tremor), a store clerk, a foreigner who couldn't tell Yankee from Secesh, and a "green" Kentucky boy. Her disguises were never penetrated, even when she came up against other spies in the job she was given as the war proceeded: rooting out Confederate spies behind Union lines. Some of these stories are hard to believe, and others are patently incredible. Edmonds intended to write a sequel to *Nurse and Spy* to settle once and for all what was fact and what was fiction, but if she wrote it, it has not yet been found. For all these women, it will take some serious historical research, as Richard Hall and some others have begun to do, to find out how far the truth goes. However, it is not the truth but the stories that created the legend that influenced the public and writers of fiction in the nineteenth century.

The stories told by the two foremost female spies, Edmonds and Velazquez, about how their careers ended reveal the two directions women's condition was headed in the late nineteenth century, back toward the past and ahead toward the future, the opposing directions I postulate as part of the cause for the rise of the confidence woman. Edmonds depicts herself as a woman of the nineteenth century who stepped out of her self-sacrificing "true woman" role only as long as she had justification for doing so. Her career ended honorably, she explains in her memoir, when she became ill with an unshakable fever. However, the comment she makes on her condition reveals how conscious she was of the

---

70. Ibid., 106–20; Velazquez, *The Woman in Battle,* 185; Garber, *Vested Interests,* 49.

feminine stereotype, and possibly how she was required by her publisher or by her own psychology to return herself to that stereotypical category and render her war career a mere anomaly: "All my soldierly qualities seemed to have fled, and I was again a poor, cowardly, nervous, whining woman."[71]

Edmonds's words show that she apparently ended up going in the direction of the past, pulled down by the powerful stereotypes of the nineteenth century; Velazquez's words, however, point in the opposite direction, toward the future. She, according to her story, which does not end with the end of the war, became rich as a blockade-runner and counterfeiter—all for the war effort, of course. After the war, as I have mentioned, she took off for Europe while working on the assignment for the Federals of, fittingly, catching herself. She traveled from Europe to South America to the Far West, during which time she was married and widowed for the third time; she married again in the Far West, her fourth husband a man rich from mining. To the end, a comment she made about herself while she was a spy held true: "I had an unlimited faith in my own tact and skill, and did not doubt my ability."[72] Velazquez was poised to become a twentieth-century confidence woman, her forceful rhetoric foreshadowing that of con women to come.

The actual life stories of these two women complicate that picture. Edmonds did not sink into a "cowardly, nervous, whining" condition; rather, she deserted the army because she was sick—"I simply left because I could hold out no longer, and to remain and become a helpless patient in a hospital was sure discovery, which to me was far worse than death,"—went on to write her bestseller, continued to nurse wounded and ill soldiers, married, and twenty years later, "still a feisty feminist," in Hall's words, "campaigned" for a pension and received it. For Velazquez, there is not much historical data to compare her autobiography against. How she lived and what she did after publishing her story still remains for historians to discover, although it appears that she continued her adventures—in South America and in the West. Until Richard Hall's study in 1993, Velazquez's story was considered by historians to be "fiction," "tawdry,"

---

71. Edmonds, *Nurse and Spy,* 359. In a similar turnabout, Pauline Cushman, although she was made a major, ended her life in poverty, a seamstress, according to Kinchen.

72. Velazquez, *The Woman in Battle,* 294. Many of the women who took part in the Civil War as soldiers and spies were quite young—Boyd, Edmonds, and Velazquez were all just twenty years old or younger when their careers began. In *The Pictorial Book of Anecdotes of the Rebellion,* p. 206, we even get a story of a twelve-year-old girl, "Charles Martin," joining the army as a drummer boy (p. 206). "Frank," of the Eighth Michigan, according to the same book, was only seventeen (p. 622).

"exaggerated," effectively silencing her for twentieth-century readers.[73] Perhaps it is Edmonds, after all, who points forward and Velazquez who can signify the silenced confidence woman whose story was suppressed.

The Twentieth Century: Criminal Confidence Women Speak

The soldiers and spies are a unique group of confidence women who felt free to publish their experiences in the nineteenth century as part of the Civil War literature. Their confidence skills take second place to their patriotism in their stories; they wrote with the zeal of a great cause. It is not until the twentieth century that other kinds of confidence women began to write their autobiographies, although confidence men had been doing so long before. The soldiers and spies could excuse their deceptions as a necessity of war. It is not surprising, then, that the earliest memoirs by criminal confidence women likewise took a self-effacing tone in an effort to subsume the criminality of their actions under a moral message. Sophie Lyons published her memoirs in 1913, after she had given up her career as a criminal confidence woman and become a real estate agent; she gave her book the title *Why Crime Does Not Pay*. She returns to the moralistic truism that crime does not pay as a kind of pious refrain throughout the book. Her autobiography is in effect a con game itself, but not a very effective one, for the moral tone is obviously an overlay to a story of self-congratulation and storytelling fun.

Immediately the autobiography begins to deconstruct, for the title page proclaims that *Why Crime Does Not Pay* was written by Sophie Lyons, "Queen of the Underworld." The gap between the presumed moral message against crime and the obvious admiration for the acknowledged "Queen" of crime in this way reflects the contradiction that runs through the book, and is in the tradition of "immoral reform" literature described by David Reynolds. Readers were to believe that Lyons, basking in her château on the Riviera, wearing her diamonds and her lace, styled a "Queen" by her admirers, was going to explain to them why crime does not pay.

The publisher's introduction to *Why Crime Does Not Pay* continues the adulation. Lyons is a "Thomas Edison" among criminals because of her inventiveness

73. Hall, *Patriots in Disguise,* 92 (quotation from a letter written to request the pension), 92–96, 207.

and a "J. P. Morgan" because of her financial success. She is "the most remarkable and the greatest criminal of modern times"; she is "conspicuously beautiful," and "many of the most daring bank robberies were, indeed, planned by her and to her quick brain and resourcefulness the burglars often owed their success." Finally, as an ironic culminating tribute, the introduction states, "It has been said that she has been arrested in nearly every large city in America, and in every country in Europe except Turkey."[74] For Sophie Lyons, crime *did* pay. It made her rich, off and on throughout her life, and it made her a celebrity to the end.

But Lyons begins her narrative by playing the abused child growing up in the 1850s and later plays the tender-hearted mother. She disguises herself in the book as a victim always giving of herself. As a child, she was taught to slit purses to help support the family. She picked pockets instead of going to school. If she failed to get enough money, her stepmother would pinch her or stick a pin in her. Apparently, Sophie, a winning child, was quite adept at her job. Jay Robert Nash, in his encyclopedia of female criminals, describes Sophie Lyons as a natural. Lyons herself says that it was "my stepmother, who forced me to do wrong."[75]

All of the data I will be working with in my examination of Sophie Lyons's autobiography is very uncertain. In her book, Lyons does not give dates very often, saying instead "One December." I have no way to verify whether she gives her exploits in chronological order—or whether they happened at all. I use Nash as my outside source because he does give some dates and presumably has based his discussion on newspaper articles from the time period. But his seven-page entry on Lyons in *Look for the Woman* gives no documentation, although there is a six-page bibliography at the end of the encyclopedia as a whole. Therefore, when I give a date for any event in Lyons's life, it is meant to be approximate, based on what Lyons and Nash tell me. For more precise data, historians will need to reconstruct her record from whatever documents they can find. For my purposes, the precise dates are not essential because I am dealing with the legend of Sophie Lyons, although it is clear that Lyons did indeed live in the late nineteenth century and did earn her title as "Confidence Queen."

Later, representing herself as a young mother, Lyons shifts the responsibility to the gang she worked with. "The first few years of my married life were divided between my little ones and the necessary exactions which my career imposed

---

74. From the introduction, by an anonymous author, to *Why Crime Does Not Pay*, 7, 8, 9.
75. Lyons, *Why Crime Does Not Pay*, 13. Subsequent page citations from this book will be given parenthetically in the text.

on me. . . . my desire was to be with my little ones, but the gang of burglars with whom I was associated had learned to make me useful, and they insisted on my accompanying them on their expeditions" (pp. 15–16). Yet it appears that, far from being an unwilling accomplice, Lyons was the engineer of many of the robberies in which she was involved and apparently enjoyed her work, as evidenced not just by her publisher and her biographer, but by her own statements later in the book.

Nevertheless, in the first chapter, Lyons persistently displaces her desire for money onto her husband and claims a passive role in her own career. She declares, "Ned Lyons was hungry for money . . . and his continual activity took me away from the children much of the time" (p. 16). If the men in her gang were arrested, she "was relied upon to get them out of trouble. This took time, money, and resourcefulness, and kept me away from my little ones against my will" (p. 18).[76] Those "little ones" never appear clearly in her story, although she gives precise details about many of her jobs. Lyons apparently sent the children to Canada to be taken care of and, except for a story about how she wrested her daughter from a family that "adopted" the girl after the nuns who had been taking care of her found out that her mother was a thief, there are no details of her relationship with her children and no description of the daughter. She and the other "little ones" remain an abstraction.

Most of *Why Crime Does Not Pay* is devoted to detailed descriptions of crimes that in fact paid very well, no matter how the criminals squandered the money later. Lyons tells of a bank-sneak job she and Johnny Meany pulled off, supposedly to pay for a home for herself and her children. Lyons gives no dates for her escapades or arrests, but apparently this episode occurred before she went to Sing Sing in 1871. Her language in describing the crime is zestful; her role was creative and active and obviously gave her satisfaction. Lyons went every day at noon to a small bank, pretending to be a widow and flattering the elderly cashier who was alone in the bank at that time of day. Her purpose was to determine whether it would be safe for Meany to sneak in and steal the cash while she distracted the cashier. She writes about the event with a sentimental flourish: "Alas! how well I remember how that vain old man enjoyed his innocent flirtation" (pp. 30–31). When the day arrived for the robbery, she contrived to

76. I should note here that the question of children is quickly dispensed with in the soldiers' and spies' stories, too. Velazquez says her child died before she joined the war. Pauline Cushman gave her children up for adoption. It would be enlightening to find out the actual familial relationships of the confidence women of all sorts.

drop some silver coins, causing the cashier to get on the floor, thereby allowing her to determine if all was clear behind the counter. When the cashier arose, she gave Meany the signal to enter by a back way and then kept the cashier occupied by showing him a picture of a child in her pendant locket. The picture was small, so the cashier had to bend to be able to see it. Deftly, Lyons created an image of herself as the pretty, bereaved woman and doting mother who values the attentions of a kind man. While she played that role, she kept tabs on the robbery: "I listened as I kept up a rapid fire conversation to hold the attention of the aged cashier." She says with a note of pride, "With increasing vivaciousness, I rattled along" until the job was done. She and her confederate left town quickly. "I am just vain enough," she comments with a coy modesty, "to think that the old cashier was probably very reluctant to believe his pretty widow had a share in the robbery" (pp. 33–34).

This particular crime grossed $150,000, but netted Lyons only $20,000 as her share because some of the loot was in securities that could not be cashed at face value. One would think that $20,000 in the 1860s or 1870s would have been enough to keep a mother and her children quite well for some time. However, although Lyons declares that she intended to go straight, she relates that before long, the money was gone for her husband's bail and to pay his gambling debts. When she tried to find a job, she explains, "nobody believed in my sincere desire to abandon my early career and lead an honest life. . . . But my home and my little ones, dearer to me than life, what was to become of them?" (p. 36).

Such is the structure of the book: a lively narrative, detailing the disguises and deceptions Lyons used, then a sudden moralizing *mea culpa,* a kind of pious deception that did not work well for Lyons. Her book did not sell very well, perhaps because of the constant moralizing interruptions in the story. Despite the rhetoric, Lyons herself was clearly not as meek a woman as she sometimes pretends to be in her story. She records one instance when she discovered a double-cross by a fence for stolen paintings. In her description, her language is fiery, all the righteousness gone: "Quick as a flash, I pulled out the revolver I always carried in those days; shoved it right under Sheedy's nose, and said: 'Come, Mr. Sheedy—hand over the original paintings I left with you, or I'll blow your head off!' " Her comment on her own behavior here belies the pretended meekness elsewhere in the book; she says, with obvious pride, "He was considerably amazed at this warlike nerve" (p. 55).

Lyons's explanation of the escape from Sing Sing is likewise relatively self-congratulatory. She gives a long description of the deceptions she and her husband played, then mentions the fleeting enjoyment their escape brought before ending the section with a sudden return to the pious note: She shows her husband and herself driving off in a carriage and proceeding to rob a bank in Canada. After several months of high living—several years, Nash says—quickly glossed over in her account, she says that the two are found and returned to prison (in 1876, according to Nash). Lyons concludes, "We had nothing to show except the fleeting satisfaction of a few days with our children" (p. 78).

Much of Lyons's narrative is taken up with descriptions of the activities of other criminals, as she displaces the focus from herself. Other criminals' escapes from prison occupy many pages of the book, giving an insight into where Lyons's loyalties really lay. The story of "Sheeny Mike" is a good example. Sheeny Mike apparently used a ruse similar to that chosen by many women who were escape artists: he escaped from prison by feigning sickness. In his case, he made himself actually ill by drinking soapsuds so that he could not eat. To cinch his release, he scraped his side raw and rubbed salt and pepper into his wound to make it fester. The prison doctor asked for his release since he would surely be dead soon. Unfortunately for Mike, the doctor was right: the soapsuds fatally undermined his health. Lyons describes the escape in a tone of reverence for the criminal's desperate refusal to be held captive. His willingness to suffer great pain to gain his freedom recalls the "blistering" and eye-peppering Emma Edmonds went through to carry off her disguise for more altruistic reasons. Lyons's admiration for Mike's persistence even in the face of great pain makes him as much a hero for Lyons as Edmonds might be for us.

Although Lyons often downplays her own role in schemes, she overflows with praise for other criminals, women in particular. One of her chapters is entitled "Women Criminals of Extraordinary Ability with Whom I Was in Partnership." Her greatest praise goes to Carrie Morse, whom Nash calls Carrie Mouse, a woman Lyons claims outwitted even her. Lyons remarks upon her "well-bred cordiality which was such an important part of her stock in trade" (p. 90). Morse always dressed in the height of fashion—a Parisian hat with plume, high heels, diamonds. "In every detail," Lyons describes, "her well kept hands, her gentle voice, her superb complexion, and the dainty way she had of wearing her mass of chestnut hair—she was the personification of luxury and refinement" (p. 90). Lyons gives Morse the genteel image so often described by Thomas Byrnes. As she puts it, Morse looks as if she could be the "wife of some millionaire" (p. 90). Lyons uses much the same mythic language in talking about Carrie Morse that Jay Robert Nash would later use to describe her. She says, "I sat spellbound by her magnetic power—patiently listening to details [about a proposed bank for ladies] which were all Greek to me and getting from every word she uttered renewed confidence in the reality of the financial castles in the air which were to make us both millionaires" (p. 92).

It is fascinating to watch one con woman conning another, even as that con woman tries to con us. For Lyons would have the reader believe that she was "dazed" by Morse's scheme and that she never meant to steal from anyone who would be hurt by the loss. The chapter becomes a test of our discernment, our ability to recognize the disguise of innocence that Lyons is using on us at the same time we admit that she had in fact been tricked herself. Morse took Lyons in by her appearance of wealth, although the jewels and clothing were all bought on credit. Morse took in the rich women she intended to bilk by transforming a common brownstone she had rented near the business district into a bank— brass rails, huge vault, old men as bookkeepers, wooden bars painted to look like iron. The "New York Women's Banking and Investment Company" opened, apparently in the early 1890s, with Lyons posing as Mrs. Celia Rigsby, figurehead president. Her job was to look very rich and very sincere when hesitant women came to check out the legitimacy of the bank. With Lyons in her office, the old men at their books, and beautiful Morse behind the desk, their "bank" was a perfect setup. "Don't you know," Lyons quotes Morse as whispering, "there's nothing that inspires people's confidence like old men? . . . And the next best thing to an old man is a pretty woman" (p. 95).

Lyons tells us she felt some twinges of conscience as she preyed on her own kind. When "a poor, bent old widow" came to invest her life's savings of $500, Lyons advised her that "it would be much wiser for a woman in her circumstances to keep her money in the savings bank." Lyons pulled Morse aside later and declared, in an illuminating show of swindlers' honor, "I'm willing to help you swindle women who can afford to lose money, but I positively will not have any part in taking the bread out of the mouths of poor widows. . . . Sooner than do that I'll starve—or go back to robbing banks or picking pockets" (pp. 98–99). Lyons did not get much out of this scheme besides a wardrobe of good clothes and a fine place to live for a while, for Morse double-crossed her, taking off with the proceeds once the bank was found out and netting $50,000. When Lyons met her again, Morse was running a crooked matrimonial agency. Yet at the end of this story, to which Lyons devotes many pages, she tells us that Morse died in poverty and had been in and out of jail, so surely crime does not pay. However, we are aware that a good many young women in the 1890s lived in poverty every day and died without ever having had the chance to see what $50,000 could buy.

Lyons enjoys telling stories about the women who supposedly tricked her. One familiar name is Ellen Peck, whom Lyons joins Byrnes in calling a confidence queen. Lyons says in admiration, "At one time, when she was in her prime, she was defendant in twenty-eight civil and criminal suits" (p. 114). In regard to Peck's ability to inveigle Lyons into joining her in some schemes, she says, "Then along she would come with some story, oh, so plausible!—and I would swallow it as readily as I had the previous one and as much to my sorrow" (p. 115). After the spirited details of the scams she and Peck shared, the regret and piety expressed in many of these statements ring false, especially at the end of the section, where Lyons expresses the fervent hope that Peck will read her book and reform.

The tone of Lyons's book is energetic and at times almost joyous. She delights in contrasting women's prowess with men's, and highlighting female ingenuity. For instance, she points out that male bank robbers could relatively easily disguise themselves as policemen and other officials; female bank robbers, in contrast, most often disguised themselves as ordinary women. Once Lyons pretended to be a Quaker farmer's wife—dirty milk can, vegetables, basket, broken English. She ended up having to spill milk on the man she was distracting, although "if necessary I would have grabbed him about the neck and held him by force until my companions escaped" (pp. 182–83). In this vein, Lyons tells the story of a con artist who played the naïve woman in a $3 million Manhattan Bank heist. The woman dressed herself "elegantly" and went to case the bank in the guise of depositing a few hundred dollars. Lyons speaks admiringly of the woman's skill: "She made clear to everyone her charming ignorance of banking. She was as amusing as pretty, and before long she was talking to President Schell himself," who obligingly showed her the doors and combination lock to quell her naïve fears. "With innocent baby stare," Lyons continues, "she noted the make of the lock and its date" (pp. 151–52).

Here is an example of a confidence woman telling a story about someone very much like herself, expressing the admiration for the nameless woman's actions that she feels for her own ability. Lyons, like the unnamed woman, often used her "baby stare" in a pantomime of innocent mindlessness; the women's "charming ignorance" was in effect the commodity that they sold. Lyons was a professional who could switch disguises and types of innocence at will. She could be a crippled old woman, with wrinkles and a wandering mind, as easily as a brainless beauty or the clumsy dairy maid. Once, she escaped from jail, where she was being held on suspicion of robbery, by switching clothes with a drunk woman. "In the morning I pretended to be half sober and protested violently against being thrown out in the cold. But they pushed me out onto the sidewalk, much to my outward grief and inward joy" (p. 249).

This is the Sophie Lyons who "reformed" when she was no longer young, in the middle 1890s, and who went on the stage, a celebrity, lecturing to earn money to help other criminals go straight. Nash speculates that Lyons left crime not because of any real transformation but because she had become too well known to succeed as a con woman any longer. By 1897 she had switched from crime to real estate—and writing. Her publisher proudly announced the appearance of her book as the "'Confidence Queen' ends her twentieth tour of the world."[77] By the end of her autobiography, Lyons has quite dismally failed to show the reader why crime does not pay.

The interaction between Lyons and her publisher is in itself quite revealing. If we believe May Churchill, who mentions in her own memoirs that the reformed Sophie Lyons was indeed insufferably stuffy, it is possible that Lyons was confused by her newfound righteousness rather than playing another outright game. Perhaps Lyons did hope that Ellen Peck would read her book and reform. But there is no question that the publisher, Ogilvie and Company, had no such agenda. Appended to the 1913 edition are several pages of advertisements for other books published by Ogilvie. One in particular underscores an attitude toward criminality that was a powerful force in the American imagination. It promotes two novels about "Arsene Dupin, Gentleman Burglar," and the publisher describes Dupin as "noble, charming, chivalrous, delicate. Thief and burglar, robber and confidence man, anything you could wish, but so sympathetic—the bandit!" The tone is coy, rather embarrassingly so. Obviously the publishers expected people to enjoy "charming" thievery. The final sentence of the ad makes the attitude even clearer: "If you appreciate skill, ability, resourcefulness, and a battle between master-minds, do not fail to read these two books." These are exactly the qualities Ogilvie and Company hoped to sell in the Lyons autobiography. But at the end of the century, women were still too much associated with moral uplift to allow for a straightforward account of Sophie Lyons—the bandit—so she supposedly aimed for uplift by adding moralization. Ogilvie and Lyons tried to have it both ways and failed.

77. From the publisher's afterword, a series of news releases, 267.

By 1928, however, some things had changed. The autobiography of Chicago May makes no pretense to the moral uplift of Lyons's book. Within the first few pages, Churchill fiercely claims her own agency in her choice of career: "I cannot blame my life of crime on bad conditions at home," she admits, explaining that she was raised in a strict but reasonably warm Catholic home; furthermore, compatriots did not lead her astray: "I never hunted with the pack. This may have been because I was proud of my ability and thought most other crooks were not my equal. I worked hard to make myself a master workman. . . . I was an individualist." Unlike Sophie Lyons, May Churchill had no desire to pretend that she had maternal feelings or that she had any "womanly" desire to make someone a good home. Likewise, she never pretended to be religious. She says of her childhood schooling in a convent, "Most of our lessons were of a religious nature, or in the nature of womanly occupations, both of which I despised. . . . Among other things, I was dreadfully afraid of having a baby." This fear seemed to be a fear for her spirit rather than for her body, for she associates her attitude with a remark her brother made about a girl who was considered "wayward," suggesting that girls are tamed by pregnancy. The brother said, " 'Well, she hasn't had a baby.' "[78] Churchill's comment is, "This made a deep impression on me," as if waywardness were something to be valued, something to be guarded against motherhood.

The tones of these two criminal autobiographies seem very different at first— Lyons's apologetic, Churchill's defiant. Yet the energetic, straightforward rhetoric of the crime stories themselves in the two books is much the same. Lyons and Churchill are similar, as a pair, to Emma Edmonds and Loreta Velazquez. Lyons, like Edmonds, feels the need to excuse her "unwomanly" behavior; Churchill, like Velazquez, does not flinch from taking credit or blame for her own decisions. Churchill's autobiography is likewise much more enjoyable to read than Lyons's. The title, *Chicago May: Her Story*, emphasizes Churchill's point of view, whereas Lyons's *Why Crime Does Not Pay* emphasizes moralistic hindsight. Because Churchill is out to tell the story of one of her personas, the infamous Chicago May, she treats her life as a fiction. Jay Robert Nash considers the book highly unreliable, a romantic story she concocted on her deathbed, although he also calls her "Queen of the Badgers." Her avowed purpose is to sell enough copies so that she can go straight—not for any moral reason, but because "age and suffering" have brought her to this "business decision." She

78. Sharpe, *Chicago May*, 18, 14, 202.

is fifty when she writes the book, having been harrowed by twelve years in an unsanitary prison. She claims her story is "straight" as well, for as she says, "I despise a hypocrite."[79]

Churchill sets her story up as a bildungsroman—the education of a confidence woman. "I was a prize-graduate of the Chicago School of Crime," she declares. "My post-graduate work was done in New York and London." Churchill continues this analogy intermittently through the book, always considering her work a career for which she received professional training and earned professional wages. She names her teachers—Dora Donegon, Nora Keatings, Minnie May, and Mary Ann the Gun—and makes a point of defending pickpockets as criminals worthy of respect. As she judiciously puts it, "The school staff always insisted that each branch of the profession was as important as every other branch. . . . allowance being made for the personal pride of the performer." Churchill declares herself "one of the brightest students," saying that she "took summer courses in schools in Milwaukee, Denver, San Francisco, and elsewhere, always managing to pick up enough extra-scholastic work to pay for the tuition."[80]

The names of female con artists come easily to both Lyons and Churchill. I find it interesting that David W. Maurer, a journalist who studied confidence men and con games, wrote in the 1940s that there were few confidence women: "The only full-fledged con woman whom I have been able to turn up, who is recognized by male colleagues everywhere as a competent professional, is Lilly the Roper, who is now over 50 and has spent her entire life on the grift [making her a turn-of-the-century con woman]. . . . Early in life she made a reputation as a pickpocket and had her own mob."[81]

Maybe the problem is that Maurer defines confidence women by their acceptance among their male counterparts, or maybe the relationship between women and men in the 1940s was different than it had been before. Maurer quotes an old man who says he used to know lots of good women "grifters"—those who live by their wits, not by violence, "like Ollie Roberts in St. Louis." These women "were roping for panel stores, and some of them were good. But most of them have passed on. Some of them should have been on the pay-off. They were natural ropers." The old man speculated that in the 1940s the women didn't get a chance

79. Nash, *Look for the Woman,* 80; Sharpe, *Chicago May,* 12, 14.

80. Sharpe, *Chicago May,* 15, 34–35, 36.

81. David W. Maurer, *The Big Con: The Story of the Confidence Man and the Confidence Game,* 190.

to learn whether they were any good. Maurer contends that many confidence men marry women who are "in one way or another connected with the grift," but most of these women do not take part in their husbands' con games. He affirms that "some of the best pickpockets are women. . . . As big-time professional thieves, some of them are unsurpassed, and the small-time thieving rackets are overrun with them. They are well-represented in flat-jointing [various cons used at circuses and fairs] and in some other branches of the short con," but he states that the big con games are reserved for men. How much of this statement is prejudice on Maurer's part, I cannot say. He gives only a paragraph or two to confidence women in his entire book.[82]

Maurer's study was published just twelve years after *Chicago May: Her Story*. It seems incredible that all the women Churchill knew so well would have disappeared so quickly. It also seems incredible that Maurer had never heard of Chicago May, although her career effectively ended in 1907, according to Nash, when she was jailed. However, Churchill should have been well enough known for Maurer to mention her, especially given the violence in her life. She once marred a man's face with a red-hot poker on little provocation and was eventually thrown into jail for being embroiled in the shooting of her former lover, Eddie Guerin, who was shot in the foot. Churchill's story, unlike Sophie Lyons's, does not avoid showing the sordid part of her life as a confidence woman. She wrote about her fine dresses and diamond earrings in close conjunction with a tale about the man she connived into coming to her room, her "creep joint," where her confederate waited behind a false wall or in a trunk to creep in and steal the man's wallet while Churchill played the piano or distracted him more amorously (although she claims her victims seldom "got very far" before the money was taken and she had gotten rid of them through some ruse). She says boldly, "I had always a certain refinement until driven into a corner. Then I was rough and coarse. I caught them all: university professors, ministers, priests, gamblers, country yokels, sports, 'gentlefolk,' and visiting grandees from foreign parts." At one point she states outright, "There was no rancor in my heart against individuals; but I did have a deep and abiding certainty that society, as such,

---

82. Ibid., 189–90. In *The American Confidence Man* (1974), Maurer again does not seem to find confidence women or give space for discussion of them. However, Erich Wulffen, in *Woman as a Sexual Criminal,* devotes an entire chapter to "female swindlers and cheats" in Europe in the early twentieth century. The European confidence woman needs a separate study.

was my enemy."[83] This attitude in itself might be enough to cause chroniclers to omit her.

A few times in her autobiography, Churchill makes a political statement, coming close to identifying herself as a rebel—something Sophie Lyons never does—yet the sentiments seem to be more rote than felt. "I am absolutely convinced that most people commit crime because of economic necessity," she states, and, "Most criminals are such because they think they can get what they think are necessities more easily by crime than by honest work" (p. 56). For her, "necessities" apparently included lavish meals and expensive jewelry. She tells us that her own introduction to crime was quite unrelated to economic necessity; her first husband was a bank robber she married at age fourteen: "In my own case, animal spirits, and romantic, chivalrous love, carried me through the entry-way of crime" (p. 57). This story is perhaps apocryphal, however, because Nash says that Churchill (née Lambert) came from Ireland at age fifteen and immediately got a job as a chorus girl under the name Latimer and then began to work in the infamous "tenderloin" district. As with Lyons, the discrepancies between the autobiography and Nash's undocumented account call everything into question.

It is hard to determine just how much a rebel May Churchill really was. She did not have "economic necessity," since she could have remained in Ireland with her reasonably affluent family, or, according to her autobiography, lived with her uncle in Nebraska. And later, she could have stayed with her husband of only a few months and his family, the wealthy Sharpes. But she decided against these options and since she "despised" what she called the "womanly occupations," few of which would have paid well, anyway, she did not consider them or any other legal route. When she later held a job as an actress, she laughed at the low wages since she was able to make much more as a confidence woman (p. 53). According to her autobiography, her first husband was lynched as a member of the Dalton gang when she was fifteen, and she found herself on her own. "I was a widow at fifteen," she says, "alone in Chicago, . . . [but] it never occurred to me to look for honest employment." She defends herself thus: "I never committed a crime against an individual unless he or she was trying to take advantage of me. . . . If a man, for instance, tried to buy my body, it was up to me to pretend

83. Sharpe, *Chicago May*, 47, 33. Subsequent page citations from this book will be given parenthetically in the text.

to go along, but to do my best to thwart him and to make him pay dearly" (p. 12). There is a bitterness behind her actions that appears to be directed at the double sexual standard, at the limited career opportunities for women, and at an unfair wage system. Yet her response is destructive, especially to herself: unlike Lyons, Churchill never amassed a fortune, and she spent a decade in a British prison, where she barely survived.

Despite Churchill's generally apolitical actions, however, she had some acute insights. For instance, in prison she was careful not to complain about conditions because women who did were committed for life to Broadmoor, the mental institution. She says in regard to her heavy punishment, "If you molest society tackle the poor only, and you will get much lighter sentences" (pp. 193–94). She believed that she was sent to prison not for participating in shooting Guerin's toes, but for all the men in high positions she had embarrassed in the past. Perhaps her insights were in part due to her unconventional self-education, which reminds me of Lyons's fierce desire to learn. Churchill used her time in prison to read, and her taste is revealing. She used her confidence skills to make it appear that she had done her quota of prison work early so that she then had time to read Balzac, the *Decameron,* Oscar Wilde, the Old Testament, Gibbon, Lewis Carroll. She recalls, "All the classical novelists were mine for the asking, if I did not ask for more than my allotment of two a week: Brontë, Elliot [*sic*], Fielding, Thackeray, Scott, Dickens, Hawthorne, Emerson and dozens more. . . . I reveled in Dickens, especially Oliver Twist, and the parts in other of his books about crooks and lawyers." She read and acted out plays by Shakespeare; her favorite poets were "Burns and Tom Moore. . . . The one socked Church, State, and hypocrites; the other was the sentimental lover of his Green Isle and its people; both talked about every-day things in every-day language" (pp. 232–33). It is interesting that so many of the authors she read were social critics, satirists with a humor akin to her own.

Like Lyons, Churchill wrote about other confidence women with admiration. She especially respected Annie Gleason, a "penny weight expert" who could memorize the cut of a jewel exactly and have a glass substitute fashioned in order to make a switch. Gleason used her confidence skills to get herself into jewelry stores and close enough to the gems in question to do her work. Churchill says of her, "She was my friend, and I admired her. She was clever and beautiful, and never got any credit for either. I, who was a second-rater in both respects, was always in the public eye" (p. 244). This is perhaps the single outstanding time in her autobiography that Churchill evinces some humility.

Her praise for another woman, whom she calls only by her first name, May, is likewise great. "What that baby did not know, in that game," she says about May as a beggar, "wasn't worth knowing. . . . If she did not have an infant in arms, she was the wan, pathetic wife of a crippled husband, dutifully sticking by him in sickness and sorrow, for the edification of a world which was too lazy to investigate for fraud and too ashamed to appear niggardly. Sometimes she herself was crippled; sometimes only blind. Her voice was worth a mint, so meek, so modest, and plaintive" (p. 300). Churchill here describes an accomplished confidence woman who created an image of herself quite different from her own or Sophie Lyons's, but who still stayed within a stereotype of womanhood. Churchill's cynicism about the people who gave May alms sets her apart from Sophie Lyons and the other confidence women who wrote their own memoirs.

Her crude comment on Sophie Lyons's reformation is especially telling. She had great respect for Lyons's ability to get herself out of a jam by pretending to be "quality," but she found her hypocritical and catty after she went straight and "got religion." "She was a wonderful woman," Churchill says, "and I really think her reformation was on the level. At the same time, however, I think she had bats in her belfry" (p. 248). Still, she cited Lyons as an anomaly among confidence women, because even though she died from having her head bashed in by thieves she had been trying to reform, "she died rich" (p. 246).

Each of the confidence women who wrote about her life—Emma Edmonds, Rose Greenhow, Belle Boyd, Loreta Velazquez, Sophie Lyons, and May Churchill—had her own version of her motives. But the women are extremely similar in the bravado they display in the course of a tale and in their descriptions of their techniques of deception. Reading what the confidence woman has to say of herself makes her seem more real than reading what the historians say about her, yet the reader is left with a sense that the woman behind the mask might well be wearing another one that we cannot easily see through. Still, it seems clear from these memoirs that the confidence woman is not the freak, the eccentric that Nash would make her. She is rather a woman who from the beginning makes her decision in defiance of social norms and then boldly carries it through.

5

Literature: Muting the Voice

---

ecause the criminal confidence woman, the soldier and spy, and the adventuress were potent forces in the late nineteenth century, one would expect them, correspondingly, to show up frequently in literature. However, such is not the case. Although the confidence woman does appear in popular fiction, the image never had the kind of currency the confidence man did; in much serious literature it is as if she never existed. Instead we get a Hester Prynne, who certainly had the drive and the intelligence to be a confidence woman, but who stands instead as a representative of a womanhood that suffers patiently, that endures. Although she dares to imagine a society in which women would be free to choose their own lives, she quickly recants and lives out her days silently resisting the society she essentially conforms to. We also get pictures of women like Edna Pontellier in Kate Chopin's *The Awakening* who defy their society by committing suicide, and women who are deformed and battered by their society, dying or retreating to a Quaker home like the hunchback Deb in Rebecca Harding Davis's "Life in the Iron Mills." We also get images of women who triumph over the restrictions of their society because of their extraordinary talent, like Anna Prince in Sarah Orne Jewett's *A Country Doctor* and like Ruth Hall in *Ruth Hall,* by Sara Willis Parton (who used the pseudonym Fanny Fern). There are women like Aunt Fortune in Susan Warner's *The Wide, Wide World,* crabbed by the drudgery and penury of their lives, and there are women like Trina in Frank Norris's *McTeague* who are driven insane by the lust for money. But not so often is there a woman who resists her condition by playing tricks, by disguising herself in order to perpetrate some scheme, by being a confidence woman.

158

The image is not entirely missing, of course. We get a few stories of criminal con women and a few glimpses of women as spies. But confidence women have not become a part of the literary tradition the way confidence men have. I have talked about society's need to silence confidence women because they were so disruptive to the gender ideology of the time. And I have talked about how that silencing was accomplished: people pretended they didn't exist or transformed them into stereotypes that were easier to deal with. In nineteenth-century literature, we see the transformation taking place; rather than the criminal confidence woman or soldiers or spies, the main form of the confidence woman we meet is the adventuress. Otherwise, we find instead of the confidence woman the escape artist and the everyday pretender. The confidence woman's voice is not entirely absent in nineteenth-century literature, but it is muted.

A few criminal confidence women do appear in relatively obscure works. For instance, Bret Harte tells the story of Polly Mullins in his "An Ingenue of the Sierras" (1896). Harte's Polly is a character similar to the real-life Sophie Lyons. She participates in a robbery by bringing the stolen gold with her—hidden among her trousseau—and sets up the transfer to her male compatriot in the theft by waving a handkerchief out the stagecoach window for him to see. Her personal appeal is reminiscent of many of the criminal confidence women the informal histories describe. "Quite a prairie blossom! yet simple and guileless as a child," says Judge Thompson, one of the passengers in the stagecoach who refuse to believe that Polly Mullins is a trickster/thief.[1] Yarba Bill, the driver, is not so easily taken in. He suspects Polly from the first, noting that she drops her ring to manipulate the judge into lighting a match just at the spot where Yarba Bill had warned everyone that any light would alert lurking highwaymen.

It is the reaction of Yarba Bill to Polly despite his suspicions that is most interesting. He describes the humor and the charisma that we find again and again in the historical accounts: "She appeared to be a well-matured country girl, whose frank gray eyes and large laughing mouth expressed a wholesome and abiding gratification in her life and surroundings." When confronted with Yarba Bill's accusations, Polly becomes the timid, innocent young girl—the "ingenue"—by admitting that she had indeed given a signal, but it was to her fiancé, and that she was running away from a cruel father to marry the man she loved. She speaks "with the slight but convincing hesitation of conscientious truthfulness" and praises her "fiancé" with "the wholesome ring of truth." All the while, of course,

---

1. Bret Harte, "An Ingenue of the Sierras," 459.

Polly has been stalling, waiting for her accomplice to arrive and get the gold, so her wholesomeness is an act, like Sophie Lyons's pretending to be a "pretty widow." Yarba Bill says, "She took us all into her confidence with a sweeping smile of innocent yet half-mischievous artfulness." And when at one juncture she bursts into tears, he acknowledges that this was the clincher: "I think this simple act completed our utter demoralization! We smiled feebly at each other with that assumption of masculine superiority which is miserably conscious of its own helplessness at such moments."[2] Polly Mullins succeeds in transporting the stolen gold right into the hands of the infamous Martinez. She is the confidence woman come decisively alive in fiction.

Susan Kuhlman, in her study of the confidence man, makes an interesting point about this story. She says that Harte wrote the story late in his career and that in it he satirizes many of the sentimental conventions he normally used as stock-in-trade. Kuhlman reminds readers that Harte was often criticized for "relying on hackneyed formulas to evoke tears or smiles on demand," but asks, "What, then, are we to think when Harte creates a con-woman protagonist who relies on the same hackneyed formulas to pull off her game?" Whether the confidence woman in real life makes a satirical comment on the cherished stereotypes about women and chivalry is debatable. That she does so when she enters fiction is more certain. As Kuhlman notes, the possibility that Polly Mullins is, using Belle Boyd's words, "laughing up her sleeve" at the men caught by their own sentimental categories "increase[s] the stature of the Ingenue."[3] In serious literature, at least, some authors appear to understand that the confidence woman is an iconoclast by her very nature in a society that presumes women incapable of the ingenuity necessary for the confidence arts, in a society that does not allow itself to "see" her.

This is not to say that American fiction did not see other kinds of female criminals. The dime novels, which became so popular by the second half of the nineteenth century, thrived on stories of murder and mayhem, and showing women perpetrating the horrors made the stories all the more popular. In the dime novels we do not see the humorous, beautiful con artist. We find instead the kind of woman who represents people's fear of women's excessive violence and cruelty, those attributes propounded by Caesar Lombroso's psychology. If there is cunning, it is of a murderous sort, as such a psychology would suppose. An

2. Ibid., 459, 461, 463.
3. Susan Kuhlmann, *Knave, Fool, and Genius: The Confidence Man as He Appears in Nineteenth-Century American Fiction,* 45.

example of this kind of cunning woman is Belle Gunness, a real woman whose murders were turned into sensational fiction. She used a technique similar to that of the Poillon sisters. She wrote ads to get suitors and then developed romances through the mail, writing loving letters that promised a storybook marriage—if only the mortgage could be paid. The suitors would come, bringing money for the wedding and extra for the debt, but unlike the Poillon sisters, who would manage to make the suitor break the engagement and pay for it, Gunness would drug her victims, kill them, and, being a hog butcher by trade, cut them up into parts. Over the years, she stole as much as $30,000. At the end of her career, when it looked as though she were about to be discovered, she escaped immediate detection by first intimating to the sheriff that a hired hand might burn her house down, then luring a beggar woman to her house, killing and decapitating her and throwing her own dental plate into the house so that the body would be identified as hers, and then burning the house down with her own children in it so that the police would be distracted by hunting for her murderer. The plan worked. Only on the insistence of her disaffected male accomplice did the police check out the house and surrounding buildings. They found assorted parts of fourteen bodies buried in the hog shed.[4]

Belle Gunness is the kind of cunning woman who gets recorded in the dime novels, not for her skill at deception, but for her savage, grotesque murders. Such criminals were acceptable because they fit the prevailing view of female psychology. Remember that despite G. T. W. Patrick's argument that most women are unfit to be criminals, he makes one reservation, saying that when women *do become* criminals, they are hopelessly depraved. Caesar Lombroso likewise gives grisly accounts in *The Female Offender* of women poisoners and of mothers murdering their children, but no detailed accounts of women swindling. The fact that Belle Gunness makes it into the dime novel but Cassie Chadwick does not suggests that the good humor, extravagance, and intelligence of a Cassie Chadwick or a Sophie Lyons were more dangerous to nineteenth-century American society than the depravity of a Belle Gunness, because the one upholds the stereotype of woman as childlike and primitive, unable to control her emotions, while the other evinces too much an attitude of choice, of perfectly rational but criminal decision.

A nonmurderous criminal confidence woman motivated by greed appears very seldom in literature, and then only in passing; she is rarely the main character. A typical example of such a secondary character is Stephen Crane's description of a

---

4. Nash, *Bloodletters and Badmen*, 236–38.

criminal confidence woman who appears rather inconspicuously in *Maggie: A Girl of the Streets* (1893). She appears as Nell, Pete's old paramour, who maneuvers him into getting so drunk that he can no longer guard his money. Given Crane's effort to make *Maggie* a realistic representation of the lives of men and women of the underclass, including prostitutes and petty criminals, it is significant that Nell is the only confidence woman portrayed. Maggie herself is an honest young woman who becomes a prostitute; she does not play games. The other women in the bar scene with Pete are perhaps small-time adventuresses because they get free liquor from him, but they "[scream] in disgust and [draw] back their skirts" when Pete falls into a drunken stupor on the floor; they quickly leave.[5]

Nell, however, "the woman of brilliance and audacity," has been the instigator of the scene, always urging Pete on, promising him the women's support. At one point, Pete is distracted from his liquor by the rude remarks of a male waiter who sees how he is being taken, but Nell intervenes. "'Never you mind, Pete, dear,' said the woman of brilliance and audacity, laying her hand with great affection upon his arm. 'Never you mind, old boy! We'll stay by you, dear!'" She gives an "oration" to the other women too, urging them to "stay by him," a necessary maneuver if Pete is to get drunk enough to pass out. When he finally does and the other women leave, Nell starts picking up the money Pete dropped as he fell, "stuffing [the bills] into a deep, irregularly-shaped pocket," reminiscent of the secret pockets of the shoplifters. When Pete snores, she looks at him and laughs. "What a damn fool!" she says, and leaves him there on the barroom floor.[6] Nell manipulates the situation by getting the women to stay and by getting Pete to trust in their and her affection. Her moment of unmasking reveals that she has been a confidence woman all along. That even Crane sees confidence women playing such a small part in the life of the city, despite what we know from Herbert Asbury and other informal historians, is strong evidence that criminal confidence women truly were invisible, and explains why that image appears so rarely in serious novels.

Short stories are more likely than novels to spend some time on the type. Artemus Ward's "The Octoroon" (1883) is, with Bret Harte's "Ingenue," one of the most obvious examples of a short story giving some description of a criminal confidence woman. The "Octoroon" is the female accomplice of "a man in black close," who begins the con against Artemus, a variation on the

5. Stephen Crane, *Maggie: A Girl of the Streets*, 74.
6. Ibid., 72, 74.

badger game. His role is to do the fast-talking, setting Artemus up by gaining his confidence: he "seemed to be as fine a man as ever was in the world." Her role is to "bust in 2 teers" and evoke Artemus's pity with her forlorn beauty. Like most confidence women, she uses her appearance, her clothing and demeanor, as her disguise. Artemus even names what she wears, a "More Antic Barsk" with all the "trimmins." He is equally drawn to her beauty: "her Ise & kurls was enuff to make a man jump into a mill pond." The woman manipulates her looks well, for Artemus lays down his fifty dollars "ker slap." But she gives the game away when she tries to do more. She calls him "old rats" and puts her head on his shoulder. Artemus is "astonished to heer this observation, which I knowd was never used in refined society," and roughly pushes her away.[7]

It is ambiguous whether the con woman makes a mistake or purposely changes the game, because she immediately switches from the "ladylike" ruse to the "hysterical female" one (qua Mary Hansen, who would extract money from strangers for "train fare" by making hysterical scenes in public places), asking him in a "wild voise" to elope with her. When Artemus pushes her away again, she "set[s] up the most unarthly yellin and hollerin," drawing the other passengers by the "rumpus." But it is the man in black clothes who articulates for the crowd what is going on, that Artemus is "insulting" his niece. Artemus hands over another fifty dollars to buy the pair off and only hours later realizes he has been "swindild."[8]

We should note how the criminal confidence woman changes as she moves from the rhetoric of history to the rhetoric of literature. Byrnes characterized the confidence women he had known as "she of the ready fingers and fluent tongue."[9] Yet the Octoroon's tongue can only unmask the game, not create it. Historical con women, as far as that history is known, usually worked alone, and all the verbal manipulation, all the confidence winning was theirs. In most badger games, although a male accomplice was involved, the man usually did not appear until the end. Ward's "The Octoroon" does let us hear the confidence woman and see her in action; however, in Ward's rendition the man is the central figure and obviously the brains behind the act.

Neither Harte's "Ingenue" nor Ward's "Octoroon" demonstrates the criminological theory of the day that one can spot a female criminal by her physiognomy,

---

7. Artemus Ward, "The Octoroon," 44, 45, 46.
8. Ibid., 46, 47.
9. Byrnes, *1886 Professional Criminals,* 31.

that criminal women are, in theory, always disfigured or masculine-looking. Apparently the confidence arts do not, in literature, suggest an atavistic regression in woman; to the contrary, criminal confidence women who appear in fiction are apparently beautiful, witty, and intelligent. Also—and this is an important point—one is apparently more likely to find a criminal confidence woman in a story by a man than in one by a woman.

But it is hard to make any theoretical statements about the criminal confidence woman as an image in nineteenth-century fiction because she appears there so rarely. It is more instructive to look at the other forms the confidence woman takes and at the ways her image has been diluted. Popular literature by men and some women relatively often deals with adventuresses, who do not break the law outright. Serious literature, on the other hand, is more likely to include images of escape artists and everyday pretenders—both images of women using confidence arts who are not confidence women themselves. Escape artists and everyday pretenders fit more easily into the accepted stereotypes of, on the one hand, women as pure angels who use their wits to evade being sullied and, on the other, women as manipulators, participating in daily deceptions. Interestingly enough, however, the fiction rises above the stereotypes by giving these women some of the characteristics associated with criminal confidence women and spies: the characters who use confidence arts to escape often have humor, intelligence, courage, and charisma—they are not just victims. Likewise, the everyday pretenders often rise above the self-serving, ill-intentioned manipulations of the stereotypically deceitful woman and deceive for altruistic reasons or harmlessly out of some small pride.

Louisa May Alcott created some strong examples of adventuresses in her "blood and thunder" novels. Jean Muir in "Behind a Mask," a novelette Alcott wrote early in her career (1866), is a confidence woman fully confronted and made the focal character. She is an adventuress, an actress turned gold digger, who has a surface refinement, an outstanding ability to be what anyone wants, and a calculating mind that foresees almost every contingency. Jean does not break the law, but she manipulates a series of people by donning multiple womanly disguises until she wins the love of the richest man on the scene. She would be a "proficient" gold-digger, using Betty Van Deventer's criteria, because she is so adept at applying one technique or the other to win over the men and women necessary to her enterprise.

Jean is absolutely calculated about her actions. She enters the scene in a disguise that Alcott reveals almost immediately: the thirty-year-old divorcée, the ex-actress pretending to be a winsome and harmless young woman of nineteen, just coming into the family as governess, goes to her room and takes a swig of alcohol, takes out her false teeth, and doffs her wig. Jean is outstanding among primary female characters for being so unqualified a fake—and for enjoying it so. She has all the attributes of a confidence woman: a great mimetic ability, excellent foresight, a charisma no one seems to be able to withstand, and an infinitely calculating intelligence, working day and night in her self-interest. As do the informal historians, Alcott presents Jean Muir as larger than life. When Jean discovers that Gerald Coventry likes to hear her sing, she sings as sweetly as anyone could imagine possible, singing as if to herself but always when he is somewhere nearby. She is ever vigilant, positioning herself exactly where she needs to be in every situation. She is beautiful. She is witty. And in her heart she is certainly greedy, but never malicious.

Right from the start, Jean zeroes in on the desires of the three men she successively manipulates into falling in love with her: Gerald's desire for a woman of spirit to mock him out of his passivity and sting him out of his cynicism; Edward's desire for a dependent and helpless woman to help him become a man and take responsibility for his own life; Sir John's desire for a good, steady young woman of noble blood to marry him and cheer his old age. Jean becomes all these women, thoroughly convincing each man of her utter truthfulness, much in the same way Madeleine played on the men who came to the house run by Madame C—. Alcott does not show us much of the other, the real woman Jean is, the woman "behind the mask," except by letting us read her highly scornful letters to her female accomplice, written in the mocking tone familiar from Velazquez's autobiography, and by letting us overhear her inner debate about which of the Coventry men to target and what to do when the scheme seems about to fail.

Alcott presents Jean Muir as a professional who is proud of her own ambitions and enjoys the game. A symbolic event occurs when Jean participates in a tableau. The tableau was a regular form of entertainment for the middle class, as explained in detail by Karen Halttunen in *Confidence Men and Painted Women,*[10] but in the hands of an expert confidence woman such as Jean Muir it could become a powerful manipulatory device. By the end of the series of tableaux, she has convinced Gerald that he loves her passionately, stage one in her plan to marry Sir John.

---

10. See Halttunen, *Confidence Men and Painted Women,* chapter 6, on parlor theatricals. Halttunen makes explicit the connection between *tableaux vivants* and the "genteel performance" on pp. 183–86.

Jean makes Gerald believe that he loves her by convincing him that *she* loves *him*. She does this by using one of the tableau scenes to her advantage; in it she "allows" her passion to show, supposedly a revelation of her true feelings. She and Gerald are to portray a painting in which a woman lies dying in the arms of her lover. Jean uses the attitude for all it is worth: "Her head was on his breast, now, her eyes looked full into his, no longer wild with fear, but eloquent with the love which even death could not conquer. The power of those tender eyes thrilled Coventry with a strange delight, and set his heart beating as rapidly as hers had done. She felt his hands tremble, saw the color flash into his cheek, knew that she had touched him at last, and when she rose it was with a sense of triumph which she found it hard to conceal. Others thought it fine acting; Coventry tried to believe so."[11] In Edith Wharton's *House of Mirth,* Lily Bart uses the tableau to show the self that is deeper and more beautiful than a hypocritical society will admit, an act that is truthful. Jean Muir uses the tableau to turn the act back on itself: in an act she reveals a seeming truth, but that truth is an act of its own.

Jean Muir is the epitome of the fictional confidence woman: she plans her complex game down to the finest detail and evinces pure joy in her scheme. Her letters to her confederate show the laughter behind her manipulation: "Early in the morning I ran over to see the Hall. Approved of it highly, and took the first step toward becoming its mistress, by piquing the curiosity and flattering the pride of its master. His estate is his idol; I praised it with a few artless compliments to himself, and he was charmed. The cadet of the family adores horses. I risked my neck to pet his beast, and he was charmed. . . . Monsieur is used to being worshipped. I took no notice of him, and by the natural perversity of human nature, he began to take notice of me." The passage shows Jean's humor, her understanding of human nature, her careful planning, her ability to take advantage of passing situations, her daring, and her egoistic pride in her machinations, all marks of the confidence woman. By the end of the story, Jean Muir's success is unconditional. Alcott has her caught, these same damning letters in the hands of the Coventry family, everyone telling Sir John he has been duped. But Alcott does not let conventional society prevail. Sir John is adamant in his love for and trust in Jean, and Jean triumphantly throws the evidence against herself into the fire. The narrator tells us that the new Lady Coventry, upon hearing her husband say, "Come home, love, and forget all this," despite the recriminations of the rest

11. Alcott, "Behind a Mask; or, A Woman's Power," 53.

of the Coventry clan, breaks into a smile because the words and her husband's ordering "Lady Coventry's carriage . . . assured her that the game was won."[12]

Alcott created many adventuresses in her thrillers, often devising games that rely on transformations of character and age, like the one in "Behind a Mask." Virginie Varens, an actress suspected of murder in Alcott's novella "V. V.; or, Plots and Counterplots" (1865), thoroughly understands the power of dress to effect a transformation in people's perception of her. When she wishes to appear as the respectable Mrs. Vane, a widow, she successfully disguises herself by wearing attractive but subdued clothing, in direct contrast to the fanciful clothing in which we first see Virginie. To make the theme of disguise clearer, Alcott has Virginie go through a symbolic change of clothing in chapter 8. Early in the chapter she looks like a "slight blooming girl of eighteen" and is surrounded by a "gay confusion" of clothing items. She is dressed in a "jaunty hat" with a feather, "scarlet boots with brass heels," a short skirt, a "blue-and-silver hussar jacket," and a "flame-colored silk domino." Her purpose is to rekindle the passion of her murderous husband Victor without compromising herself too far. She succeeds, and as the segment ends, she is smiling with a "conscious power."[13]

The scene that immediately follows is Virginie in her other mask, as Mrs. Vane. She is attempting to throw Earl Douglas off the scent, for he has almost convinced himself that Mrs. Vane is indeed the same Virginie who was implicated in his cousin's death. Virginie as the widow Mrs. Vane is also trying to prompt Douglas to marry her. Suddenly the blooming eighteen-year-old looks "thirty if she is a day" because she wears a black dress with "nunlike simplicity" under a "great mantle of black velvet." "The heavy folds of her dress," Alcott writes, "flowed over her feet. . . . she was very pale, her eyes were languid, her lips sad even in smiling, and her voice had lost is lightsome ring." That evening Mrs. Vane is careful to wear as her only ornaments a pearl brooch Douglas had given her and, in a semblance of innocence, her wedding ring. The juxtaposition of the two scenes emphasizes the power of appearance and underscores how useful a disguise clothing is to the confidence woman. It also raises the question of how aware women writers were of that power. Elaine Showalter, in *Alternative Alcott*, questions how far Alcott admitted the subversiveness of her own work. She says, "The masks that proliferate in Alcott's stories represent her own perennial effort to conceal the deeper meanings of her work from herself, as

12. Ibid., 99, 104.
13. Alcott, "V. V.; or, Plots and Counterplots," 100, 102.

well as from others."[14] But the "deeper meanings" are there—in this case in the presentation of a confidence woman—no matter how conscious of them Alcott allowed herself to be.

Because women have so long been equated with their appearance, a skillful woman can manipulate the responses of her viewers with relative ease. The manipulation of dress is in essence the manipulation of the presumptions and prejudices of the viewer. Feminist critics of the cinema and art have shown the power of the image, of how woman is seen. Recently, Martha Banta in *Imaging American Women* has shown how woman is trapped in the image, equated with her visual representation, which typically follows the stereotypes. People respond to the image created by a woman's appearance rather than to the woman herself. However, appearance is not a trap for all women. Confidence women like Cassie Chadwick, the Contessa, and Belle Boyd in history and Jean Muir and Virginie Varens in fiction went to a great deal of trouble to present an image that would elicit the responses they desired, implying that confidence women and the writers who presented them were at least subliminally aware of the prejudices they provoked or satirized.

Alcott is unlike most nineteenth-century writers in making the confidence woman figure the protagonist of her fiction. But adventuresses appear in other works as well. For instance, Mrs. Larue in John William De Forest's *Miss Ravenel's Conversion: From Secession to Loyalty* (1867), although never a professional actress like Alcott's characters, plays roles for sheer fun, an adventuress out for excitement alone. In one scene, when she wants to get into the good graces of the army chaplain, a passenger on the boat she is taking away from New Orleans, she not only acts demurely with "nun-like airs" but also is careful to don a "prim, broad, white collar, like a surplice" when she goes to speak to him. (Compare Virginie's "nunlike simplicity.") In this scene, we see Mrs. Larue's intelligence and humor: "Her manner to the chaplain was so religiously respectful as to pull all the strings of his unconscious vanity, personal and professional, so that he fell an easy prey to her humbugging." Mrs. Larue is every inch a confidence woman, even though she is not interested in monetary or social advancement, and the narrator does not hide his admiration and approval of her: "To one who knew her and was not shocked by her masquerades nothing could be

14. Ibid., 104, 103; Elaine Showalter, ed., *Alternative Alcott,* xliii. I find it hard to believe that Alcott was as unconscious of her meanings as Showalter implies. See my discussion of "A Marble Woman" later in this chapter.

more diverting than the nun-like airs which she put on *pour achalander le prêtre.*"
Later, the narrator tells us, "Carter [a man she is manipulating even as she manipulates the chaplain] and she laughed heartily" over her attitude with the chaplain,
for "it was an easy amusement to her to play a variety of social characters."[15]

Mrs. Larue is playing a game with Colonel Carter throughout the voyage. She
has already successfully maneuvered Miss Ravenel into marrying Carter, and
now she is trying to win Carter's attentions herself, just for fun. She and Carter
sail on the same ship headed north, and she makes him feel that he must be with
her if she is to go on deck, must be her protector, although as the narrator points
out she could have taken care of herself admirably had he not been on board. Mrs.
Larue woos Carter with her body and with her words. She speaks in French of her
loneliness and her need to love even as she makes her bodily presence felt. She is
eminently fluent. Carter tries to escape her by telling her that she is taking unfair
advantage of his nearness. In response, she "put on a meekly aggrieved air, drew
away from him, and answered, 'That is unmanly in you. I did not think you could
be so dishonorable.'" Carter "was deeply humiliated, begged her pardon, swore
that he was merely jesting, and troubled himself much to obtain forgiveness." He
ends up putting his arm around her and kissing her cheek the next night "in his
efforts to obtain a reconciliation."[16] Mrs. Larue's skills are well developed: she
can make a man apologize for thinking himself seduced. An expert confidence
woman, she gains her goal without seeming to have engineered it.

An outstanding quality of Mrs. Larue's personality is the relative absence of
malicious intent. Although she manipulates Carter into being her lover, she is
ready to drop the liaison immediately when someone could be seriously hurt.
As soon as Mrs. Carter is brought to childbed, Mrs. Larue falls into the role
of her female confidant and helper, breaking off with Colonel Carter without
hesitation. The narrator emphasizes her unusual and essentially good-hearted
nature: "Mrs. Larue was a curious study. Her vices and virtues (for she had
both) were all instinctive, without a taint of education or effort. She did just
what she liked to do, unchecked by conscience or by anything but prudence. She
was as corrupt as possible without self-reproach. . . . She took a pride in making
conquests of men at no matter what personal sacrifice."[17] The passage shows a

---

15. John William De Forest, *Miss Ravenel's Conversion: From Secession to Loyalty*,
353–54.
16. Ibid., 350–51.
17. Ibid.

rather begrudging admiration, careful to undercut Mrs. Larue's active choice by reducing her strategies to "instinct." But the descriptions of her machinations with Colonel Carter and with the chaplain belie the "instinctual" nature of her art. De Forest's treatment of Mrs. Larue is a good example of how the image of the confidence woman is raised in fiction above the often sordid reality of her historical counterpart.

Although it is possible to find examples of criminal confidence women in nineteenth-century literature if one looks with a certain amount of assiduity, and although one can with a little less trouble find some adventuresses, the majority of female characters who use confidence arts are not confidence women at all, but are only akin to them, fitting into the category of escape artists and everyday pretenders. However, the attitude and the language of the escape artists in particular is very reminiscent of such historical confidence women as Loreta Velazquez and Sophie Lyons. On the one hand, writers have muted the confidence woman's voice by displacing the image away from the sordid; on the other hand, they have brought significant elements of the voice onto the page by retaining the vigor, the imagination, the humor, and the creative courage of the historical confidence woman.

A perfect example of this displaced voice occurs in the popular novel *The Hidden Hand; Or, Capitola the Madcap* (1859), by E. D. E. N. Southworth. Capitola Black is a "madcap" because she so enjoys adventure and playing tricks. If trouble doesn't find her, she will go out of her way to find it. Her very birth is an adventure of disguise, for her mother convinces the midwife to pretend Capitola belongs to some other woman and thus help the baby girl evade the clutches of the evil Le Noir.

Capitola goes through an ironic initiation into womanhood when she is thirteen. Alone in the city, she discovers that she cannot survive as a girl: no one will let her shovel sidewalks or black boots because of her gender. On the edge of starvation, Capitola realizes that she can control her own fate by a simple change of clothes: "I thought to myself if *I were only a boy,* I might carry packages, and shovel in coal, and do lots of jobs by day, and sleep without terror by night! . . . and then, all of a sudden, a bright thought struck me: and *I made up my mind to be a boy!*" (Southworth's emphasis). The social statement is clear, as is Capitola's decisiveness. She tells the judge, after she has been arrested for transvestism, "The only thing that made me feel sorry, was to see what a fool I had been, not to turn to a boy before, when it was so easy!"[18]

18. E. D. E. N. Southworth, *The Hidden Hand; or, Capitola the Madcap,* 46–47.

How much power a change of clothing can give a woman is evident in the response of the pawnbroker who exchanges a suit of boy's clothes for Capitola's own: "I went into that little back parlor [at the pawnbroker's] a girl," she tells the judge, "and I came out a boy. . . . Well, the first thing I did was to hire myself to him, at a sixpence a day, and find myself [*sic*], to shovel in his coal." Even though the pawnbroker knows Capitola's sex, he hires her for a job for which he would normally hire only a boy. The clothes themselves in a way *are* gender. Simply to dress oneself as a boy manipulates gender stereotypes and expectations, as Velazquez and Edmonds both discovered. Capitola Black is initiated into womanhood by putting on a mask and by discovering the power it gives her to work out her desire. At first, her primary motivations are to avoid starvation and to avoid "danger from bad boys and bad men," but when she discovers the freedom her new identity gives her, there is motivation enough in that: "And from that day forth I was happy and prosperous! . . . I carried carpet-bags, held horses, put in coal, cleaned sidewalks, blacked gentlemen's boots, and did everything an honest lad could turn his hand to! And so for more'n a year I was as happy as a king, and should have kept on so, only I forgot and let my hair grow."[19]

Like many of the women who disguised themselves as soldiers, Capitola is caught only when she is personally recognized, for the police officer who brings her in says that the long hair alone would not have made him realize her gender, but that it helped him recognize the little girl he had previously known. Capitola's joy and success in her work remind one of Ragged Dick, her young male confidence-artist counterpart. The difference is that her success ends when her mask comes off. Ragged Dick goes on to prosper as a man; Capitola Black is on the verge of being sent to prison for daring to dress like a boy.

In history, women like Velazquez and those "passing" women Jonathan Ned Katz has documented often put on men's clothing in order to pursue careers not open to women. In literature, women dress like men primarily as a means of escape. Fear of rape and the need to earn money for food first impel Capitola to dress like a boy, her discovery of her new power coming only later. By reducing confidence women like Velazquez into escape artists, nineteenth-century writers muted the confidence woman's voice, but kept—in a whisper—its tone. On the other hand, by reshaping everyday pretenders like Murray Hall—who dress in men's clothing to pass as men for a lifetime—into escape artists, too, the writers underplay the very serious causes and effects of gender reversal.

19. Ibid., 47.

Stories about women who escape some dire peril often include another mark of the confidence woman besides disguise: the woman's ability to handle language. I have already noted that for the confidence woman silence and some appropriate pantomime, such as bursting into tears, are often her version of fast talk, but confidence women in history and in literature often also have gilded tongues. Polly Mullins, for example, convinces the men that she is eloping by using "lover-like diffusiveness" as she tells her story, and it is Mrs. Larue's erotic French speech that wins the day with Colonel Carter.[20] Capitola manipulates language early in her story, too, when she tries to convince her guardian to give her more freedom. Living a life of ease and refinement at the home of Major Warfield, Capitola does not need to pretend to be who she is not. But it is in her nature to play games. She consistently disobeys Warfield's restrictions, and then cools his excesses of temper by using her power of mimicry.

One evening, for instance, Major Warfield rides out alone into town still angry at Capitola for some offense. Riding alone is strictly taboo for her, so she turns his own rules against him when he returns home very late: "OLD GENTLEMAN," she says "with a sharp stamp of her foot," "Tell me instantly, and without prevarication, where have you been?" Major Warfield is of course taken aback. Capitola strides across the floor and shakes her fist. "DIDN'T you know, you headstrong, restless, desperate, frantic veteran! didn't you know the jeopardy in which you placed yourself by riding out alone at this hour? Suppose three or four great runaway negresses had sprung out of the bushes—and—and—" Warfield finally catches on to what she is doing and is delighted. "Oh, I take! I take! ha! ha! ha! Good, Cap, good!"[21] Capitola has the sense of humor and the daring of an adventuress like Jean Muir, without being one. She exemplifies the lusty spirit, the mimetic talent, and the fluency of the confidence woman, without any stigma attaching. Southworth discovered a way to give confidence women their voice by an act of ventriloquism.

Confidence women also revel in the control they have when they play their games. In part the excitement of this control comes from beating a social system that tries to deny women their independence and tries to tell women they have no head for carrying out complicated schemes. In *The Hidden Hand,* Southworth takes on this issue by throwing Capitola Black into situation after situation that

---

20. Harte, "An Ingenue," 463; De Forest, *Miss Ravenel's Conversion,* 349.
21. Southworth, *The Hidden Hand,* 127–28. Subsequent page citations from this book will be given parenthetically in the text.

demands her outsmarting the men who have come to do her harm. For instance, she quickly outmaneuvers the criminals who first try to abduct her: she sees Black Donald's henchmen under the bed and succeeds in locking them in the room without their catching on until the police can take them away. When Black Donald himself, a man she admires because he is a master of disguise, appears in her room at midnight, she escapes his clutches by using all her confidence arts. She says to herself, "Nothing on earth will save you, Cap, but your own wits! . . . All stratagems are fair in love and war—especially in war, and most especially in such a war as this is likely to be—a contest in close quarters for dear life!" (pp. 384–85).

Immediately she begins her plan. Rather than screaming (which would have been useless in the nearly empty house) or fainting, as most sentimental heroines would have done, Capitola throws herself into a chair as if she'd expected Black Donald all along, saying, "Well, upon my word, I think a gentleman might let a lady know when he means to pay her a domiciliary visit at midnight!" (p. 385). Black Donald, being a confidence artist himself, sees through the disguise, refusing to be the "gentleman" she is trying to manipulate him into being. The banter continues, each trying to circumvent the tactics of the other, and Black Donald comes close to winning. But Capitola has one lucky secret Black Donald is unaware of: there is a door under her rug that opens into a presumably bottomless pit. Capitola holds her own in this scene with Black Donald in a rapid exchange of talk about how much she admires him all the while she is setting the fatal trap.

Much of Capitola's manipulation is ultimately an effort to keep from having to send Black Donald to his death. She keeps trying to give him an out verbally, even as she sets up the room physically for the final action. She moves a table and her chair off the hidden trap door; Black Donald moves his own chair after her, until he is "luckily" situated directly above it. Thinking that her only strategy is to make him believe she likes him and therefore to let down his guard, Donald is very sure of himself: "All your acting has no other effect on me than to make me admire your wonderful coolness and courage; so, my dear, stop puzzling your little head with schemes to baffle me" (p. 388).

At last, Capitola clears all the furniture away, so that Donald sits alone on the rug. She leans on the back of his chair and tries to talk him out of his evil design, but finally stands back, her toe on the trap-door latch, hidden by her skirts. When it comes to the test, Capitola has the courage to make her decisive move, reminding us of women on the battlefield who must either fight the enemy or die.

Southworth consistently presents Capitola as a heroine precisely because she is so adept at disguise, fast talk, and quick maneuvers, and because she is both courageous and good-hearted. Capitola has to do some quick thinking when she sees the kidnappers under her bed and when she finds Black Donald in her room. In a similar instance she dons a quick disguise to rescue herself from Craven Le Noir, pretending to go along with his advances until she can race off on her own horse after putting his horse outside his reach. One could say that the novel is built on a series of confidence tricks: the switch at her birth, her dressing like a boy, her helping Clara Day, her various escapes, and finally her part in the rescue of Black Donald from the local prison. It is through such a character as the good-hearted Capitola that we hear the confidence woman, transformed, speak.

The voice that Southworth gives to the confidence woman is a complex one. It doesn't remain on the surface of disguise and banter, but begins to dip into the psychology of conning as well. Southworth recognized that the inability to see a woman is sometimes attached as much to her personality as to a general stereotype. She deals with this idea in the scene in which Capitola Black and Clara Day switch places: the quiet Miss Day is being held prisoner in the Le Noir mansion, awaiting her enforced marriage to Craven Le Noir, when Capitola arrives. Capitola changes clothes with Clara and instructs her on how to look like Capitola as she leaves the house. Clara is normally the epitome of blond-haired, blue-eyed Christian humility, whose first answer to her problem is to contemplate suicide; but Capitola tells her to have "courage, self-control and presence of mind" and, in order to make the identity switch complete, to "walk with a little springy sway and swagger, as if you didn't care a damson for anybody" (pp. 306–7). Clara does so and even imitates Capitola's temper, wheeling her horse and raising her whip, to avoid discovery. Southworth explains this transformation by remarking that "nearly all girls are clever imitators" (p. 308).

When reading the autobiographies of historical confidence women, we are readily struck by the humor and self-admiration of the narrative voice. In *The Hidden Hand* a similar tone comes across. Capitola thoroughly enjoys her role as escape artist and master of disguise. In the scenes following her rescue of Clara Day, when she has taken on Clara's clothing and identity and has been taken to the chapel to be married to the evil Craven Le Noir, Capitola is in her element. She has no trouble, of course, pretending to be the weeping Clara and succeeds in carrying off her ruse until she can reveal her true identity with a flourish. Using her typical sense of humorous timing, she waits until the priest asks her in front of the congregation if she will have Craven Le Noir as her wedded husband. She tosses off her veil and says, "No! not if he were the last man and I the last woman on the face of the earth, and the human race were about to become extinct, and the angel Gabriel came down from above to ask it of me as a personal favor" (p. 315). In a characteristic final salute, Capitola thumbs her nose at her would-be captors.

Amid the ensuing confusion, Capitola expresses the similarity between the confidence game and a play, between being a confidence woman and being an actress, in her answer to the Le Noirs' bafflement at her disguise: "It means confusion! distraction! perdition! and a tearing off of our wigs! It means the game's up, the play's over, villainy is about to be hanged, and virtue about to be rewarded, and the curtain is going to drop, and the principal performer—that's I—is going to be called out amid the applause of the audience!" Then, more seriously, "It means that you have been outwitted by a girl" (p. 316).

The similarity of conning and acting is quite clear historically: many confidence women in history were actresses at some time in their lives. Edmonds and Velazquez brought the production of themselves as artifacts to an art, making the connection between the confidence arts and acting an obvious one. Pauline Cushman, another spy who dressed like a man, was an actress before she joined the war. Belle Boyd went on the stage afterward.[22] May Churchill and Victoria (Claflin) Woodhull were also professional actresses at one time in their lives. In literature, many female characters who give voice to the confidence woman have been actresses by trade, too: for example, both Jean Muir and Virginie Varens have to hide their associations with acting, and the narrator in *Miss Ravenel's Conversion* says that Mrs. Larue "would have made a capital actress in the natural comedy school." The stage was just opening up for women in the late nineteenth century, and its allure of freedom and spirit was obviously compelling. Furthermore, some historians have suggested that most middle-class women in the nineteenth century had to be a species of actress in their everyday lives. Karen Halttunen describes the nineteenth-century middle-class parlor as a kind of stage. Although it is usually dangerous to use metaphors to describe historical reality, her interpretation helps to clarify some of the themes in nineteenth-century fiction. Halttunen suggests that once one entered the parlor in the nineteenth century, one was on view. The back kitchen and upstairs

22. See Kinchen, *Women Who Spied,* for the stories of many women spies, including Pauline Cushman. Two other spies, Charlotte Moon and Elizabeth Van Lew, also used many of the same tactics Edmonds and Velazquez did, involving changes of class and ethnicity.

bedrooms were dressing rooms and work rooms, but in the front parlor, the "genteel performance" went on "as if by magic." Visitors to the front parlor were actors and audience at once, Halttunen contends, and everyone knew the "laws" that guided the play.[23] However exaggerated this conception of social life might be as an explanation of how people actually lived, it at least explains the sense of theatricality that runs through so much nineteenth-century fiction. Was Southworth consciously making a critique of her society by creating a character who sees herself as an actress and who uses the devices of a confidence woman? We can't tell. But she did give voice to a spirit that was very much alive in the nineteenth century.

Alcott uses the idea that women's lives are a performance in many of her works. In "Pauline's Passion and Punishment" (1863), the entire game is a performance. Pauline is trying to make her old lover regret that he left her. When her husband/accomplice asks her why on their honeymoon she spends so much time in a hammock showing her affection for him by her fond looks and tender actions, she answers, "This week has seemed one of indolent delight to you. To me it has been one of constant vigilance and labor, for scarcely a look, act, or word of mine has been without effect." Pauline has made a stage of her hotel suite and is performing for a one-person audience, her old lover, whom she has caught spying on her from his own room: "Now do you comprehend why I remained in these rooms with the curtains seldom drawn? Why I swung the hammock here and let you sing and read to me while I played with your hair or leaned upon your shoulder? Why I have been all devotion and made this balcony a little stage for the performance of our version of the honeymoon for one spectator?"[24] The way Pauline stages her little drama is reminiscent of Jean Muir's manipulating the tableau. Both women use their histrionic ability in their own service, one to gain social position, the other to get revenge.

Alcott and Southworth both created characters who are brilliant examples of how the confidence-woman image appears in nineteenth-century fiction, as adventuresses and escape artists. Other, more subdued characterizations appear as well. Hope Leslie, for instance, in Catharine Sedgwick's 1827 novel *Hope Leslie,* is an escape artist who uses disguise, fast talk, and good humor. She uses her confidence skills reluctantly, however, preferring to be straightforward and

23. De Forest, *Miss Ravenel's Conversion,* 353; Halttunen, *Confidence Men and Painted Women,* 107.
24. Alcott, "Pauline's Passion and Punishment," 134, 135.

honestly courageous. Still, in some situations, being straightforward simply will not work. In such a case, Hope Leslie is willing to use her other skills, as in her run-in with a band of drunken sailors.

Finding herself on an island on which a "horrid crew" of sailors wakes from a drunken sleep to pursue her, Hope escapes in a boat, only to find that the boat she has pushed off in has a sailor in it too. "Luck" favors Hope: the sailor lifts his head to see her just as she kneels, "clasp[s] her hands, and breathe[s] forth her soul in fervent thanksgivings." Although Hope at this point is unaware of her companion, he opens the way for her game of deception by presuming that she is either the Virgin Mary or some saint. The narrator notes that in her flight, Hope's hair has fallen "in graceful disorder about her neck and shoulders, and her white dress and blue silk mantle had a saint-like simplicity."[25] The similarity among Mrs. Larue's studied "nun-like airs," Virginie Varens's "nunlike simplicity," and Hope Leslie's "saint-like simplicity" points to the virginal stereotype that quick-witted women can manipulate for their various purposes.

Unlike later in the story, at this point Hope must be pressed by circumstance into her confidence role. Whereas Capitola never has a doubt about taking on her various roles, Hope has to ponder whether she should play the masquerade that the sailor Antonio begins. Twice she smilingly tells Antonio that he is mistaken when he tries to name her, but he only presses on in his search for her supernatural identity. When he finally hits upon the idea that she is Petronilla, his personal patron saint, and lets slip his name as he praises her, Hope at last makes up her mind. She plays the part of the Catholic saint with finesse, remonstrating with Antonio about his "vile comrades" and reminding him that he has been jeopardizing his "eternal welfare." She even throws in some Latin she has learned from her tutor and blesses a holy relic of Petronilla's that Antonio has about him, a classic example of fast talk. To salve her own conscience, she adds to his relic box a bracelet with a diamond clasp for his "spiritual and temporal necessities." With some prompting, she manages to get Antonio to take her to the pier in town, where she completes her masquerade with a warning: "I give thee my blessings and my thanks, Antonio, and I enjoin thee, to say nought to thy wicked comrades, of my visitation to thee; . . . Reserve the tale, Antonio, for the ears of the faithful who marvel not at miracles."[26] Manipulating Antonio

25. Catharine Maria Sedgwick, *Hope Leslie; or, Early Times in the Massachusetts,* 240, 241.
26. Ibid., 243.

into keeping her visit quiet, Hope has not only achieved her escape, she has also covered her tracks.

This kind of necessary conning is different from the more meditated sort, for it depends on spur-of-the-moment decisions and fortuitous circumstances. Hope's reluctance to use the stereotype Antonio puts on her sets her apart from the confidence women who choose on their own to don a mask, but the confidence skill itself is similar.

For all her reluctance to use disguise, Hope Leslie finds herself in situation after situation that calls for her to do so. As the novel goes on, she becomes more accustomed to playing tricks and manipulating words, always for altruistic reasons. Like Capitola Black, she is both escape artist and rescuer, the latter role making her feel more comfortable about using deception, as when she attempts to rescue Magawisca, the novel's heroic Indian woman, from prison and certain death. From a reluctant deceiver earlier in the book, Hope turns into a high-powered, fast-talking pro in the jailhouse. The jailkeeper wants to see her permit to visit Magawisca, a permit Hope does not have and could never get. Her solution is to accuse him of ill-treatment and to burst into tears; her "womanly" solution works. But inside the cell she is all business, wasting not a moment of the short time they have together. She has to convince Cradock and Magawisca to obey her without question and has to physically dress Cradock like Magawisca in the midst of his complaints. She arranges the cell to look as it had before the switch and instructs Magawisca to walk with a Cradock-like shuffle and Cradock to breathe more quietly.

On the way out, the jailkeeper several times tries to check "Cradock's" face in the lamplight, and each time Hope foils him, finally resorting to putting the light out by "accident." Despite the suspicious circumstances, she wins the jailkeeper's confidence by a constant patter of conversation, centering now and again on his grandchild. When she and Magawisca are gone, the jailkeeper says to himself, "It is marvellous . . . how this young creature spins me round, at her will, like a top. I think she keeps the key to all hearts."[27]

Women cross-dressing as men in order to escape is a motif that occurs in many nineteenth-century works by both men and women writers. The light-skinned Roxanne in Mark Twain's *Pudd'nhead Wilson* (1894) dresses like a dark-skinned black man in order to elude her slave master, although her change in color had

27. Ibid., 314.

as much to do with her invisibility as her change in sex. Clotel, in William Wells Brown's novel *Clotel; or, The President's Daughter* (1853), dresses like a white man to get to the North just as Ellen Craft, her model in history, did. Ellen Craft's husband felt that he had to downplay her decision to dress as a white man by saying that she would not have done so if there had been some simpler means of the couple's attaining their freedom. Such an apology does not seem to have been necessary in the literature of the time. In *Clotel*, the idea of the disguise is the woman's, and there is no narrative voice apologizing for her action. To emphasize Clotel's agency even more, Brown makes the man with whom she escapes a friend, not her husband. In addition to engineering their own escapes, female characters sometimes dress like men to rescue their lovers or husbands. Mary, Clotel's daughter, exchanges clothing with her lover, George, in prison so that he can escape hanging. It is Mary's idea and no apology is offered. She has to persuade George into going along with her ruse. George finally puts on her clothing and gets by the guard by pretending to weep, as Mary often had after her visits, a handkerchief at his face.[28]

Hope Leslie gives the reader two disguise situations, one doomed and the other successful. In one, Roslin, a former mistress of Sir Philip Gardiner, an evil man who is courting Hope Leslie, dresses like a boy and acts the part of Sir Philip's page. Her motivation is love, jealousy, and a pitiable obsession with a man who is not honest enough to tell her to leave. Roslin comes to a bad end, killing Sir Philip, a hooded woman she thinks is Hope, and herself in a fearful explosion. In the other disguise situation, Magawisca, who has great power among her people, dresses "down," pretending to be an old Indian peddler woman. With this disguise she can come into the very house of the enemy and face a woman who would have turned her in immediately if she had recognized her. But no one sees the old woman as a person, so Magawisca, in effect invisible, can leave her message for Hope in safety.

Such wonderful escapes and disguises form a recurrent theme in American literature. Although historically such bold actions were typical mainly for criminal confidence women and female spies, in literature the women who perform these confidence tricks are depicted as sentimental heroines. In *Hope Leslie,* Hope's motivations are thoroughly pure and altruistic, creating an impression quite different from that of a Sophie Lyons, a Chicago May, or even a Loreta

28. William Wells Brown, *Clotel; or, The President's Daughter,* 167–70, 226.

Velazquez. Still, she "spins [one] round, at her will" as they did, an image that is qualitatively different from other sentimental characters, like the submissive Ellen Montgomery in *The Wide, Wide World.*

However, the transformation of criminals and spies into sentimental heroines was not absolute. When the story was written and who wrote it are important factors in whether its heroine was sentimental or realistic. *Hope Leslie, The Hidden Hand,* and *Uncle Tom's Cabin* (which includes another angle on the escape artist) all create the sentimental heroine as escape artist and all were written before the Civil War, the historical watershed I have marked for the flourishing of the confidence woman. On the other hand, the works that depict criminal confidence women and adventuresses—the short stories by Harte and Ward, De Forest's novel, Alcott's books, and Wharton's *The Custom of the Country,* in which Wharton creates an unparalleled confidence woman in Undine Spragg— were written later in the nineteenth century or early in the twentieth century. Perhaps before the war, because criminal confidence women and adventuresses were not as numerous as they were during and after it, fiction writers were reflecting what they saw, women of spirit and ingenuity using their skills for moral purposes. Or perhaps before the war the imperative to show such women as moral was more forceful. At any rate, it appears that the form the confidence woman takes in nineteenth-century fiction is in part determined by when a book was written: escape artists early in the century; adventuresses—and a few criminal con women—later. Also it appears that until the turn of the century, the gender of the writer made a difference, too: most of the stories and novels that show criminal con women or adventuresses before Wharton were written by men—or by a woman using a male pseudonym (Alcott wrote her thrillers as A. M. Barnard). The pressure on women writers to avoid describing this highly disruptive character type was apparently very strong.

So it comes as no surprise that Harriet Beecher Stowe, writing just ten years before the war, would refrain from describing a confidence woman but would feel free to create an escape artist. In *Uncle Tom's Cabin,* Cassy is the escape artist who rescues herself and Emmeline from the clutches of Simon Legree. Stowe adds a layer of meaning to the escape-artist figure by making her both a woman and a slave, who is perpetrating a complicated, well-thought-out act that neither a woman nor a slave was considered capable of devising. Cassy's escape plan is extremely complex; unlike Capitola Black or Hope Leslie, she does not have to come up with a lightning-quick scheme, but she does have to figure out all the contingencies beforehand. This is in line with the foresight necessary to carrying off a confidence game. Being an actress, the confidence woman understands the importance of having the right props. She sets her own stage carefully in order to help her direct the action of the play that she and her antagonist are in: Sophie Beck created the facade of a prosperous company in the apartment she rented; Velazquez would seek out the enemy in a disguise of her choice in order to control the situation; Chadwick made sure the lawyer saw her enter and leave the Carnegie mansion.

In *Uncle Tom's Cabin,* Cassy has to arrange circumstances perfectly by setting up both the physical and the psychological environment. She plans the escape with extreme care, playing not on Legree's assumptions about women and slaves but on his superstitions and his guilt for a past atrocity. She leads Legree to believe that he has a ghost in the garret, putting a bottle neck in a knothole to produce wails and shrieks, and she stirs Legree's imagination by leaving books about murders and other horrors in his path and by looking at him with a "fearful light in her eye."[29] Meanwhile, she is stocking the garret with provisions and clothing so that she and Emmeline can live there undetected until they make their escape.

Stowe describes Cassy's manipulations as a "game," in the last stage of which Cassy makes herself "unusually gracious and accommodating in her humors; and Legree and she had been, apparently, on the best of terms." Cassy's plan is complex, from the setup through the false escape to the denouement. Cassy physically disguises herself as a ghost by donning a white sheet and is bold enough to enter Legree's bedroom and speak in a spectral voice, driving Legree to "rave and scream."[30] From the very beginning, Cassy has manipulated the situation to be in her favor. The thought that she might be behind the terrifying apparitions never enters Legree's mind.

Fiction writers often emphasize the control that escape artists have over their actions. In this case, Cassy took a series of complicated steps to ensure that control. She had to prepare the upstairs room for a long stay and for the final escape, including making ghostly noises—by moving furniture around and creating the wailing with the bottle neck—beforehand so that her own movements later on would be assigned to a supernatural cause. She had to figure out ahead of time that the safest place to hide would be in the house itself. She had to premeditate her plan to physically appear to Legree as a ghost to prepare him and anybody else

29. Harriet Beecher Stowe, *Uncle Tom's Cabin,* 430.
30. Ibid., 431, 450.

on the plantation to misinterpret her and Emmeline's departing figures. Finally, she had to steal a roll of Legree's money for future use in the getaway. All this imaginative foresight is in direct contrast to the standard nineteenth-century understanding of women's psychology and is a surprise not only for Cassy's opponents in the book but for the nineteenth-century reader as well. One of the assumptions about women in the nineteenth century was that they are creatures of the moment, unable to carry out a plan even if they could devise one, because of a basic emotional instability. The root cause, according to psychologists, was woman's subordination to her body, specifically her reproductive system. In a culture that believed women to be passive, Cassy's adventurous intelligence is quite unexpected. That Cassy is black upsets a double prejudice, making her actions even more of a shock.

Capitola Black, Hope Leslie, and Cassy are three of the relatively few escape artists we find in nineteenth-century fiction. Although they are not confidence women per se, they do evince many of the characteristics of historical confidence women, especially soldiers and spies. They have an energy and imagination that thrive on danger. Women like Stowe's Cassy and Southworth's Capitola have something urgent in their natures that makes them begin a confidence game with zeal, even though the motive is escape. Certainly the confidence woman's voice has been muted in the escape-artist image, but we can still discern it. The women writers who were daring enough to create such characters were picking up on the urge of many American women to fight against societal strictures by turning the stereotypes inside out.

But a more common character that arises in nineteenth-century literature is what I call the everyday pretender. This is a woman who practices small deceits. She is not a confidence woman in any way comparable to the criminals and adventuresses, but she symbolizes the most remote limits of the type. Such characters do con the people in their lives, just as the women who passed for men and the lesbians who passed for straight did, but they do not feel the joy of the game that is basic to the confidence artist. Still, such an image of deception is important because it disrupts the transparent honesty and sincerity that were supposedly the marks of a "true woman." The everyday pretenders are certainly not criminals; they are usually not even driven by any great desire. For the most part, they simply want, as Madge Preston with her abusive husband wanted, to keep up appearances.

Harriet Prescott Spofford, in her story "Mrs. Claxton's Skeleton," gives an example of a woman who presents one face to the world and keeps another to herself. She lives with a man who considers himself a member of the elite and therefore expects his wife to be submissively obedient to his whims. Mrs. Claxton rebels and refuses to bend to him. However, the outside community does not know this, for she practices an everyday deception by her demeanor: "For all her sweet smiles and her tranquil manners out-doors, she was an exceedingly wretched woman within the house," the narrator says.[31] The deception does not go on only out-of-doors; Mrs. Claxton works around her husband by using tears and the appearance of patient submission despite the fact of her unbending will. By the end of the story, the deceptions can stop: in a dangerous flood, her husband comes to realize that he is not as significant as he had thought and she comes to realize that she really does love him. Everything ends happily.

Louisa May Alcott is more cynical about the effects of such constant deception on a woman's character. She shows the psychological damage that can be wreaked by the demand for daily performance. In "A Marble Woman" (1865), she makes her strongest, clearest statement. The protagonist, Cecil, plays her whole life as a performance, hiding her love for her guardian because he seems to wish it. She becomes "marble" in order to please him. That her demeanor is a conscious act, conscious for both the character and the writer, becomes apparent when her guardian, now her husband, finds himself embarrassed at a party by her coldness and asks her to show some life, pointing to a vibrant woman at the party: "Imitate Mrs. Vivian if you can; I want to try the effect upon these gentlemen." She holds up her fan a moment, then drops it to show not a calm, perfect statue as before but "a blooming, blushing face, with smiles on the lips, light in the eyes, and happiness in every tone of the youthful voice." When she is finished, Cecil asks, "Was my imitation a good one? Is that what you wish me to be in public?"[32] Her long-term act is also successful, but only at great cost to herself—she maintains her constant performance by taking opium. Such stories as "A Marble Woman" remind us that the women who consciously deceive every day are not necessarily going to be as visible and as unique as the criminals, the adventuresses, the soldiers and spies, and the escape artists. But the stories of these women are perhaps even more significant for a society that silently coerces many women to wear masks.

In nineteenth-century literature, such continual, everyday deceptions occur frequently: Iola LeRoy's mother passes for white in *Iola LeRoy* and tries to pass

31. Harriet Prescott Spofford, "Mrs. Claxton's Skeleton," 146.
32. Alcott, "A Marble Woman; or, The Mysterious Model," 184.

her daughters as white, too. (Passing becomes an even more frequent topic after the turn of the century. Nella Larsen's *Passing* is a novel that centers on the issue, and Fannie Hurst deals with the problems passing raises in family relationships in *Imitation of Life*.) In the 1870s Harriet Beecher Stowe wrote a whole novel on a woman's everyday deception about her age, *Pink and White Tyranny*.

Not all stories about everyday pretenders show the pretense to be harmful to the woman's soul, however. Mary Wilkins Freeman is just as likely to put a positive note on the act. A good example is her wonderful story of everyday deception, "A Gala Dress," in which Emily and Elizabeth Babcock pretend to the community that they have two silk dresses when in fact they have only one: they never go out together, and one wears a bit of velvet with the dress, the other wears lace—which means resewing the dress every time the switch is made. The lie grows larger as time goes on. A neighbor is jealous that the women have such fine dresses and neglects to warn Emily that she is about to step into some firecrackers; the result is a hole in the bottom of the dress. To keep the deception going, Elizabeth puts a black crepe flounce on the dress, explaining that she is in mourning for her aunt. The upshot is that the aunt really does die and leaves both Emily and Elizabeth her black silk dresses. To round the happy ending off, the two women give their old, burnt dress to the jealous neighbor.

One of the interesting things about this story is the double message it gives. At first it seems that it will be a moral tale about the dangers of lying and of using deception out of pride. But it ends up showing that the lie is successful, that the con has worked, not only to the benefit of the women involved but to the benefit of others in the community. This is reminiscent of Alcott's "Behind a Mask," in which Jean Muir wins but everyone else wins, too: Gerald comes to see who he really loves, Edward learns to be a man, and Sir John gets the loving companion he always wanted. This kind of multiple success is common to many nineteenth-century stories about confidence women or their sisters, in contrast to what often actually happened. Historically, criminal confidence women came to relatively bad ends, no matter how successful they were during the greater part of their lives. The story of a criminal confidence woman is often a story of a woman spending time in jail again and again, or at least coming up for trial. Even adventuresses like Tennessee Claflin, the clairvoyant and magnetic healer, had to keep on the move to evade the law and an unhappy populace.[33] Criminal

33. See Johanna Johnston, *Mrs. Satan: The Incredible Saga of Victoria C. Woodhull*, 23–24, 31–32.

confidence women's deaths were often rather grotesque: Cassie Chadwick died in prison, a pathetic figure, three years after she was arrested for her ten-year spree; Sophie Lyons had her head bashed in by thieves; Kitty Adams, who falsely claimed to have tuberculosis to get out of prison, died ironically enough of tuberculosis that she caught in prison. That some nineteenth-century authors rewrote the lives of confidence women, albeit not specifically "criminal" ones, to end with success instead of tragedy is an important comment on how they used fiction to invent their worlds. Since they sanitized the confidence woman's motivations, they perhaps felt justified in cleaning up her fate.

These relatively happy endings occur not only in short works, but in novels, too. The everyday ruse and all the convolutions of the deception become the focal interest, leading to the positive ending. A good case in point is Freeman's novel *Jane Field* (1892). It is the story of an old woman who uses an everyday deception—against her own conscience—in order to save her daughter. Jane's daughter, Lois, is coming down with consumption but cannot give up her teaching position in a school located in a dangerously damp and unhealthy place, Green River, because she has no money. Jane herself had had money at one time, but had lent it to her sister, Esther Maxwell, whose husband lost it all in a bad business deal. Esther and her husband are both dead at the time of the story, so the money will not be repaid. Jane had asked Mr. Maxwell, the husband's father, to help out the dying son, but he wouldn't. And he also refused to repay his dead son's $1,500 debt to Jane. The story begins when old Mr. Maxwell dies and leaves his money to Esther, his daughter-in-law—if she were alive—and to his niece Flora if Esther were dead. Jane decides to perpetrate a con in order to get her money back and save her daughter: she pretends to be Esther, saying that Lois is her niece. This would seem to be the perfect example of a story about a confidence woman, except that Jane Field simply doesn't have the flair. She arouses the entire community against her when she does not invite people over for lavish meals; they accuse her of niggardliness when her real problem is her scruples: she refuses to touch any more of the inherited money than the $1,500 that is rightfully hers, and won't spend any of the money at all until the monthly allowance accumulates to that point, even though Lois has to go out to sew and even though they are starving.

A confidence woman with scruples? No, Jane is an everyday pretender. She never even disguises herself as Esther outright; she just lets people assume who she is, since she and Esther always did look alike. Lois also has to deceive if she wants to save her mother from prison but is very upset at having to do so;

she fears her mother and despises her—even bolts her bedroom door against her. Finally, Jane breaks down, experiencing a kind of insanity of remorse, and goes house to house to announce that she is not Esther after all.

Apparently the game has failed because Jane is not brave enough to go through with it. Her scruples are unproductive: her principles about property take precedence over her relationships. But once again we get a double message from the story. The hatred of the community, the painful breach between mother and daughter, the deceitful stealing from the rightful heiress—the innocent Flora—and Jane's mental breakdown seem to indicate that deception is wrong, even in order to save a daughter's life. Yet the story ends with Lois becoming healthy despite having to work—she would have died in Green River, it is almost certain. Her mother has succeeded in saving her life. Also, Lois ends up marrying a relatively rich man—related to the Maxwells, no less—so she will be comfortable for life. Even Flora ends up happy, marrying the man she loves and being accepted by her mother even though her mother had been against the match. Actually, Flora's mother was an everyday pretender herself, pretending to the community that she had known of and approved Flora's secret marriage when she hadn't. Jane protects this deception, and Flora's mother later does not press charges against Jane. The final positive result is that Flora says Jane should keep the money, since she herself doesn't need it.

Such a story raises the question of how the confidence-woman image affected nineteenth-century women's writing. The clearest point is that writers admitted deceptions occurred and that they had an ambiguous attitude toward them. In an unjust world, perhaps women had to deceive. But certainly they weren't supposed to enjoy their deceptions, even if the end result were good. Another point is that it was more acceptable to write about everyday pretenders than about adventuresses and criminal confidence women because the motivations were more pure—saving a marriage, saving one's daughter, saving one's own small dignity. Unlike the image of the confidence man, which was writ large in the nineteenth century, the confidence woman appears in the fiction in a displaced form, questioning the stereotypes of women, but asking the questions in a whisper.

Among the diverse images of women in most nineteenth-century literature, from sentimental heroine to deformed victim to hardworking survivor, one attribute remains constant: the woman's straightforward honesty. Of course, there are little lies, minor deceptions, small thefts—Hester Prynne's pretending she does not know Dimmesdale intimately (*The Scarlet Letter*), Ruth Hall's using a pseudonym (*Ruth Hall*), Deb's stealing the overseer's wallet to give it to the man she loves ("Life in the Iron Mills"). But to find a Chicago May or a Cassie Chadwick or even a Loreta Velazquez is quite unusual. Male writers perhaps realized that the confidence woman could not be controlled and therefore was too dangerous to introduce into a story. Female writers perhaps realized that the confidence woman could too easily be misinterpreted as an example of the misogynistic stereotypes of the scheming and lying woman. Probably, most women writers had a different agenda; they had to rehabilitate women from the image of weakness and inconsequentiality too often associated with them by creating strong, positive female characters. Creating such female characters was in part an internal revolution, a way for women writers to overcome their own sense of social inferiority. Women had to create female heroes first; they were not ready to confront the antihero.

We ought therefore to recognize the intellectual courage of men and women who dared to create the confidence woman at all, even in sanitized form. Edward Friedman studies, in *The Antiheroine's Voice,* the changes through the centuries in female characters of the picaresque tradition, "from the condemnation to the exaltation of nonconformity, and from imposed silence to forms of eloquence." *Moll Flanders* is a transitional book, Friedman says, in which society and conformity win out on the surface but in which we hear Moll's voice, rather muffled perhaps, but not totally silenced. Erica Jong's recent novel *Fanny* represents the liberation of the antiheroine, Friedman asserts, for "the implied author takes the protagonist's side against the prevailing social philosophy," letting the antiheroine at last speak for herself out loud.[34]

The novels in nineteenth-century America that allow the confidence woman to appear are in a transitional stage similar to that of *Moll Flanders.* They tone the confidence woman down, overwrite her struggle against society by making order prevail and by manipulating her motivations and techniques to keep them within accepted bounds. Her voice is there, in some pieces of American literature—her extravagance, her humor, her self-assurance, her delight in her own schemes and successes—but that voice is muted even in the most daring works.

34. Edward H. Friedman, *The Antiheroine's Voice: Narrative Discourse and Transformations of the Picaresque,* xv.

6

The Writer as Confidence Woman

Afdter seeing the interesting productions of confidence women who became writers, constructing memoirs and autobiographies that are in part pure fiction, it is time to look at the works of some writers who became confidence women—at least metaphorically. In the nineteenth century, certain topics were very touchy: discussions of race, gender, class, prostitution, women's education, and abusive marriage relationships all demanded a certain finesse, especially if the writer was a woman. The more stereotypes were challenged in daily life, the stricter censorship of fiction became. A woman writer could lose her reputation—a dangerous thing in a time when marriage was one of the few ways for a woman to become financially secure—if she spoke too loudly about women's rights. Or she could face rejection from publishers and see her work go unpublished.

A. W. Abbot, in an 1851 article on "female authors" in the *North American Review,* states, "It may be said that in taking *any* public stand for praise or blame, a woman risks more than a man" (Abbot's emphasis). Later in the article he speculates on the reason for the number of women writing: "We trust the appetite for bookmaking notoriety is not so alarmingly on the increase among our fair friends, as from the mere number of names we might forebode. In many of these female authors we recognize an earnest and holy spirit and true aim, inconsistent with a petty love of display." The implication is that a woman may write as long as she stays within certain acceptable subject areas and uses an acceptable tone, showing her "holy spirit." Women who dare to write about anything unholy are, to use Abbot's words, "shrews," "vixenish," falling into the "Amazonian mania." Abbot declares that he would prefer a plague of cholera to the "rage for public speech and action, and for turning the world inside out and upside down" that some "strong-minded women" evince. According to Abbot, women didn't need to "advocate their own claims or be each other's champions" because they could depend on men's "chivalrous disposition" to do the job for them.[1]

On the other hand, Nathaniel Hawthorne, in an 1855 letter to William D. Ticknor, deplores the shallowness of most women's writing, declaring, "Generally women write like emasculated men." It is only when "they throw off the restraints of decency, and come before the public stark naked, as it were— [that] their books are sure to possess character and value." Women were caught between two conflicting attitudes: their writing was shocking if it was not "holy," but it was "emasculated" if it was decent. The sexual metaphors Hawthorne uses are revealing. Apparently, for him, a woman writer's personal reputation was intrinsically tied to her writing. The double bind women faced is exemplified perfectly in a judgment Hawthorne pronounces, in another letter to Ticknor, written in 1857, about the poetry of a Mrs. Howe: " 'Passion Flowers' were delightful; but she ought to have been soundly whipt for publishing them."[2]

Obviously, a woman who wanted to speak her mind about women's condition in her writing—about unequal laws, about the sickness at the heart of many male-female relationships, about racial prejudice and religious intolerance, or about the emptiness of many women's lives—could not do so directly without risking being seen "stark naked" or being considered a "shrew," if her books were published at all. In the face of this, several women, including Marietta Holley, Elizabeth Stuart Phelps, Frances E. W. Harper, Harriet Beecher Stowe, and Elizabeth Stoddard, tried a different avenue. Under the cloak of holiness and decency, they told the unholy truth, tricking their readers into considering ideas they would not have considered by choice.

Pseudonyms as Masks

Many women writers in the nineteenth century felt the need to use pseudonyms. Novels that were acceptable from the hands of male authors would have been shocking if the author were suspected of being a woman: Charlotte Brontë's *Jane Eyre* is a famous example. In America, one of the best-known cases of a woman using a male pseudonym is Alcott's calling herself A. M. Barnard when

1. A. W. Abbot, "Female Authors," in Lucy M. Freibert and Barbara A. White, eds., *Hidden Hands: An Anthology of American Women Writers, 1790–1870*, 359–61.

2. Freibert and White, eds., *Hidden Hands*, 357.

she published her thrillers. Alcott apparently recognized the daring nature of her stories about the confidence women Jean Muir, V. V., and Pauline and used one of their typical ruses as a mask for herself. Elaine Showalter in *Alternative Alcott* suggests that Alcott the writer had, in effect, two selves: Alcott's thrillers, full of passion and perfidy, are in marked contrast to the children's books that made her famous, as if she did not feel safe admitting that it was she who was allowing the voice of the confidence woman to be heard. A pseudonym is an alias, reminiscent of the multiple aliases of Sophie Lyons and Chicago May; that the pseudonym is a man's name reminds us of the disguise of masculinity Edmonds and Velazquez used to enter the man's world. In any case, it is a deception freely chosen by the author and is one example of the writer as confidence woman. Mary Kelley argues in *Private Woman, Public Stage* that many women writers of the nineteenth century led dual lives: they were often the main financial support for their families and yet strove to maintain the role of "angel in the house"; she argues, further, that this is why many of these same women used pseudonyms: to protect their families from public knowledge of their financial arrangement.

An intriguing analogue to this pseudonym usage is the famous case of Patience Worth. In 1913 Pearl Pollard Curran began writing poems, stories, even a six-act play, as a medium for a spirit named Patience Worth. Pearl sat at the Ouija board and spelled out reams of poetry and fiction, supposedly composed by a woman who had lived and died in seventeenth-century England. Patience composed; Mrs. Curran transmitted; Mr. Curran recorded; Mrs. Curran got the royalties. This is an extreme case of separating the unassuming woman from the prolific and aggressive writer. According to Joseph Jastrow, a psychologist who wrote a study of human belief in 1935, Curran was a "gifted and intelligent but moderately schooled, middle-class young woman, with rather limited advantages." Patience Worth herself "compose[d] with amazing facility." So much so that Jastrow comments, " 'Patience Worth' has become an enterprise." Apparently, Curran believed that she herself did not write the books from which she earned her living; she was merely the medium through which Patience Worth spoke. Jastrow argues that by using Patience Worth as a "mask" Curran could allow herself to speak out. It was not a "trick authorship, but [was] an interesting form of release."[3] This is a confidence game played by the subconscious, making Curran an unconscious con woman. Curran's game in the early twentieth century helps us understand the need of some nineteenth-century women writers to retain their less dramatic disguises.

3. Joseph Jastrow, *Error and Eccentricity in Human Belief,* 178, 178, 186, 191.

Other spiritualists were perhaps more aware of the trickery in their literary productions. Madame Blavatsky, the founder of modern-day Theosophy, for instance, wrote letters herself that she later claimed had been written by a "Tibetan Religious Man." Ellen G. White, the Seventh-Day Adventist, no matter how sincere she was about having visions, was insincere about how she put those visions into words. It is clear that she plagiarized most of the works she wrote, although she denied doing so. It is equally clear that she made a lot of money from the sale of the religious books she wrote.[4]

The Novel as a Confidence Game

I find it fruitful to analyze certain nineteenth-century novels by women writers as confidence games: the writer seems to take on the role of a con artist playing a confidence game on the reader. In these novels, the novelist uses a traditional plot and sometimes a traditional character to disguise the thematic game, but in such a way that the game is clear to any reader who decides to play. The game often has a structure similar to the typical one used by historical confidence women, including a moment of recognition of the sting.

Carol Pearson and Katherine Pope have suggested that many women writers in the nineteenth century disguised their opinions in their writing, using a verbal "camouflage." In books by such writers there is a disunity between themes and plot assumptions that "enables authors to camouflage feminist ideas in acceptable, protective wrapping." A literary confidence game, however, is of a different order. It entices readers into slowly undoing the wrapping and confronting the subversive themes of their own accord. Wolfgang Iser points out that the most serious literary works are built on blanks and indeterminacies that make reading a "game of the imagination." The reader creates the meaning of the text out of the various perspectives the writer gives. Geoffrey H. Hartman, too, speaks of literature as a game that demands the participation of the reader: "Thus the skill or will of the interpreter is essential: his skill in playing, his will to find or else to impose a meaning. Goethe calls this literary game a 'passionate divination.' It brings ear and wit into play."[5] Literary confidence games, a particular kind of writing, also depend implicitly upon the participation of the reader.

4. Kurtz, *The Transcendental Temptation*, 343 (Blavatsky), 274 (White).
5. Carol Pearson and Katherine Pope, *The Female Hero in American and British Literature*, 175; Wolfgang Iser, *The Act of Reading: A Theory of Aesthetic Response*, 108; Geoffrey H. Hartman, *Saving the Text: Literature/Derrida/Philosophy*, 135.

In *The Confidence Man in Modern Fiction,* John Blair argues that the con artist "serves as figure for the writer" and "stirs up the most troublesome moral, aesthetic, and epistemic uncertainties of our time."[6] When women write novels that trap readers into recognizing the uncertainty of many dearly held assumptions about gender, race, and class, the writers are con artists themselves. Essentially, in a literary confidence game, a writer uses a literary convention as a disguise to give the reader a sense of security; then the writer adds something unusual, a twist that does not belong in the convention, to signal the reader that rules will be broken. If the reader agrees to read on, the first stage of the game has begun. An old adage has it that one cannot con an honest person. Once the reader has agreed to go along with the "twist," there is a certain amount of complicity in the act of reading further. In a literary confidence game, the writer purposely sets out to play a game on the reader, to lure the reader ever farther away from the protective assumptions of some basic prejudice into the realm of a new vision. For some writers, the new vision is a vision of women's equality. For some it is a vision of racial respect. In any case, the game cannot go on unless the reader agrees to participate. The writer's task is to encourage that participation. This form of subversion is qualitatively different from the subversions of much women's writing because it is a *game.* Without the signal, without the complicity, the novel is not a confidence game. Obviously, not very many books fit this description. I have found five in my study of nineteenth-century women's literature. I am sure there are more, but I doubt that there are many more.

As far as I can determine, women did not begin writing the literary confidence game until the second half of the nineteenth century, although novelists began giving confidence women some voice as escape artists at least as early as Catharine Sedgwick's *Hope Leslie* in 1827. Before such novels could appear, it was necessary for women to develop a strong self-image as professional artists. Nina Baym suggests that the era of "woman's fiction," 1820 to 1870, was a time of growth and that "women authors tended not to think of themselves as artists or justify themselves in the language of art until the 1870s and after."[7] Most of the women's literary confidence games that I have found were written in the 1860s or later. Harriet Beecher Stowe (*Oldtown Folks*), Marietta Holley,

6. Blair, *The Confidence Man in Modern Fiction,* 11–12.

7. Nina Baym, *Woman's Fiction: A Guide to Novels by and about Women in America, 1820–1870,* 32.

Elizabeth Stuart Phelps, Frances Harper, and Elizabeth Stoddard all wrote their confidence-game novels from 1860 onward.

We have already seen how by the 1860s and later the stage was set for confidence women in their various guises to appear. Women writers were ready to be confidence women, too, because at the same time that their belief in their own artistic powers had grown strong, social restrictions that made it dangerous to "throw off the restraints of decency" still held sway.

The Basics of the Game

A literary confidence game is a particular kind of fiction, recognizable by having at least these five parts: disguise, a lure, the enforcing of a reader's complicity, a signal that the game is under way, and the sting. The disguise consists of a subversive theme masquerading in a traditional form that supports the status quo. The reader assumes from the outset that the novel will stay within the bounds of the convention, but there is an alluring difference. The novel suggests that it will step outside those bounds, just for a moment, just for the titillation of it, and the reader either follows the lure or closes the book. As Blair says, a confidence man will "cheat only those who are themselves ready to cheat" and "the victim must agree in advance to participate in the trickery."[8] For a novel to be a confidence game readers' cooperation is a precondition; readers help to set their own trap.

For the game to work, there must be a signal at some point that the conventions—both social and literary—that readers confidently believe in do not apply in this case. Yet readers must be so engaged by this point that they read on anyway, implicating themselves more and more in the subversive themes of the text. One of the reasons readers go forward is that the disguise continues, allowing readers to pretend that nothing has happened, that no game is occurring. Iser explains that "the game will not work if the text sets out to be anything more than a set of governing rules." Readers must be "willing to participate," or they will "opt out of the game."[9] If they wish, readers can ignore the game cues, often to the very end, because, as Iser explains, readers construct the meaning of the book only from the cues that are recognized. Ignoring the cues would be a form of opting out. But if readers stay in, even subliminally, they finally

8. Blair, *The Confidence Man in Modern Fiction*, 12.
9. Iser, *The Act of Reading*, 108.

realize that the "sting," the denouement, a wounding of consciousness—to use Geoffrey Hartman's words—has occurred. Sometimes the sting can be pointed to in the text: a particular scene or shift in language forces the disguise to drop and makes it clear to readers that they have been "caught." However, if readers have become embroiled in the story there is no way out other than reading to the end and admitting that some previous assumptions about society need refinement or rejection. Sometimes the sting is more elusive, spreading out over a series of scenes, but is felt nonetheless.

A confidence game naturally results in anxiety. Jacques Derrida explains that we search for a "center" in a text, a "reassuring certitude" that is "beyond the reach of play." The center helps us overcome our anxiety, "for anxiety is invariably the result of a certain mode of being implicated in the game, of being caught by the game, of being as it were at stake in the game from the outset."[10] In a novel that is a confidence game, readers depend on a center made up of assumptions about their society, but at the moment of the sting those assumptions overturn, leaving readers anxious because they have indeed been "caught." However, the psychological wounding is also pleasurable. For readers recognize their own part in setting the trap.

A good example of how a confidence game works in a social interaction is the game William Thompson played in the 1840s. The term *confidence game* was used for the first time, as far as historians can tell, to describe what Thompson did. Thompson would stop a stranger on the street and ask if the stranger had enough confidence in him to give him his watch. When the stranger handed over his confidence and his watch, Thompson would walk away laughing.[11] The "center" the stranger depended on was Thompson's middle-class appearance. The effect of the game was not just a lost watch, but anxiety because there was no truth to hold on to. The stranger had discovered that the appearance and tone of respectability were not a guarantee of honesty. He had been "caught by the game," and his own belief in respectability had been "at stake" all along. The stranger had had to trust Thompson and hand him the watch of his own free will; there was no force involved. That was the stranger's act of complicity: he broke the rules, however slightly, by trusting someone he did not know.

---

10. Jacques Derrida, "Structure, Sign and Play in the Discourse of the Human Sciences," 279.

11. For the Thompson story, see Lindberg, *The Confidence Man in American Literature*, 6, and Halttunen, *Confidence Men and Painted Women*, 6.

Afterward, he could complain of Thompson's actions only by revealing his own foolishness.

In a literary confidence game, the pleasure lies in recognizing our own foolishness even as we anxiously watch our original assumptions turn inside out. Literary confidence games have been written by men and women alike: most of the foremost male authors of the nineteenth century—Poe, Melville, Twain, and James—wrote one or more of the type. But the literary confidence game is particularly suited to women writers because, as Patricia Meyer Spacks argues, the "mode of indirection" is a common characteristic of women's writing. Because confronting an issue head on, both domestically and politically, so often failed amid the social restrictions on women in the nineteenth century, women sometimes used a less direct assault and won the point. Spacks describes Mary Ellmann, the twentieth-century polemicist, as a writer who uses "indirection" in an unusual way. I would argue that Ellmann has learned the tricks of a confidence woman. Spacks describes Ellmann's *Thinking about Women* as "evasive" and highly provocative. Her "mode of indirection is of course itself a particularly effective kind of evasiveness. Claiming so little, Mrs. Ellmann is difficult to attack; implying so much, she is difficult to refute."[12] Spacks puts Ellmann in a "new category" because her evasiveness has impact, unlike the evasions many other women writers use in a simple effort to play it safe or to avoid facing their own anger. Ellmann is evasive on purpose; indirection is her consciously chosen method of making a point. Readers must fill in the gaps, make the statements Ellmann refuses to, and so close the trap on themselves. Making readers fill in gaps in ways they normally would not is a kind of game. The evasiveness is not meant as escape but as a leading toward an idea. One might think of the Socratic method as a form of this purposeful indirection, leading the pupil to see things in new ways without stating the proposition clearly from the outset. The literary confidence game uses indirection as its technique.

Pearson and Pope's "camouflage" was tempting for women writing in the nineteenth century because a more straightforward approach to dangerous issues like wife-battering, suffrage, and property rights would often go unread, killed by early reviews. If the piece did sell, the writer could easily suffer social ostracism, her moral reputation called into question, a serious consequence for women in that time. Unfortunately, the result of such camouflage was all too often what Annis V. Pratt calls "the drowning effect": the socially unacceptable ideas are

12. Patricia Meyer Spacks, *The Female Imagination,* 26.

so well hidden in the text that they are barely audible under the conventional "drums."[13] The confidence game is a productive alternative to a camouflage that hides one's ideas, one's outrage. A writer could circumvent her own camouflage by luring readers through it, into actual confrontation with the issues they would not have faced on their own.

Novels That Are Not Confidence Games

In a patriarchal society such as existed in nineteenth-century America, it was sometimes dangerous to tell the truth. Therefore many women opted instead to stay within the bounds set by the literary conventions they used. For many, one of their first purposes, after all, was to sell books and so to support themselves and often their families, as Ellen Moers has shown.[14] Instead of writing novels that were confidence games, they wrote novels that stretched the conventional limits but stepped back at the end. Although characters like Louisa May Alcott's Jo are relatively rebellious, *Little Women* is an example of a book that does not play a game on its readers. It sold over 38,000 copies in one year and made a small fortune for Alcott; from the proceeds she was able to pay off the family debts and move with her family from the "poverty of dirty High Street" to the "riches of Pinckney Street."[15] Unlike her decidedly unconventional "blood and thunder" novels, which often use confidence women as main characters, and unlike the more subdued but still outspoken *Christy, Little Women* does not take the reader very far. Ultimately, its moralistic tone affirms the status quo; Jo's running and daring simply make her a better wife for the father-figure, Mr. Bauer, and a better mother for "her boys." There is no disguise here, no sting. Alcott's book is a clear example of what a con game is not.

Another kind of novel that is not a confidence game is one that does indeed use "feints, ploys, masks, and disguises" (to use Annis Pratt's terminology), but in order to "drown" the subversive ideas, not to lure the reader in.[16] Unorthodox major characters are either killed off or succumb to the stereotype at last (as Jo does); unorthodox ideas are kept in the realm of the minor characters, where

---

13. Annis V. Pratt, "The New Feminist Criticisms: Exploring the History of the New Space," 182.

14. See Ellen Moers, *Literary Women,* 85.

15. Madeleine B. Stern, *Louisa May Alcott,* 196, 198.

16. Pratt, "The New Feminist Criticisms," 183.

they can be criticized from a safe distance. Pratt explains that this "drowning" can go so far as to conceal the writer's provocative ideas from herself. Such a use of masks and feints is not a confidence game; its purpose is to avoid confrontation.

Susan Warner's *The Wide, Wide World* (1850) is such a book. Ellen Montgomery successfully suppresses her anger, her originality, and her independent spirit, but minor characters exhibit many of the qualities that Ellen fears in herself. Nancy Vawse, for instance, stays somewhat unregenerate to the end. She has the spirit and ingenuity Ellen tries to rid herself of. No one in the novel likes Nancy, with the possible exception of her grandmother, Mrs. Vawse, who lives alone on the mountain and is a figure of wisdom and self-definition. Nancy is not meant to be admired by the reader; she is clearly meant as an example of what Ellen could but should not become. The narrator, for instance, describes Nancy as "a restless spirit," and Christian-hearted Mrs. Van Brunt calls her "a regular bad girl," Mr. Van Brunt using the tag "that wicked thing."[17] Yet many readers find Nancy refreshing if naughty: her antics in Ellen's sickroom, for example, are a rich mixture of care, curiosity, and mischief; Ellen's hypersensitivity to Nancy's tricks makes the reader uncertain about whose side to be on.

Nancy comes to visit Ellen out of a kind of friendship and adolescent curiosity. She tries to help Ellen get up and walk, since Ellen has been in bed for two weeks, but Ellen fights her, which makes it appear that Ellen could have walked if she had tried. Ironically, we find later that Ellen had walked to her chair and sat up for a while the day before. Nancy has a "mischievous twinkle" in her eye as she threatens to tickle Ellen if she does not cooperate. Ellen, typically, decides to be passive. The difference between the two personalities is remarkably clear in the scene. Nancy's "quest for amusement . . . had so much of lawlessness that Ellen was in perpetual terror." Nancy's "lawlessness" reaches its height when she opens a door that Ellen never had the gumption to look behind on her own, goes up to the attic, and takes some of the hickory nuts Aunt Fortune had hidden away. She commences cracking and eating the nuts "on the clean white hearth," generously offering some to Ellen, who righteously refuses and worries about the "dreadful muss."[18] Ellen's compulsive cleanliness and overly nice sensibilities put Nancy's free spirit in an attractive light. Nancy is Ellen's alter ego. She promises to take a ladder and climb in Ellen's window some night

17. Susan Warner, *The Wide, Wide World*, 211, 126–27.
18. Ibid., 208, 209.

when Ellen forgets to lock the casement. The psychological metaphor is clear: lawless desire cannot be locked out.

Her vigor infectious, Nancy does get Ellen to loosen up a little: "In her vexation [Ellen] was in danger of forgetting her fear." Her "vexation" is caused by Nancy's trying on her scrupulously folded clothes and tossing the items aside when she is finished admiring herself and criticizing Ellen's taste. It is again the "muss" that "worried [Ellen] to the last degree." Nancy balls up Ellen's stockings and lobs them at her. "Ellen seized them to throw back" (good, the reader says, she finally shows some spunk), "but her weakness warned her she was not able." It is her weakness that is plain here, although the reader is meant to sympathize with her. We know where our sympathy is supposed to lie when, shortly after this scene, Ellen's closest friend, the selfless Alice Humphreys, comes to see her. First Alice scolds Ellen for saying "ain't"; then, because Ellen has complained about her ill treatment at Nancy's hands, Alice admonishes her for letting Nancy into her life in the first place.[19] Obviously, no game is intended; Nancy's unconventional behavior is to be criticized and Ellen is to subdue any similar urges.

However, Nancy's personality shows a complexity that must interest the reader on her side. At one point, Ellen gets "fretted" enough about what Nancy is up to, to get out of bed after all and come looking. Nancy's response is to worry about "those dear little bare feet." She carries Ellen back to bed "as if she had been a baby." Shortly thereafter, there ensues a fight over the gruel Nancy has been heating for Ellen. "Between laughing on Nancy's part, and very serious anger on Ellen's," they succeed in spilling most of the meal on the bed. Here is the contrast between the two personalities: "Ellen burst into tears. Nancy laughed." Nancy finally does resort to tickling in an effort to put Ellen into good humor, but Ellen "writhe[s] in hysterics" instead. When Ellen is "rescued" by Mr. Van Brunt and Nancy is sent packing, Ellen's tearful request is that Van Brunt read her a hymn.[20]

Although Ellen does not want to admit it, Nancy with all her faults is one of the few true friends she has. However, Warner does not seem to recognize the ambiguity of her own characters. She describes as a triumph how Ellen, after   . years of hard work, succeeds in making herself a perpetual adolescent, malleable enough to "deserve" marriage to John Humphreys. Warner might be said to play

19. Ibid., 210, 221–22.
20. Ibid., 211–12.

a con game on herself. She convinces herself, following the teachings of Thomas Harvey Skinner, her Presbyterian pastor, that Ellen is better at the end than at the beginning, raising her masochistic self-abnegation to a Christ-like stature. Jane Tompkins finds evidence of feminine solidarity in the book, in, for instance, the early scene in which Ellen and her dying mother share a ritual tea. The "routines of the fireside acquire sacramental power," according to Tompkins. But the ritual seems compulsive rather than creative: "Then she knew exactly how much tea to put into the tiny little tea-pot [note the repeated diminutive], which was just big enough to hold two cups of tea. . . . How careful Ellen was about that toast! The bread must not be cut too thick, nor too thin . . . and she herself held the bread on a fork, just at the right distance from the coals. . . . When this was done to her satisfaction (and if the first piece failed she would take another)" she would finally make the tea. This is "one of the pleasantest" moments in what is a mightily confined day.[21] If there is subversive material in *The Wide, Wide World,* it is there despite Susan Warner's best intentions. Perhaps for this reason the book sold more than any other single book in American history before it, over one million copies, and brought Warner enough money to "have provided a lifetime of comfort." Ironically enough, Warner's father thereafter—"in one of his unsuccessful projects"—lost the money earned from this conventional woman's book.[22]

Warner had convinced herself to *believe* in the restrictive stereotypes her public expected, and she did quite well under their dominion. Once she took Ellen Montgomery through the struggle to suppress her spirit, Warner rewrote the character as Fleda Ringgan in *Queechy,* but this time without the spiritual turmoil and therefore without needing a Nancy. Fleda begins where Ellen ends, and she too never achieves womanhood. Susan Warner did not write novels that are confidence games. She is the kind of writer Patricia Spacks has described as full of "self-doubt," needing to "escape" her own anger.[23] When the writer conceals her anger from herself, she cannot lure the reader into recognizing that anger's validity. A writer who will be a confidence woman cannot doubt.

Confidence alone, however, does not make a writer a confidence artist. A writer must purposely decide to play a game on the reader, to use disguise.

---

21. See Freibert and White, eds., *Hidden Hands,* 220, on Warner's relationship to Thomas Harvey Skinner; Jane Tompkins, *Sensational Designs,* 168–69; Warner, *The Wide, Wide World,* 13.

22. Freibert and White, eds., *Hidden Hands,* 220.

23. Spacks, *The Female Imagination,* 28.

Melville's *Pierre* is a good example. *Pierre* follows the conventions of the sentimental novel, but it takes the conventions to such an extreme that there can be no question the conventions are being satirized. In fact, the satire is so clear that readers are not really fooled for long; the conventions themselves are the disguise Melville uses to "hide" his satire of them. At the other extreme are books that do not use disguise at all, as camouflage or as game. Harriet Wilson's *Our Nig* (1859) is a strong example of that sort of novel.

Wilson, a black woman writing before the Civil War, knew that a white audience would not like to hear what she had to say about the position of lower-class free blacks in the North, but she desperately needed to write a book that would sell enough copies to support herself in her illness and to support her sick child. "I am forced to some experiment which shall aid me in maintaining myself and child without extinguishing this feeble life. . . . I sincerely appeal to my colored brethren universally for patronage," she says in the preface to *Our Nig*, as straightforwardly as anyone could.[24] But perhaps because Wilson was so open, not just about her need, but about her vision of the plight of blacks in the North, her book suffered a fate worse than Alcott or Warner might have imagined possible.

From the outset, Wilson refused disguise. The title alone doomed the book: *Our Nig; or, Sketches from the Life of a Free Black in a Two-Story White House, North. Showing that Slavery's Shadows Fall Even There,* by "Our Nig." The term *our nig* is a cynical exposure of the racist paternalism of the North, and if the cynicism in that term is not clear, the cynicism in the subtitle is inescapably so. According to Henry Louis Gates Jr., Harriet Wilson wrote one of the first, if not the first, books in English by a black woman, yet she has barely been heard of since the ill-fated publication of her book, until her recent rediscovery. Gates tells the story of what happens to a book that takes on the dominant culture so openly. Wilson's book, privately published, was not reviewed. Sales were killed before they could begin. Wilson's seven-year-old son died six months later, and Wilson, even though she was too ill to sew or do other work, never wrote for publication again.[25]

Gates argues that one blatant unorthodoxy Wilson dared was to describe without hesitation a relatively happy marriage between a black man and a white

24. Harriet E. Wilson, *Our Nig; or, Sketches from the Life of a Free Black, in a Two-Story White House, North. Showing that Slavery's Shadows Fall Even There,* preface.
25. See Henry Louis Gates Jr.'s introduction to *Our Nig,* by Harriet E. Wilson, xii–xiii.

woman. Miscegenation alone was a sensitive topic in the pre–Civil War years, but taking for granted that such a mixed marriage could be pleasant and productive went far beyond the bounds of what people would accept as true about white-black relations. Yet this marriage occurs in the first pages of the book, merely one of the vehicles for getting the real story going. Frado, the daughter of this marriage, is abandoned at a white northern woman's house. The novel traces how pretty, free-born Frado is immediately turned into a drudge, how she is physically, emotionally, and spiritually abused by a northern middle-class white woman, and how she finally stands up in courage to threaten violence against her tormentor. Again, there is no disguise. By the end of the book, as Gates shows, the reader is aware that Frado's story is Harriet Wilson's fictionalized autobiography; the final line ("Still an invalid, she [Frado] asks your sympathy, gentle reader") indicates a shift by implication from third- to first-person point of view, making a full circle back to the preface.[26]

Wilson is unorthodox in other ways too, Gates argues. She substitutes her love for and devotion to James, the white woman's son, for a Christianity she has found color sensitive and hypocritical, but she pretends that she has taken that religion to heart, going so far as to pretend conversion. Furthermore, a black confidence man appears in the book, tricking both Frado and the abolitionists into believing that he is an escaped slave who goes on abolitionist lecture tours for the cause rather than for money. Samuel is a free black man who marries Frado and then deserts her, leaving her in ill health and dire need, an ending very different from the conventional white woman's novel.[27] Harriet Wilson does not lure the reader into confronting these unconventional ideas; she just tells the truth. The result is a book that was silenced at its birth, leaving Wilson in poverty and seclusion.

The long-term result is even worse. Gates documents how Wilson's head-on approach effectively made the book drop out of literary history. In all the literary histories of America written since 1900, Gates finds *Our Nig* listed only five times, despite its obvious historical importance. In these five sources, Wilson is misrepresented variously as white or male or both. Her book gets no more than passing mention, and if it gets that, the focus is inevitably on the miscegenation. Yet Gates argues that Wilson "*created* the black woman's novel . . . because she *invented* her own plot structure," one founded on the effects of poverty and

26. Ibid., xxix, 130, xxxvii–viii.
27. Ibid., xlix–l.

class distinctions, in contrast to the typical women's plot described by Baym, in which a young woman faced with innumerable troubles rises to triumph through her own courage and intelligence. Gates believes that Wilson began the "Afro-American literary tradition."[28] Wilson should have been read, for her ideas, her unconventional characterization, her plot, but she was not—not then, nor for the hundred-odd years that followed.

Alcott and Warner were right in their belief that a book that broke the conventions outright would lack commercial appeal. Before the 1860s women tried various methods for dealing with their subversive ideas: (1) they camouflaged them, often ending up hiding them too well; (2) they denied their own intent, avoiding the problem altogether; or (3) they wrote their ideas straightforwardly—and lost everything. But there was a fourth alternative, which Alcott exhibited an awareness of in some of her works other than the *Little Women* series. A woman could tell the truth, if she would but, as Emily Dickinson would say, "tell it slant." The women who chose the fourth alternative—to tell the truth in such a way that most readers could not escape it even as the writers protected themselves—were confidence women. They built up readers' confidence in a traditionally safe form, then revealed their true purpose after the readers had already been hooked.

Novels That Are Confidence Games

Holley's *My Opinions and Betsy Bobbet's*

The best way to understand how a novel works as a confidence game is to look at a clear example. Marietta Holley (1836–1926) provides us with one in her first Samantha Allen book, *My Opinions and Betsy Bobbet's,* published in 1872. Holley was one of the first American women humorists and was vastly popular, both here and in Europe. Much of her popularity resulted from the confidence games she played.

Holley's writing mixes humor and social protest; her humorous writing was from the woman's point of view. Carrie Chapman Catt herself wrote that Holley "did more for the suffrage cause than anyone except the regular leaders."[29] Her

28. Ibid., xxxi–iv, xlvi, xlvi–xlvii.
29. Quoted in Jane Louise Runner Pierce, "Marietta Holley's (Josiah Allen's Wife) Techniques of Humor," 65.

humor is in the American humorist tradition, having an ill-educated narrator, Samantha Allen, comment in her rustic dialect on an odd assortment of characters. The social protest is essentially feminist. Holley relieves the "anxiety" caused by letting the subject matter have too much "play" for the humorist conventions she uses by supplying an ostensible center, folksy Samantha and the humorist tradition itself. The Samantha Allen books are confidence games, drawing readers into contemplation of ideas they might not have listened to if they were presented in a more straightforward way. There is never a question about the political stance of the books. Walter Blair, in *Horse Sense in American Humor,* says that in Holley's books "the propaganda [for women's rights] was brilliantly handled. . . . there can be no doubt that Samantha did more for the cause than many hard workers ever accomplished by serious speeches and arguments."[30] Such a generalization cannot be proven, but certainly Holley's books, with their blatant feminist opinions, were much more successful than the straightforward seriousness of a book like *Our Nig* (although one must also consider that the race issue was much more touchy than the feminist one at the time).

In *My Opinions and Betsy Bobbet's,* the disguise is clear. Marietta Holley, the writer, was an elegant single woman fond of French dresses; Samantha Allen, the character, is a 200-pound farmer's wife who takes pride in her clean house and good cooking and who always appears in apron and housecap. Samantha is so seemingly tradition-bound that she signs her books "Josiah Allen's Wife," taking no identity for herself. Holley explains her choice of signature for the character in an article for *Harper's Bazaar*: "Probably I thought that it would soften somewhat the edge of unwelcome argument to have the writer meekly claim to be the wife of Josiah Allen and so stand in the shadow of a man's personality."[31] This is a disguise within a disguise: Holley is not like Samantha Allen, and Samantha is not really content to be a man's shadow. The disguise is also in the loose plot, the series of laughable characters, and the dialect, all indicating that the book is for fun, not to be taken seriously, and all indicating that the humorist tradition is something the reader can rely on, no matter how far the unconventional topics might go. Furthermore, the humor is not only disguise, but lure. The reader is drawn into the book by laughter.

From the very beginning, the reader's complicity is demanded. In the preface, Samantha tells the reader that a "voice" kept telling her, "Josiah Allen's wife,

30. Walter Blair, *Horse Sense in American Humor,* 238–39.
31. Quoted in Pierce, "Marietta Holley's," 16–17.

write a book givin' your views on the great subject of Wimmen's Rites." The
idea "skairt" Josiah enough to make him "[start] off on the run for the camfire
bottle."[32] His worry is that he will have to pay someone to read the book. Readers
are to have a good laugh, but they must be willing to consider the topic of women's
rights, a subject even the militant women's groups shied away from by this
time in the century, focusing instead on the less controversial subject of "social
housekeeping." Therein lies the complicity. Once the reader agrees to step this
far beyond the bounds, the game has begun.

Immediately, Holley steps back from her subject to ease the readers on. The
first chapters lead us into Samantha's life, beginning in the sentimental vein:
"The first minute I sot my grey eye onto Josiah Allen I knew my fate. . . .
I married Josiah Allen . . . from pure love" (p. 2). The chapter ends with a
reassurance that Samantha's thoughts about women's rights will not be overly
scandalous: Samantha contends "that this book shall be a Becon light, guidin'
female wimmin, to life, liberty, and the pursuit of true happiness" (p. 20). Her
first "solem' warnin' to [her] sect" is that second wives should not allow their
husbands to compare them to the first wife. "On this short rule hangs the hope
of domestick harmony" (p. 20).

Holley is building the reader's confidence in the inoffensiveness of Samantha's
ideas. For seven chapters Samantha talks about dresses and children and cooking
in her inimitable way. For a full chapter she ridicules Betsy Bobbet, in the
true misogynist manner, for being a bluestocking. Betsy writes horrible poetry
("Gushings of a Tendah Soul"), and, Samantha says, "she is awful opposed to
wimmin's havein' any right only the right to get married. She holds on to that
right as tight as any single woman I ever see" (p. 27). At the same time, even in
these chapters meant to calm any anxiety on the reader's part, Holley continues
her feminist argument, albeit in a low key. Men talk about "its bein' [a woman's]
duty to cling to man like a vine to a tree." Samantha makes them "drop their
heads before [her] keen grey eyes" by asking, "which had you ruther do, let
Betsy Bobbet cling to you or let her vote?" (pp. 27–28).

Such a question is a signal to the reader that the game is proceeding and
that the serious point is about to be made. In chapter 8, Holley writes "An

32. Marietta Holley, *My Opinions and Betsey Bobbet's: Designed as a Beacon Light to
Guide Women to Life Liberty and the Pursuit of Happiness but Which May Be Read by
Members of the Sterner Sect, Without Injury to Themselves or the Book*, v, vi. Subsequent
page citations from this book will be given parenthetically in the text.

Allegory on Wimmin's Rights." The reader expects to laugh at the language in the segment but is not sure just how serious the "allegory" will be. As Josiah's son rides off to a lecture on women's rights, Josiah states emphatically, "I am sick of wimmin's rights, I don't believe in 'em" (p. 85). Ever eager to argue with her husband, Samantha takes up the challenge. What follows is one of the most frequently quoted pieces of Holley's work, for it is one of her strongest, most open statements of the urgency behind the women's movement. There is an interplay of serious point and humorous undercutting that keeps the reader going despite the subversive ideas. By the end of the chapter, however, the nature of the game is clear.

Josiah says that women have no business with the laws of the country. Samantha responds with a speech: " 'Of the three classes that haint no business with the law—lunatics, idiots, and wimmin—the lunatics and idiots have the best time of it,' says I, with a great rush of ideas into my brain that almost lifted up the border of my head-dress" (p. 87). And her ideas do rush on. She quotes the law "in awful accents": "You haint no business with the law, but the law has a good deal of business with you, vile female, start for State's prison; you haint nothin' at all to do with the law, only to pay all the taxes it tells you to—embrace a license bill that is ruinin' your husband—give up your innocent little children to a wicked father if it tells you to—and a few other little things, such as bein' dragged off to prison by it—chained up for life, and hung, and et cetery" (p. 88).

Samantha's "allegory" goes on in "rapped eloquence" for three pages. In the rest of the chapter, she takes on women's work, "wife slavery," motherhood, wife abuse, poor wages, and the paradox that men like Josiah tell women they think of them as no "more nor less than angels any way" (pp. 89–98). The scene ends with Josiah refusing to get Samantha the wood she needs, a contradiction of the division of labor Josiah has been arguing for, as she points out; then she "said no more, but with lofty emotions surgin' in [her] breast [she] took [her] axe and started for the woodpile" (p. 98).

In a literary confidence game such as Holley's, readers can choose to ignore the serious point, pretend that a game is not being played. Always the readers can escape, but only at the price of deceiving themselves. The humor allows the escape here, and Samantha does too, for despite her unconventional views, she never asserts her own rights in an improper way. Perhaps the escape route is what helps make such novels the popular successes they are. Here is the fourth alternative to "drowning" one's opinions, losing the opinions altogether, or being honest but unread. For Holley's statement is made, and if the readers have not refused to recognize the game cues, their understanding of women and society must change.

Phelps's *Dr. Zay*

Holley's Samantha Allen books make clear what a confidence game consists of, but they are so distinctive that it would be instructive to see how a confidence game works in a more typical nineteenth-century novel. Elizabeth Stuart Phelps's *Dr. Zay* (1882) is a more typical literary confidence game. Phelps wrote it five years after her first major work, *The Story of Avis*, using a similar subject: the effect of marriage on a strong, creative woman. But the structure of *Dr. Zay* is quite different from that of the earlier, straightforward story—although each is a bildungsroman—and in many ways *Dr. Zay* is more effective. Phelps begins the game in *Dr. Zay* by setting up the reader's expectations for a certain kind of story, a romance: a doctor and patient fall in love. The "fictitious reader," a construct Iser describes as a "perspective" from which the story is told, knows the conventions of such a story and pushes the story on to its fitting conclusion, even as the actual reader begins to feel that such a conclusion would not be fitting for this character at all.[33] The love story is the disguise *Dr. Zay* uses and carries through to the end. However, there is a difference in this love story, for the doctor is a woman, and her patient is a man. That reversal is just one of many in the novel. Another, more important one is that Dr. Zay herself, Atalanta, is of heroic proportions and her would-be lover, Waldo Yorke, is sickly and incompetent. Herein lies the lure of the game and the reader's complicity. The reader must secretly enjoy reading about a dominant woman and a weak man and must be willing to accept the reversed roles.

That the surface love story is not, to use Iser's term, the actual "aesthetic object" of the book is clear. Michael Sartisky, editor of a 1987 edition of the novel, says that "Phelps invites her readers into the embrace of a comfortable romantic tale, only to gracefully invert the prevailing conventional social assumptions about the roles of men and women, matrimony and professions, Atalanta [the Greek hero] and her suitor."[34] The inversion is a signal that the game is going on; if we continue reading despite the inversion, we are complicit in accepting,

33. Iser, *The Act of Reading*, 35–36.
34. Ibid., 95; Michael Sartisky, afterword to Elizabeth Stuart Phelps, *Dr. Zay*, 307–8.

at least this far, a major shift in the prevailing assumptions about the roles of men and women. Perhaps this explains from another perspective why women began to write the novel as confidence game consistently in the second half of the nineteenth century. Before that, the reader would not have taken the lure. Society's view of the proper roles for women was changing in the last decades of the century, in part because the women's movement had begun.

One way to understand how *Dr. Zay* works as a confidence game is to use Iser's ideas about background and foreground. The background in *Dr. Zay* is the love story, with all the expectations that go with it. The foreground is the shifting meanings of Dr. Zay's strength and Waldo's relationship to it. "In the literary text," Iser argues, "not only is the background unformulated and variable, but its significance will also change in accordance with the new perspectives brought about by the foregrounded elements; the familiar facilitates our comprehension of the unfamiliar, but the unfamiliar in turn restructures our comprehension of the familiar." The interplay of love story and the story of a strong woman who is quite fulfilled without a man creates the game and the "anxiety" of the text. By the end of the book the "foreground" has made us see the meaning of the love story in quite a new way. According to Sartisky, readers come away from the book with an "uncomfortable feeling that something is awry," not just in the story but also in society.[35] By the end of the book, our whole way of understanding the relations between men and women and between women and work seems askew, creating that epistemic question Blair finds in all confidence games. Making us "anxious" about a love story that ends happily by all conventional signs is the most important effect of the game in *Dr. Zay:* readers lose confidence in some fundamental assumptions about women's place in society.

Zaidee Atalanta Lloyd—Dr. Zay—is a strong, intelligent, courageous woman who has a wide practice for little pay in the New England hinterland. This fact alone makes the book unusual. Although in the 1880s, according to Sartisky, there was a short-lived upsurge of women doctors, those pictured in literature were usually not very admirable: Henry James's Dr. Prance in *The Bostonians,* for example, and William Dean Howells's Dr. Breen in *Dr. Breen's Practice.* The woman as doctor is a threatening symbol because doctors represent rationality and sturdy fortitude, presumably male attributes. If a woman can be a successful doctor without being "unsexed," gender assumptions must come into serious question. Sarah Orne Jewett, of course, drew an estimable woman doctor in

35. Iser, *The Act of Reading,* 94; Sartisky, afterword to Phelps, *Dr. Zay,* 306.

Anna Prince (*A Country Doctor*), and Phelps herself created a strong female doctor earlier in her short story "Zerviah Hope," although Dr. Marion Dare was not the main focus. In *Dr. Zay*, however, in a style reminiscent of *The Story of Avis,* the female doctor is almost superhuman: "The doctor had on her linen dress and sack, and her figure absorbed the July morning light. Her color was fine. She was the eidolon of glorious health. Every free motion of her happy head and body was superb. She seemed to radiate health, as if she had too much for her own use, and to spare for half the pining world. She had the mysterious odic force of the healer, which is above science, and beyond expression, and behind theory, and which we call magnetism or vitality, tact or inspiration, according to our assimilating power in its presence, and our reverence for its mission."[36]

Such hyperbole is part of the game strategy of *Dr. Zay*. For the reader must never doubt Dr. Zay's complete competence and full psychological and physical strength. The reader enters the story when Dr. Zay is at the top of her powers: before long, she saves a lumberman from drowning by heroic persistence and unquestioning faith in her technique; she sets bones and stops arterial bleeding without a qualm; she is called at all hours of the day and night to deliver babies, fight typhoid, still fears; blizzards cannot stop her. This exaggerated characterization sets the reader up for the sting, the moment when Dr. Zay loses her soul, at our (or the fictitious reader's) request. The story is not told from Dr. Zay's point of view, an important difference from the strategy in *The Story of Avis,* this novel's double. It is told from the point of view of her would-be lover, a patient who lives in the same house with her as he recuperates from an accident and who thus has knowledge of Dr. Zay's comings and goings. Waldo Yorke is aptly called an "emotional egoist" by Sartisky, for Waldo languishes in an essentially spiritual disorder. Dr. Zay's medicines have much less effect on him than does her physical presence, and Waldo demands her presence as much as he can. Waldo wants Dr. Zay to tend him like a sick child. He acts like a child: willful, petulant, and charming by turns. Dr. Zay tries to ignore his demands on her, but he retaliates by making himself sicker.

This is what Sartisky calls the "role reversal." Waldo is dependent on Dr. Zay physically and spiritually. "The terrible leisure of invalidism gaped, a gulf, and filled itself with her. . . . He lay there like a woman, reduced from activity to endurance, from resolve to patience." Waldo's faintings and weakness are of the type usually ascribed to women in nineteenth-century fiction. Dr. Zay, on

36. Phelps, *Dr. Zay,* 98–99.

the other hand, is "preoccupied," a standard male failing in such writing. We see her most clearly in her office surrounded by her "vials" and "her ledgers and note-book, and one or two volumes of Materia Medica . . . bookcases, all full,"[37] certainly not the usual paraphernalia to be found in the private room of a romance heroine. Such obvious inversions of the normal love-story character positions are recurring signals that the game is taking place. Again and again the reader is asked to condone such unorthodox roles, bringing the reader ever deeper into complicity. Accepting Waldo as weak and admiring Dr. Zay as a professional and a full human being, yet wanting them to live together happily ever after in the end, at once implicates us and catches us in the game. This is a standard tactic of a literary confidence game. The lure and the potential complicity are always present, making readers continually assent to their own active participation.

Waldo wants Dr. Zay to love him, and he manipulates her any way he can to get her to do so. Dr. Zay wants to heal Waldo and then dismiss him. That is the central struggle of the story. That we do not want Dr. Zay to turn Waldo away, even though he is such a flawed person, is the point. Phelps is not setting out to make statements about the "great Cause" of women. Rather, she wants to make us feel that the whole sentimental love story is wrong for Dr. Zay and women like her, and that Dr. Zay's final delusion of finding a happy marriage— that "miracle"—with Waldo is tragic. Waldo has nothing to offer Dr. Zay. She is all dedication, studying when she isn't out helping someone, digging her way through snow drifts to make her rounds. He is a lawyer without clients, living off his mother's money, a specimen of "inherited inertia. . . . Atrophied ambition. Paralyzed aspiration," as he himself admits. When Waldo offers Dr. Zay his love, she tells him he mistakes nerves for passion and will be set right when he feels better. The reader suspects she is right, although that would ruin the love story. But Waldo "experience[s] the terrible acceleration of . . . passion" when she refuses his love. He, in a mode similar to Ostrander in *The Story of Avis,* cries, "You would not want to give up your profession. . . . You should not give it up! I would not ask it." Her response is "a slow, slight smile curl[ing] the delicate corners of her lips."[38] The reader understands why she smiles: Dr. Zay's personal strength and sense of self are ineradicably tied to her profession; that Waldo would even consider that she would confer upon him the power to make her forfeit her identity is unthinkable to her and to the reader. She smiles at the

37. Ibid., 119, 121.
38. Ibid., 166, 212–13 (Dr. Zay's answer to Waldo's profession of love), 208, 209.

absurdity of the thought. Thus the story should end, with the two irreconcilable characters going their separate ways.

Still there is that pull of the sentimental tradition, that an unmarried woman must be in want of a husband. The reader on the one hand realizes that Waldo is not equal to Dr. Zay—Sartisky calls him a "straw man"—but, on the other, feels dissatisfied to see Dr. Zay remain single when a lover is so near.[39] So Phelps, having taken the game this far, gives us an alternative ending. She lets us taste what our sentimental desire leads us to and so accomplishes the sting. By the end of the novel we no longer desire marriage and love for Dr. Zay if Waldo is to be the partner; rather, we are horrified by what it inevitably must do to her, although Dr. Zay herself appears to have high hopes.

Up to this point, the game strategy has been built on the structure of the book and on simple inversions of roles. But the final thirty pages become a strategy of language. Waldo comes back to Maine, restored, with his passion undiminished. Dr. Zay sees his "fine shoulders," and "her will, like a drowning thing, seem[s] to struggle" with the "mistiness" that image brings to her eyes. Waldo considers her "a beautiful wild creature. . . . Who was he that he should think to tame her? Yet, should a man let go his hold on a moment like this?"[40] The scene is a passionate one, fitting for a popular romance, although it is perhaps more sexually loaded than most such scenes are, but the language and its implications are jarringly inappropriate for describing Dr. Zay. It is unpleasant to see her will "drowning," for her will has been her distinction and glory throughout the novel. And for Waldo, that piece of self-centered fluff, to think that he can "tame" her is insufferable.

Phelps draws out the final love scene for thirty pages, an "uncomfortable" ordeal for anyone who has taken the bait. That is the purpose. Waldo has "an imperious step"; Dr. Zay "lower[s] her head . . . like a caged thing." Dr. Zay, against all reason, other than that Waldo does, after all, have fine shoulders and that Dr. Zay has been celibate for all of her twenty-nine years, admits that she loves him after he tells her that she does and that she fears him because of it. Constantly Phelps reminds us of the difference between these two characters. Dr. Zay says, "You do not understand how to talk to a woman! . . . It is presumptuous. It is unpardonable. You torture her. You are rough." He comes

39. Sartisky, afterword to Phelps, *Dr. Zay*, 292. Sartisky offers a cogent explanation of the book as a subversive text, although he sees Phelps as being much more ambivalent than I do.

40. Phelps, *Dr. Zay*, 227.

closer and says "deliriously," "How beautiful you are." Waldo is still Waldo, wrapped up in his own desires. Phelps uses words like *torture* and *rough* to emphasize the violence of the scene. Dr. Zay's will must be shattered if she is to fit the shape of the sentimental tradition. Yet in this novel the reader fights that denouement because it is so out of character for Dr. Zay. In other novels in which the main character has denied her genius all along and has been confined by social expectations at every turn, the protagonist meets her tragic end, or the obligatory "happy marriage," fittingly. *This* novel does not prepare us for the turnaround, even though we, using the perspective of the fictitious reader, desire it. Therefore, when we see Dr. Zay "start" as Waldo looks at her, "as if his gaze had been a blow," and when we see that she "shrank before him, a shaken creature," we are not happy. Waldo, too, has "more a sense of awe than of transport, at the sight of her royal overthrow." But he proves himself inadequate to understand her again when he listens to her "plead," "I have lost my self-possession. . . . I have lost—myself" and he experiences only joy, although he "spare[s] her for that time" and leaves, "the maddest, gladdest, most ignorant man" in town.[41] In that "most ignorant," Phelps lets slip her disguise for a moment, for the reader has been caught; the sting is complete. Phelps has made the reader feel how wrong the "womanly" role is for some women. More than any speech, this granting of the reader's sentimental desire is the feminist statement.

A literary confidence game is not different from other sorts of serious writing in kind, but in degree. Its structures and strategies are more entangling than most and its inversions constantly upset the reader's attempt at consistency-building. The result is a text that profoundly affects the way we think. Iser states that "when we are present in an event, something must happen to us. The more 'present' the text is to us, the more our habitual selves—at least for the duration of the reading—recede into the 'past.'" A text becomes "an event" when readers find themselves trapped by their own imaginations: "The discrepancies produced by the reader make him dispute his own gestalten [world vision]. He tries to balance out these discrepancies, but the questionable gestalt which was the starting-point for this operation remains as a challenge. . . . This whole process takes place within the reader's imagination, so that he cannot escape from it. This involvement, or entanglement, is what places us in the 'presentness' of the text and what makes the text into a presence for us."[42]

41. Ibid., 228, 229, 230, 231.
42. Iser, *The Act of Reading,* 123, 131.

The "gestalt" that is called into question in *Dr. Zay* is the assumed set of roles for men and women. The game leads one into creating one's own "discrepancies" between what one wants for Dr. Zay as a whole person and what the romance gestalt demands. The book becomes an event for us because we participated in its making.

Once Waldo returns, a healthy man, Phelps constantly describes Dr. Zay in words denoting weakness. She "trembles" and is "feeble," she "pants" and is "pale"—all images used to describe Waldo for the first three-quarters of the book. Yet Dr. Zay, as if caught in the gestalt of the romance herself, allows herself to believe that she can find her ideal of the perfect marriage with Waldo. Sartisky finds in this an "ambivalence" in Phelps's attitude toward marriage. However, the ambivalence is merely apparent, not real. For, deluded as Dr. Zay might be about Waldo's capabilities, Phelps is never unsure.

The final scene proves Phelps's absolute certainty that Waldo is not the perfect mate Dr. Zay seeks. Dr. Zay's trembling and pale color are a direct result of the work she has just undertaken, wresting a gun from a man in delirium tremens who was wildly shooting up his own home. Waldo, who has waited for her passively in her carriage, takes "advantage" of the situation and elicits an acceptance of his marriage proposal from her, his "darling, [his] poor, brave lonely girl." He transforms her through his words from a truly heroic person into a sentimental heroine. She asks if "it is *me* you want,—a strong-minded doctor?" His response is, "A sweet-hearted woman! It is only you," another transformation. The significance of setting the final scene under the shadow of an alcoholic on a shooting spree is made clear by an earlier statement. Waldo said, "A woman cannot follow a career without ruin to all that is noblest and sweetest and truest in her nature. . . . If I had a fair chance . . . I would compel you to feel my presence, to recognize my claim. You should be wounded by a bullet that you could not find,—." Too ill to "wound" her at the time, Waldo now takes an unfair chance and compels Dr. Zay to acquiesce to his demands when she is "worn out." The link between Waldo and the crazed alcoholic who terrorizes his family could not be more clear. There is no ambivalence here. The novel ends with Dr. Zay "gliding" into Waldo's arms, yet, as Sartisky sees it, "though concluding conventionally with matrimony, the novel simultaneously subverts it."[43] The reader must live with the result of his or her own traditional desires. *Dr. Zay* is not a novel that "drowns" its feminist

43. Phelps, *Dr. Zay,* 254, 210; Sartisky, afterword to Phelps, *Dr. Zay,* 294.

statement by clinging to the tradition of romance; it makes its statement by doing so.

Harper's *Iola LeRoy*

Although at the end of *Dr. Zay* Phelps uses language to complete the game, her strategy throughout the book relies on role inversion almost exclusively. For the game to work, the reader must recognize the conventions of the romantic novel and notice when inversions occurred. However, some literary confidence games are much more evident in the style than in the structure. Frances Harper's *Iola LeRoy or Shadows Uplifted* (1892) is a good example. Harper manipulates the language to surprise the reader into recognizing the "questionable gestalt" while simultaneously making her point and signaling that the game is on.

Harper has often been faulted for having a nearly white mulatto as the heroine of the book. But if we understand *Iola LeRoy* as a confidence game, we recognize that Iola's color is part of the lure. Without that, a concession to convention, the reader might well not begin the game, as Harriet Wilson discovered, to her misfortune. Without it, also, the plot would not work. Iola is white enough, middle class enough, and well bred enough to elicit the implied white, middle-class reader's goodwill. Iola's octoroon status is sentimentally tragic, without really undermining color distinctions.

The first stage in the game is for the reader to become interested in Iola's predicament: Iola thinks she is white and experiences life as a well-to-do white girl would; but the reader knows that she has a black heritage too, for her grandmother is black. For the game to proceed, the reader must accept Iola's black heritage and consider her a sentimental heroine in spite of it. That is the lure, the tantalizing thought that an almost white woman could be remanded to slavery, and the reader is complicit: the reader cares. Early in the book come Iola's history and her mother's, helping the reader understand the precarious nature of their freedom. But Harper needs the reader to invest more than understanding and sympathy; if there is to be what Stanley Fish calls a "transformation" in the reader's mind, the reader has to be drawn "inescapably into the world of the text" and "experience" the horror of slavery.[44] Harper accomplishes this through a manipulation of language, occurring at least three times in the novel.

44. Quoted in Iser, *The Act of Reading*, 32, 36.

The first moment that the reader's personal involvement becomes at issue is in chapter 12. Iola, at a school where she learns to be a graceful, educated, middle-class white woman, "defends" slavery in a conversation with a white girlfriend. Iola at this point is unaware that she is not entirely white. She is also unaware that her cousin, Alfred Lorraine, has found a way to revoke her mother's manumission papers, upon the father's death, and has sent men to find Iola and bring her back to Georgia a slave. The reader is aware of it all. Clearly the conversation is ironic, especially when the friend asks Iola, "Would you be satisfied to have the most beautiful home, the costliest jewels, or the most elegant wardrobe if you were a slave?" Iola answers, "Oh, the cases are not parallel. Our slaves do not want their freedom. They would not take it if we gave it to them."[45]

The irony is intellectually interesting, but the reader still does not have a gut response to what is happening to Iola. As she goes on, however, making plans for her "first season out," the reader begins to appreciate the seriousness of what is about to happen. It is here, in the midst of a rather ordinary schoolgirl conversation, that Harper makes her first major move: she switches voices, switches scenes, switches points of view without any warning, and in the switch turns the intellectual interest into an "event" the reader cannot help but "experience." The onset of the event is sudden: Iola finishes the description of her debut plans and ends her argument on a decisive note, still speaking to her friend: "I think one winter in the South would cure you of your Abolitionism." The next line is "Have you seen her yet?" (p. 99). Because no speaker is indicated for the second line, the reader assumes the words are spoken by Iola's friend. Yet the pronoun reference is unclear, putting the reader into momentary confusion. Clarity returns with the following line, however, for we discover that the speaker is Louis Bastine, an attorney sent by Lorraine to compel Iola to return to the South, where she will become a slave. The reader's shock upon learning that the speaker is Bastine constitutes the novel's game. In one moment Iola changes from a subject "I" to an object "her," grammatically and really. The shift begins an ironic juxtaposition of conversations: the relatively innocent one (the innocence of which is called into question when we see what such race prejudice as Iola's can lead to) and the villainous one. Bastine and his friend LeCroix are across town discussing Bastine's errand at the same moment Iola is defending the institution

45. Harper, *Iola LeRoy,* 97–98. Subsequent page citations from this book will be given parenthetically in the text.

that is about to enslave her. Harper makes immediate capital of the confusion caused by the text. She has Bastine say, "She is a most beautiful creature. . . . she has the proud poise of Leroy, the most splendid eyes I ever saw in a woman's head, lovely complexion, and a glorious wealth of hair. She would bring $2000 any day in a New Orleans market" (p. 99). So much for her debut. The very qualities Iola depends on to make her "coming out" a success will make Lorraine rich. Obviously, the intended purpose of her sale is also unsettling.

The two conversations are parallel in topic, however unlike they are in point of view. LeCroix says that "were it not for the cross in her blood," Iola "would be the sensation of the season" (p. 100), a clear parallel to the schoolgirls' conversation. Again, in an opinion ironically similar to Iola's own, Bastine predicts that "she will sulk and take it pretty hard at first; but if she is managed right she will soon get over it. Give her plenty of jewelry, fine clothes, and an easy time" (pp. 101–2). By the time Bastine explains how he will lure Iola back south with a story about her father's ill health, and by the time he states baldly that once she is home, he will "have her inventoried with the rest of the property" (p. 101), the reader has been hooked, heart and mind. There is no doubt that the game is occurring. The deliberate confusion of the text is a signal that a trap has been sprung, and if the reader is going to decide not to care for Iola LeRoy because of the "cross in her blood," it is time for the reader to opt out. For everything else that happens in the novel depends on the reader's empathy with a woman who is irrefutably black in part. Harper has manipulated the reader into "experiencing" the horror of what Iola is about to face, has overridden the reader's prejudice to that extent.

To strengthen the hold that Iola and her situation have on the reader's mind, Harper includes a second textual manipulation. On the train south, Iola dreams of her mother kissing her and, symbolically, of Mammy Liza holding her in her arms, only to waken to find Bastine pressing a "burning kiss" on her lips and "encircling her" with "a strong arm," making the sexual implications of Iola's new status clear. When she rejects Bastine in panic and disgust, he calls her "my lovely tigress" (p. 104). Just as the grammar earlier changed a subject into an object, Bastine's label reduces Iola from a human into an animal, a pre-enactment of enslavement.

As critics have seen, empathizing with a woman who could pass for white and could be admitted into the highest circles is not unsurpassingly hard for most readers of moderate prejudice. However, Harper has a more intense game in hand. By the end of the novel, the reader will have admitted the right of all blacks to freedom, property, the vote, education, and equal employment—not the right of mulattoes alone. The reader's empathy will, by force of logic, extend to full blacks in the uneducated, lower-class status in which slavery left them. That is the object of the game. Iola's role is lure and advance guard. Harper's strategy has to this point been linguistic, creating confusions in the text and surprising the reader by ironic juxtapositions. The focus remains on language in the rest of the novel, and it is again through language that the third important move of the game occurs: the reader comes to agree with Iola's view of human value. Iola embraces her black heritage, becoming a teacher of black children and old people because "she had no physical repulsions to overcome, no prejudices to conquer" (p. 146). Iola is in contrast to Dr. Gresham, who condescends to black people: "some of them are wide-awake and sharp as steel traps" (p. 145). He is the exemplar of the moderate white whose liberalism does not go beyond expecting those blacks who can pass to do so and marveling at any sign of Negro intelligence. It is necessary to an understanding of Harper's game strategy to note that Gresham sees a dialect difference as evidence of ignorance. Gresham's limitations are the limitations of the implied reader, and his later turnaround is similar to the reader's. Gresham gives an illuminating example of the "duncery of slavery" that is entirely linguistic. He is horrified by the depths of ignorance shown by one black person who said, "I no shum," meaning "I don't see it" (p. 145). Equating linguistic difference with "duncery" is a typical form of prejudice. Harper uses such prejudice to create the final sting.

There is no denying that Iola and her long-lost uncle, Robert Johnson, speak a "high" language. From the beginning, Robert is set off from his slave peers by his literacy and by his well-bred vocabulary. Harper is careful to explain that he learned to read and speak through his owner, Mrs. Johnson, who treated him like a "pet animal" (p. 7). The narrator too is fastidious in the use of an obviously educated diction. Only at the beginning, before meeting Iola LeRoy, does the reader hear nonprivileged black characters speak. Once the game is on, all language is "perfect" enough to be stilted, lulling the reader into confidence that the novel will ask no very difficult feats of imagination and sympathy. That is, until chapter 18.

In that chapter, just over halfway through the book, Robert Johnson goes back, after the war, to the old plantation and visits his former owner, Mrs. Johnson, who is living in bitter poverty. The old rules no longer apply in the South, and the reader will also experience an overturning of the rules established by the text. One of the expectations set up by the text is that the narrator shares the implied reader's moderate prejudices. Iola's mother is a paragon and yet rues the fact that "for her children there were no companions except the young slaves of the plantation, and she dread[s] the effect of such intercourse upon their lives and characters" (p. 82). Likewise, in chapter 1 the narrator gives the reader some comic black stereotypes. Superstition about the Yankees fulfills one stereotype, and ignorance of common things another. In preparation for the sting that will occur in chapter 18, Aunt Linda is set up in chapter 1 as an example of black ignorance. The conversation is standard minstrel comedy: " 'Why, Aunt Linda, you never saw a circus?' 'No, but I'se hearn tell ob dem, and I thinks dey mus' be mighty funny' " (pp. 11–12). The immediate purpose of Harper's use of comic stereotypes is to lure the reader into the complicity of accepting the revolutionary activities of the blacks in that chapter: secret meetings, a secret code, plans to escape to the Union army as "contraband of war." There is an interplay of stereotype and revolution, as Harper writes simultaneously for her two audiences. But the reader does not doubt that the narrator will be careful not to press our sympathy for the slaves too far. That confidence is built on the stereotypes and even more on the carefully established difference between the narrator's diction (the narrator, for instance, says that Robert is "held in durance vile" [p. 38]) and that of the slaves.

In chapter 18 the story comes full circle. The slaves the reader met in chapter 1 are now freedmen and women living on the old Gundover plantation, which they bought. We again meet Aunt Linda and Robert Johnson's old friends, but the difference is that we have experienced with Iola her transformation from respected, wealthy, beautiful white woman to a "reg'lar spitfire" of a slave who cannot be managed by her masters even by the whip (p. 38). We have applauded her for having the same sense of rebellion the slaves in chapter 1 showed. We have been made to experience the injustices and humiliations of slavery through Iola, and so have accepted her stand for the black people intellectually. When Iola rejects Dr. Gresham's offer of a life of wealth as his white wife, we respect her and agree when she says that "New England is not free from racial prejudice" (p. 117). We are ashamed of Dr. Gresham because he can only blush and be silent when Iola asks him if he'd accept their child if it were a child of color. The story has come full circle, but the reader has changed and finds shortly that he or she has been "caught by the game."

Robert goes to the plantation owned by the freed slaves: "Now the gloomy silence of those woods was broken by the hum of industry, the murmur of cheerful voices, and the merry laughter of happy children" (p. 152). The scene is idyllic and could easily describe a white New England village. The reader expects to see a community of mulattoes of Robert and Iola's stamp. The first indication that this is not so is in the dialect of the people Robert meets: "'How is yer, ole boy?' asked one laborer of another. 'Everything is lobly,' replied the other. The blue sky arching overhead and the beauty of the scenery justified the expression" (p. 153). The dialect comes as a shock, heightened by the narrator's pointing to the "expression" and commending it. These "laborers" are the people the reader is to admire. For the first time, the reader must equate "ignorant slaves" with industry. But how can the reader disagree, since he or she has been agreeing with Iola's views all along? This is the sting. The shock comes in recognizing one's own prejudices, one's own condescending reaction to "lobly." The reader knows immediately that he or she has been had, but there is no graceful way to backtrack. If the implied middle-class white readers do not want to admit that they are as prejudiced as Dr. Gresham and that Iola would have to reject them too, they must learn to respect not just mulattoes, but fully black people, too, including those who do not speak "white" language.

The rest of the chapter is an intermixture of sentimental scenes—the pretty cottage, recognition of long-lost friends—and the very people the novel brought the reader to laugh at in chapter 1. Robert lingers by "a garden filled with beautiful flowers, clambering vines, and rustic adornments" (p. 153). The reader expects to see some respectable white matron come to the door, some Irvingesque "country wife," or at the furthest reaches of imagination a pretty creole like Harriet Beecher Stowe's Lisette (*Dred*). Instead, there is on the porch an "elderly woman, darning stockings, the very embodiment of content and good humor," who says "shore as I'se born, dat's Robert! Look yere, honey, whar did yer come from? I'll gib my head fer a choppin' block ef dat ain't Miss Nancy's Bob" (p. 153). It is Aunt Linda, the same as the reader had left her, but free now, and the reader is forced to a different view of her because of what the reader has learned through Iola. Her referring to Robert as "Miss Nancy's Bob" seals the inescapability of the reader's recognizing that, as Robert said to Captain Sybil back in chapter 6, "it was [not] any worse to have held me in slavery than the blackest man in the south" (p. 44).

Harper is unrelenting in making the reader accept Aunt Linda and all the "blackest" and least-educated men and women she represents, exactly as she and they are. Robert asks Aunt Linda how she knew him. "By dem mischeebous eyes, ob course. I'd a knowed yer if I had seed yer in Europe" (p. 153). This is the set-up for another bout of the minstrel comedy that occurred so conspicuously in chapter 1. Robert baits Aunt Linda here as he did then: "In Europe, Aunt

Linda? Where's that?" Aunt Linda answers, "I specs its some big city, somewhar" (p. 153). Her ignorance has not changed since the beginning of the book. But the reader's attitude toward her ignorance has. After all, Iola is a teacher who understands that ignorance has little to do with character, and we have listened to and agreed with Iola's theories about black education. Harper reminds us of that as Linda shows her true affection for a lost friend. "Yer looks jis' splendid. Yer looks good 'nuff ter kiss" (p. 153). Linda's intelligence and thoughtfulness are clear in the conversation about freedom that immediately follows. Linda "wanted ter re'lize [she] was free" and so left Miss Nancy at the first notice she could do so (p. 154). We are brought back to Iola's earlier, complacent statement about well-treated slaves disdaining freedom. Linda, we learn, immediately engaged in free enterprise, selling pies to soldiers until she and her husband could buy the Gundover place. The chapter ends with a reiteration of the main theme: that all blacks, not just mulattoes like Iola and Robert, want and are ready for freedom. Robert asks Linda if she wouldn't "just as leave be back again" with Miss Nancy if Nancy could "take care of her." Linda shows a "faint quiver of indignation" and returns the accusation on him: "Don't yer want yer freedom?" (pp. 162–63).

The game is now essentially complete. From this point on in the novel, Harper can move into what Hazel Carby identifies as "excerpts of her speeches" on black education and on the fostering of black genius because the most important struggle has been won.[46] The reader has been made to recognize that Aunt Linda and Uncle Daniel and Mam Liza are admirable human beings who have survived slavery with their good sense and good hearts still intact. Plans for the "uplifting" of the race refer to potentials, long suppressed by slavery, that need to be tapped, without implication that the race is inferior.

It is important to notice what the book is actually saying. Iola and Robert, who both could easily pass as white and who could find status and a decent life by doing so, choose to stay by their grandmother/mother Harriet, the fully black woman who defied the whip as heroically as ever Iola did: "she snatched de whip out ob [Miss Nancy's] han' an gib her a lickin'" (p.159). This fact is radical in its implications. But Robert puts it even more plainly: "I don't think they [black people] are any worse than the white people. I don't believe, if we had the power, we would do any more lynching, burning, and murdering than they do" (pp. 170–71). Such a statement is dangerous, yet Harper does not "drown" it. She manages to speak honestly and still have her book read. How does she accomplish this?

46. Hazel V. Carby, introduction to Harper, *Iola LeRoy,* xvi.

She gains the complicity and finally the agreement, at least as far as the novel is concerned, of the reader, whose prejudices have fallen victim to her game. We are ready to see northern color prejudice in action in chapter 24, as readers were not ready to see it in *Our Nig* thirty years earlier. We are ready to listen to Reverend Carmicle, an Oxford-educated, fully black intellectual, and we enjoy the joke on Dr. Latrobe, the white man who prides himself on being able to spot "black blood" (p. 229). Finally, we are ready to accept Lucille Delaney, with her sentimental name, one usually reserved for the blond, "pure" heroine. Delaney is the fully black intellectual woman who *should* have been the heroine of the book, but who would not have been accepted by a white audience before the game was played. By having very black Lucille marry almost white Harry LeRoy, Harper comes close to the miscegenation issue Wilson tried unsuccessfully to raise. Harper carries it off because she has overturned the reader's habitual worldview and can make her own rules. She has won the right to dare.

Barbara Christian explains that Harper uses a mulatto woman rather than a fully black woman as the main character because "undoubtedly many white women could identify with the beautiful woman who looked as white as they did, who was certainly more wealthy and privileged than they were, and who, despite all this, is instantly pummeled into the pit of servitude." However, Harper goes a step further than Christian suggests and uses that appeal as a lure. Iola is a pawn in a game that finally manipulates the reader into allowing two full blacks, Delaney and Carmicle, to become, in Carby's words, "figures of the future,"[47] and, more important, into accepting Aunt Linda, back on her porch amid her flowers, free and fully human and worthy of respect, as the last image of the book.

Stowe's *Oldtown Folks*

Holly, Phelps, and Harper all make it clear that there are many ways to play a confidence game on the reader. Yet the result is always the same: the reader comes to "experience" an idea he or she would not otherwise have considered. The strategy is a gradual one; the effect is sharp. The term *sting* is an appropriate one for the moment of realization, for it signifies a wounding, a painful sensation that cannot be ignored. In a confidence game, literary or otherwise, the most serious wounding is not financial or social or intellectual, but psychological or

47. Barbara Christian, *Black Women Novelists: The Development of a Tradition, 1892–1976,* 26; Carby, introduction to Harper, *Iola Leroy,* xxiii.

spiritual. The victim must admit that he or she has been shortsighted, shallow, prejudiced, naïve. Geoffrey Hartman supposes "that words are always armed and capable of wounding," for if we read actively, "a book has the capacity to put us on the defensive, or make us envious, or inflict some other narcissistic injury." Yet reading is not mere masochism, for the very text that pains us also heals: "The medicinal function of literature is to word a wound words have made."[48] Perhaps the greater the wounding of one's flawed consciousness, the more completely one can be healed. Certainly a literary confidence game—at least for the reader who chooses to play—makes us feel our own shortcomings in a healing way.

Depending on the strategy, however, the sting can be more painful or less. Phelps and Harper make the lesson hurt. Holley's humor assuages some of the pain. In *Oldtown Folks* (1869), Harriet Beecher Stowe likewise is gentle. The idea is revolutionary enough: that the religion of the fathers is a "disease" for many women because "woman's nature has never been consulted" in it.[49] Such activists as Elizabeth Cady Stanton, with her revisionary woman's Bible, would later say the same thing under strong public disapproval. But Stowe gradually leads the reader into confronting the issue in *Oldtown Folks,* a quarter of a century before Stanton, in such a way that, although we experience the shallowness of our own prejudices, the experience purges rather than hurts.

Focusing on her strategy also helps make the shape of the book clear. The structure of *Oldtown Folks* is hard to pin down. Henry May, editor of the 1966 edition, wrote in his introduction that he was unsure whether *Oldtown Folks* is a novel or "a series of sketches, a historical essay with interpolated plot," because there seems to be so little true plot structure and because Horace Holyoke himself is so vague. On the other hand, Dorothy Berkson, editor of the 1987 edition, finds several plots: a bildungsroman plot, a courtship plot, and an adoption plot, all rather loose, although the adoption plot seems to dominate and creates a "circular structure."[50] If we foreground the minor characters, however, rather than Horace, Tina, or Harry, another, tighter structure becomes apparent in a steady progression of strong women intimately involved in their religion, climaxing in the Cloudland section and the ideas connected with Esther there.

48. Hartman, *Saving the Text,* 128, 133.

49. Harriet Beecher Stowe, *Oldtown Folks,* Rutgers University Press edition (1987), 365.

50. Henry F. May, introduction to *Oldtown Folks,* Belknap edition (1966), 43; Dorothy Berkson, introduction to *Oldtown Folks,* Rutgers University Press edition, xxxv–vi.

Stowe uses the typical disguise for a literary confidence game: she appears to write a novel that follows a readily acceptable convention. In this case, the convention is the regional sketch. Critics at the time were already "weary" of such descriptions, although the public was eager to buy the book.[51] The reader, then and now, settles back expecting to see a parade of quaint caricatures, and that is what the book delivers at first. Yet almost from the beginning, the reader is asked to take some risks. Never are we challenged by inoffensive Horace, although it is purportedly his insights and his story we are reading, but we are repeatedly challenged by the minor female characters. Aunt Lois, for example, from the instant Horace comes to his grandmother's house, steps forward as a woman of strong mind and spirit. She is not the retiring unmarried sister who lives in the shadows of the acceptably married women, as such women usually did in nineteenth-century novels; rather, she, through her "unsparing vigor" and decided opinions, has established a place for herself in her home and in the community, single and abrasive though she is.[52] Aunt Lois is the first in a steadily sharpening series of strong women that creates the underlying shape and direction of *Oldtown Folks*. The progression from Aunt Lois to Esther, the beautiful and intense soul on the verge of spiritual disfigurement by a male theology, is how the game develops.

It is clear that the crux of a literary confidence game is reader complicity. Without it, there can be no sting, no "transformation" of the reader's perception. The reader must be lured ever more deeply into accepting unorthodox ideas before the final, logical step is taken, with no recourse. In *Oldtown Folks*, the complicity lies in the reader's accepting women of strong minds and accepting their vital interest in religion. Not only are many of the women from Aunt Lois on anti-sentimental, strong, and capable figures, but they also have decided opinions on Calvinism and Christianity. This yoking of religion and strong-mindedness is a direct preparation for Esther, who is an ideal of logic, will, and selfhood going awry in her constricting environment.

Early in the book Stowe gives us a signal that the game is on. We meet Hepsey Lawson, Sam's wife. She, like Holley's Betsy Bobbet, is a caricature from a long misogynist line. She is a shrew, a nag of the infamous Dame Van Winkle sort, who harries her sociable husband dismally. Yet for an instant we see Hepsey, as we never see Dame Van Winkle, in a sympathetic light. She is "an

51. May, introduction to *Oldtown Folks*, 4.
52. Stowe, *Oldtown Folks*, 30.

early-rising, bustling, driving, neat, efficient, capable little body" who through a multitude of skills and great persistence supports her large family. Because of that glimpse of her, we take a second look at Sam Lawson's view of things and see what Dorothy Berkson calls the satire on "Sam's dogmatic assertion of his male prerogatives" despite his failings as husband and provider. We understand, then, the anger that can make Hepsey "really dangerous" when Sam tries to preach to her.[53] Our sympathy for Hepsey takes us, for just a moment, outside the bounds of convention and is one of the first steps toward the feminist statement of Cloudland.

Miss Mehitable is a clear movement forward in Stowe's characterization of intellectual, self-determined women and is a long stride from Aunt Lois and Hepsey. She illustrates the game in herself. She first appears in the meeting-house chapter as a laughable, eccentric old woman who wears "queer bonnets and dyed gowns" (p. 49). The focus is on her appearance. She is another cartoon of the disappointed and silly spinster. But slowly her characterization changes. She becomes a person with feelings and thoughts we cannot discount. By chapter 6, "Firelight Talks," her appearance and our evaluation of her have undergone a remarkable change. Now this "queer" old woman has "clear, trustworthy, steady eyes" and even a kind of "beauty," "good-goblin style" (p. 63). This supposed caricature suddenly has "a strong mind, [is] an omnivorous reader, [is] apt, ready in conversation, and [has] a droll, original way of viewing things"; her "tastes were in the world of books and ideas" (pp. 63–64).

Once again the reader is drawn into sympathy with a character to whom we have been taught to condescend. Our accepting queer old Miss Mehitable, the spinster, as a woman of ideas is a further step in our complicity. By now the reader, if the reader has been recognizing the cues, knows that this is not simply "a series of sketches" of the local-color genre.

Still, accepting Miss Mehitable is not revolutionary, for she offers no challenge to another stereotype, that intelligent women are by nature homely. We are more ready to admit Miss Mehitable's wisdom because she looks like a "goblin" and is as faithful as a "good, homely dog" (p. 63). Within the new stereotype, however, Miss Mehitable grows in the reader's respect. We come to understand her wisdom and affection in the way she handles Tina, and we are prepared,

53. Ibid., 34; Berkson, introduction to *Oldtown Folks,* xxxi–ii; Stowe, *Oldtown Folks,* 34. Subsequent page citations from this work will be from the Rutgers University Press edition and will be given parenthetically in the text.

then, to accept her introduction of the crucial issue of the book, an issue that will come to a climax with Esther. In chapter 19, Miss Mehitable writes to her brother about her spiritual malaise. She asks how she can fight existential despair, being a woman. "A man can fight this dragon as a woman cannot. We women are helpless,—tied to places, forms, and rules,—chained to our stake. We must meet him as we can" (p. 181). Although Horace justifies presenting Miss Mehitable's letter by claiming that he is merely giving background for his history, the "historical essay" disguise has faded and the philosophical and feminist heart of the book becomes audible. But note how slowly the reader has been led along to this point. The letter does not occur until almost halfway through the book.

Miss Mehitable's particular cause for "such sinking of heart, such helplessness of fear" is her sitting at the sickbed and deathbed of their brother Theodore. She asks the question that Calvinism cannot answer helpfully for "sensitive minds"; she asks "if *this* be life, whether an immortal existence is not a curse to be feared . . . and if the wretchedness we fear in the eternal world can be worse than what we sometimes suffer now" (p. 181; Stowe's emphasis). Her defiant melancholy is similar to Esther's, except that Miss Mehitable is determined to "think that God has some pity for the work of his hand" (p. 182), whereas Esther is not. Miss Mehitable writes to her implacable brother about their sister Emily, another woman who has been scarred by the "appalling doctrines" of Edwardian Calvinism, and finally admits her own conversion to Christ by means of Tina. The letter is, in the end, a ministering to her brother.

Miss Mehitable is the most fully drawn of the minor female characters, and our initial complicity is greatest in accepting her. She is a woman whom "men always admired . . . as they admired other men." She has "intellect" and yet "heart, so warm, so tender, and so true" that she is ashamed of it (p. 197). Other minor female characters also have a relationship to religion, specifically Calvinism. Miss Asphyxia is interesting in her decision to act as if she were not of the elect, since everyone tells her she is not. Miss Deborah has equally strong opinions, in her case about the glory of England and the English Church. She speaks with "zeal and earnestness" about the "horrid old Calvinistic doctrines," closely allied in her mind with "the vile democratic idea that people are to have opinions on all subjects" (pp. 265–67). Miss Deborah's ideas are "amusing" to us and to Ellery, but her sincerity causes us and him to come close to admiring her. Each of the minor characters establishes the link between strength of mind and the religious ministry or the rejection of it. Grandma Badger and her blue book,

Miss Mehitable and her newfound belief in a personal Christ, Miss Deborah and her Anglican proselytizing to the children and Ellery—all lead inevitably to Esther Avery.

That the Cloudland section is feminist, whether Stowe would have admitted it or not, is indubitable. Miss Minerva Randall is the reigning spinster figure here, one step more unorthodox than Miss Mehitable. She is practical, which Mehitable is not, and yet reads Greek and Latin flawlessly (p. 355). In her past she navigated her brother's ship home as he lay in a fever. She does not countenance any "fol-de-rol about women's rights," but believes "that if women want any rights they had better take them, and say nothing about it" (p. 355). The narrator here adds a caution to this presumption that rights are there for the taking: "Miss Minerva," Horace notes, "had not enough of the external illusive charms of her sex, to suggest to a casual spectator any doubt on that score of the propriety of her doing or not doing anything" (p. 355). Obviously, appearance plays a role in the rights it is "proper" for a woman to take. Miss Minerva's looks have "a fishy quaintness"; she is "wild and withered," "unsightly and stunted," "short, square, and broad." Even her eyebrows are described: they are bushy as a "thicket" (p. 355). Unlike Tina, who tries to take rights too, the right to minister to lost souls, the right to be a brilliant scholar as the whim takes her, Miss "Nervy" does not have men and boys interpreting her religion and scholarship as seduction.

The whole section argues against the opinion that women can so easily "take their rights." The section is the feminist center and climax of the book and is the sting of the game. Because we have accepted the intelligence, courage, and full humanity of women who are like goblins and fish, we have no stereotyped response to fall back on when we are presented with Esther. Esther is not only as intelligent, sensitive, and well read as Miss Mehitable, but she is as beautiful as Harry's mother, who dies selflessly for her unorthodox ways.

Stowe's description of Esther is intense; it brings into focus her deepest criticism of New England Calvinism and of the repressive social system that allowed such women no outlet for their vitality. Esther is a "half-spiritual organization" in whom "*thinking* [had grown] to be a disease" (p. 365; Stowe's emphasis). It is her "misfortune" to approximate Plato's "perfect human thinker," the "MAN-WOMAN," in a society that cuts women off from "outward sources of excitement" (p. 365). It is her "misfortune" to have "strong logical faculties" and intellectual tastes and perceptions at the same time as she has "exquisite moral perceptions . . . tremulous, half-spiritual, half-sensuous intuitions," the mixture rendering her "half refined to angel" like her female ancestors (p. 366). Being nearly "perfect" as a philosopher and thinker, Esther can only be "tortured" by Calvinist theology and the society that springs from it.

Stowe writes with bitterness about a theology constructed by men like St. Augustine, to whom women, trapped by their "animal nature," are specially made for the temptation of men (p. 365). This criticism is extremely unorthodox, rivaling the most daring feminist thinking of the time. Yet Stowe's book was a popular success. Stowe does not drown her religious and feminist criticism. Nothing could be clearer or more straightforward than her denunciation of the system and her praise of Esther. The reason she can make her statement and get away with it is that she has played the reader into a position from which there is no appeal. If nineteenth-century readers can accept homely Miss Mehitable, whose stereotypical role would have been as a useless spinster, not a serious and deep-thinking woman, they must accept beautiful Esther. If they admit that Nervy Randall can know Virgil inside and out, they must believe that Esther can write a "Penseroso" on the subject of God's benevolence (p. 364). If Mehitable can be wise, certainly a paragon like Esther can be so, too.

The Cloudland section denounces not only traditional theology but also the limitations of traditional education for women. Esther is not "diseased" only because of a misogynist theology but also because she has no "outward sources of excitement." For her, the perfect thinker and philosopher, such a source of excitement would be college, where ideas are not always tied to theology. Harry admits that "in these very things that I set my heart on in the college course Esther is by far my superior. . . . she was ahead of us in both Greek and mathematics" (p. 423), and yet she cannot go on to college, while both Harry and Horace can. At the moment, Esther is healing because she has found Harry's love and his intuitive religion, but she has no prospects of doing anything with her fine mind. She can be a minister's daughter and a minister's wife, but she cannot be a minister herself.

The focus on Esther disappears after her betrothal to Harry, for she has served her polemic purpose. The focus shifts to Tina, who up to this point has been a "fairy-child," amusing and intelligent but not one who makes us feel something. Our concern for Esther, however, makes us see that Tina too has something more to her than we had thought. She can write translations of the Greek and Roman poets that Mr. Rossiter must begrudgingly praise. She can minister to such diehard atheists as Ezekiel Scranton. She can write compositions on subjects like the "difference between the natural and the moral sublime." As

Esther disappears, our concern for her mental growth transfers to Tina. Horace articulates it in the chapter following the Cloudland section: "It's rather a steep thing for girls that have kept step with us in study up to this point, and had their minds braced just as ours have been . . . to be suddenly let down, with nothing in particular to do." Harry responds, "Except to wait the coming man, who is to teach her what to do" (p. 423). The obvious irony of Harry's complacent answer indicates that the sting is still in process. Every educated woman in the novel, besides Esther, is single. The idea that a man will be coming is seriously questionable. As for Tina, we have already seen the men who misinterpret her friendship and zeal as love or who take advantage of their positions of power to try to convince her to marry them. These men are incapable of teaching her how to live. The greatest irony is that Tina does wait for the coming man and ends up with Ellery Davenport, a man who has deserted his lover and their child and who has thrown over faith not only in religion but in any positive values.

Oldtown Folks is a serious game meant to make us feel the distortions of a rigid, male-centered theology and an arbitrarily limited female education. Although its strategy is gradual and its climax gentle, the book speaks its revolutionary ideas clearly and makes us listen.

Stoddard's *The Morgesons*

The wounding of consciousness in some confidence games is more difficult to describe than that in Harper's or Phelps's books, yet hurts more than in Stowe's. One feels the sting but does not quite know whence it came. Elizabeth Stoddard was very adept at this kind of game. *The Morgesons* (1862) eludes every attempt to hold it down, but creates an ache it gives no remedy for: it is bleak and wonderful and despairing at one motion. Lawrence Buell and Sandra Zagarell, who brought Stoddard to critical attention in 1984, mention the "uneasy sense" of irony in the book. This uneasiness is part of the game Stoddard plays, akin to the "uncomfortable" feeling we are left with at the end of *Dr. Zay.* That Stoddard was conscious of playing a game is evident in a letter she wrote to Edmund Stedman in 1888: "I am *not* realistic—I am *romantic,* the very bareness and simplicity of my work is a trap for its romance."[54] I would say that her work is a double trap.

54. Quoted in Lawrence Buell and Sandra A. Zagarell, introduction to Elizabeth Stoddard, *The Morgesons and Other Writings, Published and Unpublished,* xxii.

The realism makes the reader yearn for the romantic, but the romantic lures the reader into the nihilistic realism just as surely.

A descriptive passage from the beginning of chapter 2 is a good example of Stoddard's style. It is a reminiscence of Cassandra's perceptions at age ten: "From the observatory of our house we could see how the inlet was pinched by the long claws of the land, which nearly enclosed it. . . . [a] desolate coast . . . edged by beaches overgrown with pale sedge. . . . Nothing alive, except the gulls, abode in these solitary shores. . . . Now and then a drowned man floated in among the sedge, or a small craft went to pieces on the rocks. . . . the coast resounded with the bellowing sea. . . . We heard its roar as it leaped over the rocks on Gloster Point, and its long, unbroken wail when it rolled in on Whitefoot Beach. In mild weather, too . . . we still heard its whimper. . . . the inland scenery was tame; no hill or dale broke its dull uniformity. . . . Seaward it was enchanting— beautiful under the sun and moon and clouds."[55]

This description is an example of how the book's language plays the reader: always the interplay of house and sea, of "pinching" social expectations and the "bellow" of the spirit trying to break free. The images in the description are realistically coarse. But the tone is romantic; it enchants the reader as the sea does Cassandra, despite the drowned men and the "pale sedge." The description is a psychological metaphor for the alienation, the passion, and the weakness of Cassandra. The "trap," however, is that the weakness, the "whimper," wins despite the promise of the tone.

"*Morgeson—Born—Lived—Died* were all their archives," Cassandra says of her ancestors, implying that she will live more fully than they.[56] The Morgesons are the inland; Cassandra wills herself to be of the sea. Stoddard makes the reader yearn with Cassandra, no matter how perverse her desires seem. From the beginning, passion and death are linked, but we romantically applaud Cassandra's efforts to do more than just live, no matter what the cost. Yet each step she seems to take forward leads only to further alienation. Her passion turns to a death in life. The realization that Cassandra, although she attains all she desires, has surrendered to "eternal monotony" is the wounding the book produces; the bleak realism of Cassandra's end traps us at last.

In many nineteenth-century novels, the separation of self from society was a major theme, but almost wholly reserved for men. Hawthorne, with whom

55. Elizabeth Stoddard, *The Morgesons and Other Writings, Published and Unpublished,* 7–8.
56. Ibid., 9.

Stoddard was compared at the time, was one of the few writers who conceived of alienated women. Yet Hester Prynne and Beatrice Rappaccini are special cases. They both have a mark upon them which causes society to reject them. Stoddard looks at a woman who rejects society of her own accord, who suffers alienation because of her own reactions to society's demands. Kate Chopin would write on a similar theme a third of a century later, but *The Morgesons* is one of the first novels to analyze a woman's struggle with her own genius.

Such a theme, tasting more of the twentieth century than of the nineteenth, was not one Stoddard could lay out openly in 1862 and expect the public to approve. In its own way, Stoddard's idea in *The Morgesons* was as revolutionary as Harper's in *Iola Leroy*. She too wanted the reader to experience an empathy seldom dreamed of.

The novel is about many things, but one of the key ideas is made explicit near the end of the book. Ben Somers's father, speaking of Veronica and her gift for music, says, "Your sister is a genius, I think. . . . What a deplorable thing for a woman!"[57] The fate of genius when it is entrapped by the social conventions that surrounded women in the 1860s is the theme, romantic in the Jamesian sense of a striving after an intangible goal of great value, realist in the ultimate failure and the manner of failure. Cassandra is Ahab without a ship, bound to the daily round of a middle-class woman's life, with little room to grow. She is alienated not just from society—she wouldn't have minded that—she is alienated from herself. From the very beginning, Cassandra is "possessed" by her own genius, but she does not understand that. The game of the novel is to get the reader to admit who Cassandra is and to recognize the horror of her end. In the mid-nineteenth century, such a recognition, such an admittance was almost unthinkable.

For Cassandra's end, by all conventional signs, is good. She subdues her passions, chooses "duty" over self-will, inherits her father's house, and marries the man she loves. But, like Phelps's *Dr. Zay* twenty years later, *The Morgesons* succeeds in making us unhappy with Cassandra's success. The game strategy is similar to Harper's: our dissatisfaction and sudden moments of understanding result from the language. Stoddard's style in itself was revolutionary for the 1860s, according to Buell and Zagarell: "[Stoddard] anticipates modern fiction in using a severely limited mode, with minimal narrative clues . . . minimal transitions, and dramatic, imagistic, and aphoristic impact."[58] The relative absence of

57. Ibid., 242.
58. Buell and Zagarell, introduction to Stoddard, *The Morgesons and Other Writings*, xxiii.

"narrative clues" draws the reader into the text, to supply meaning. When that meaning breaks the bounds of traditional thought, the reader, complicit in the creation of the meaning, finds himself or herself "caught by the game."

The play of the language can be described as a dance of the romantic and the real. The details of daily life are realistic; the moments of insight are romantic. The submersion of insight in "duty" is realism; the potential for genius despite everything is romanticism. The reader comes to have confidence in Cassandra's "flying Spirit," which calls, "Hail, Cassandra! Hail!" Yet the book ends with Cassandra's abdication of herself, her submission to "the yearning, yawning empty void" within her.[59] If romance, as Michael Davitt Bell demonstrates, is undermined by its own claim that it is true to the human heart because it can only hint through an "arabesque" of language at the undercurrent of blackness, then Stoddard's romanticism is a trap for realism, for Stoddard puts the blackness on the surface, like the drowned man in the cove, and hints instead at the "void" beneath.

The Morgesons uses two kinds of romance as its disguise: the romance that is a love story and the romance of the growing soul. At all the major game moves, the two kinds of romance intersect. The first intersection is in Cassandra's love for Charles Morgeson. By choosing to love him, Cassandra is choosing her freedom. She defies social strictures by daring to love a man who has a "devil . . . loose in him . . . looking through his eyes . . . like a maniac who looks through the bars of his cell," a man who "menace[s]" her and who says of love, "It is life—it is heaven—it is hell" (pp. 114, 118). That Charles is married makes her choice more clearly perverse, for it is forbidden to any nineteenth-century mind and heart of proper education, and therefore, in a Byronic inversion, more truly free. Cassandra dares to recognize her physical and spiritual passion, although she does not act on it. Her daring is all of the mind. The reader cannot but admire Cassandra's strength of will, her individuality, her intense confrontation with life. That is the reader's complicity. Although Stoddard is careful to keep the reader in the game by showing Cassandra committing no outward impropriety, the range of her inner rebellion is great.

If the novel had ended with the driving accident, with Cassandra and Charles metaphorically trampled by the horses of their passion, it would have been pure romance with a moral ending. If Cassandra had lived to be reborn as a Hester

59. Stoddard, *The Morgesons and Other Writings*, 214, 250. Subsequent page citations from this work will be given parenthetically in the text.

Prynne, it would have been romance again. But Cassandra's "rebirth" is ironic, for she "crawled out of a small hole," as the doctor put it, only to renounce herself and betray the genius that set her apart (p. 121). After the accident, she is paralyzed for a time and her face is irrevocably scarred. Now begins the long journey downward, although society would call it her maturation and success.

The second intersection of the two romances is Cassandra's love for Desmond Somers. Again she breaks expectations by choosing him rather than his brother, Ben, and again she chooses a man who has "something animal" in his eyes (p. 183). Desmond is brutal to his dogs and is obscenely alcoholic, but he can speak to the "thirst that from the soul doth rise" and can bring Cassandra back to the "blue deeps of our summer sea" that is herself (p. 174). Desmond, unlike Ben, understands the tension in Cassandra's life: "Women like you," he says, "pure, with no vice of blood, sometimes are tempted, struggle, and suffer" (p. 183). His statement makes Cassandra "wince" because she knows she has been and is now tempted and because she is unsure that she has no "vice of blood" (p. 184).

That uncertainty is the seed of her weakness, and begins to grow when she wakens after the accident. She begins to identify with her mother, a woman who has suppressed her passions, symbolized by the "serpent coil" of her hair that sometimes slips from its combs, a woman who runs her household and stares at the sea and will go no further. The result of such an abdication of the self is a nihilistic boredom. Cassandra, home again, sees all activity as an effort to "narcotize or stimulate [oneself] to forget that man's life was a vain going to and fro" (p. 142). But Cassandra has been chastened by her experience with Charles and finds herself humbled by her mother's "unselfish, unasking, vital love." She knows that "there should have been no higher beatitude that to live in [its] presence" (p. 128). That "should" is her undoing. Cassandra has always broken away from the "shoulds." But when she sees her sister, Veronica, notices her "colorless, fixedly pale complexion," she feels "a contraction in the region of [her] heart, as if a cord of steel were binding it" (p. 128). The kind of love Veronica and Mrs. Morgeson represent is a love that binds and contracts, a love that looks like death.

Unlike Dr. Zay, whose spirit is broken by the man she decides to love, Cassandra breaks her own will. She takes on her mother's role after her mother dies and becomes a housewife without a husband. She dives into a selflessness that Susan Warner's Ellen Montgomery would approve, but Cassandra does not ripen in her self-abnegation as Ellen does. Instead, she loses her soul. "What a starved, thin, haggard face I saw, with its border of pale hair! Whose were those wide, pitiful, robbed eyes?" (p. 240). The reader grieves at Cassandra's submission to "duty" and recoils when she begins to label her passion for Charles Morgeson "sin" (p. 244). Stoddard keeps the romance alive in the midst of this bleak realism by showing Cassandra intermittently remembering herself and trying to "break the fetters" of her alienation. She looks on herself and sees "no change, no growth or development! The fulfillment of duty avails me nothing; and self-discipline has passed the necessary point" (p. 243). But with every struggle forward of her old spirit, some fresh reality pulls her back. The romance is a trap for the realism, and the reader is caught in it.

An example of how Stoddard plays the reader, holding out a hope for Cassandra's true rebirth and then drawing it back, occurs soon after Mrs. Morgeson's death. Life has gone back to its routine, but with an emptiness now, and Cassandra suffers in the "vacuum in [the] atmosphere" (p. 213). But she goes to the sea, for the first time since separating from Desmond, and she has an epiphany there. She walks onto the rocks and lies down to watch the seaweed in a pool: "The pool showed me the motionless shadow of my face again, on which I pondered, till I suddenly became aware of a slow, internal oscillation, which increased till I felt in a strange tumult. I put my hand in the pool and troubled its surface. 'Hail, Cassandra! Hail!' I sprang up the highest rock on the point, and looked seaward, to catch a glimpse of the flying Spirit who had touched me. My soul was brought in poise and quickened with the beauty before me! The wide, shimmering plain of sea . . . mingled its essence with mine" (p. 214). Cassandra has looked into herself and recognized her own genius, giving her "poise" and life. Out of a sense of grief and a sense of emptiness she finds herself full and cries, "Have then at life! . . . We will possess its longing silence, rifle its waiting beauty. . . . Its roar, its beauty, its madness—we will have—*all*" (pp. 214–15).

Such a vision and such a cry are the height of romanticism, and the reader thrills with Cassandra to see her back to her old demoniac self. Yet the next instant, as Cassandra returns home and meets her Aunt Merce at the door, full of talk about the servant and "cold ham," Cassandra turns her high vision of selfhood into a paltry vision of service: "I never shall have any more colds, Aunt Merce; never mean to have anything to myself—entirely, you know" (p. 215), and she curses the sea spray that flies against the windows.

Romance and realism. Which is the trap for which? While Cassandra betrays her selfhood, the moment of vision has occurred, giving the reader confidence that Cassandra can still arise.

When Desmond finally comes, after Cassandra has inherited the house, he too is broken. He has done as Cassandra has done, repressed his passions. For him, alcoholism was the outward symbol of his difference. To overcome his alcoholism he had to overcome the part of his nature that had drawn Cassandra to him in the first place. His hair has turned gray; his face is old. When he speaks, his voice is "deathly faint" (p. 250). Cassandra wishes to cry, presumably for their lost selves. The hollowness of Desmond's "My God, I shall die with happiness," spoken as "a mortal paleness overspread his face" (p. 251), is a foreshadowing of the story's end, two pages later. This long-awaited marriage gets half a sentence; the honeymoon and following two years are dispensed with in a one-sentence paragraph. Cassandra ends up sitting at the window as her mother did, looking at the sea: "Its beauty wears a relentless aspect to me now; its eternal monotone expresses no pity, no compassion" (p. 252). Cassandra Morgeson has gained a loving, although vastly changed, husband and a substantial amount of property, but she has lost herself. Desmond, too, is just a pale reminder of the passionate man he used to be.

The third and underlying intersection of the romances of love story and growing soul is Cassandra's unstated love for Desmond's brother, Ben. Ben chooses Cassandra's sister, Veronica, over Cassandra because Veronica is death and Ben cannot choose life. "Her delicate, pure, ignorant soul suggests to me eternal repose" (p. 226), Ben tells Cassandra as he tries to explain why he did not choose to marry her. Cassandra, he says, is "unlike most women": "You understand your instincts; . . . you dared to define them, and were impious enough to follow them" (p. 226).

Veronica is an ascetic beset by a strange malady that "attacks" her whenever her passions are aroused. The causes for this illness are complex, perhaps implying a desire for sexual impotence, perhaps symbolizing Veronica's active refusal to participate in a world she detests. Cassandra, revealingly, says, "I feel well to my fingers' ends; they tingle with strength. I am elated with health." Veronica replies that for herself, she "will be" ill again: "I need all the illnesses that come" (p. 67). Ben chooses Veronica because, as he says, "the man who is willing to marry you [Cassandra] has more courage than I have" (p. 226). But the reader never chooses Veronica over Cassandra, for Cassandra represents some elusive ideal. To admit that she does, even as we face what Buell and Zagarell call Cassandra's "mysterious obsessions," makes us complicit in the game.

The Morgesons ends on an extremely negative note. There is no indication that Cassandra will rediscover her old imaginative aggressiveness or that finding one's "true love" is any answer to the contradictions and trivialities of daily life. The important thing is that Stoddard has lured the reader into confronting a view of life very much in opposition to the facile optimism dispensed in the religious tracts and sentimental novels of the day. It reminds readers then and now of how difficult it is to live fully in a society that demands the repression of passion and genius. *The Morgesons* is a game that hurts.

As many scholars of women's literature have noticed, books by women very often seem confused, saying one thing on the surface, but implying something else in the way characters or scenes are constructed. In most cases, this confusion is an artistic limitation that undermines the power of the novel. Mary Wilkins Freeman, especially in *The Portion of Labor* and in *Jane Field,* is a good example of an author who often does not seem to know for sure what her point is, leaving the reader unsure at the end of her novels, too. But sometimes books are considered artistically flawed when a closer look would reveal that the supposed confusion is part of a carefully planned strategy, a planned deconstruction of a traditional pattern. Before making a judgment on a novel, one should take a moment to consider whether something that seems disjointed is not in reality a signal that the author is playing a confidence game.

7

Stowe to Wharton: A Bold Move

In 1871, when Harriet Beecher Stowe published *Pink and White Tyranny*, it was becoming understood that women played a unique role in the capitalist economy, both as unpaid worker in the home and as commodity on the exchange market. Such ideas appeared in novels increasingly as the century neared its finish. Stowe's novel was one of the earliest to explicitly compare a woman's beauty to "stock in trade." However, it was not common for writers to consider women as active agents in their own exchange, although mothers often enough engineered the sale of their daughters' futures in the marriage "market." The view had shifted by the early twentieth century; writers began to see women actively selling themselves.

As I noted in Chapter 1, Luce Irigaray asserts that "commodities should never speak, and certainly should not go to market alone."[1] In the twentieth century, writers have dared to tell stories about confidence women who do "speak" unhesitatingly and who market themselves boldly. In the nineteenth century, on the other hand, literature tended to concentrate on the women who tried to escape their role as commodity—Hope Leslie turning Catholic saint, Capitola Black dressing like a boy, Cassy pretending to be a rich white woman, Clotel dressing like a white man. These women did not "go to market alone"; rather, they took themselves off the market, or at least changed their market value. Twentieth-century writers became more ready to examine different kinds of women, those who did not escape the market but who packaged themselves

1. Irigaray, *This Sex Which Is Not One,* 158.

for sale to the highest bidder. It is no longer only the escape artists and everyday pretenders but also some confidence women that we see in twentieth-century autobiography and fiction, women who have analyzed their economic role and try to control it, rather than trying to run away from it.

In the early twentieth century, the autobiographies of the professional confidence women, Sophie Lyons, May Churchill, and Madeleine (sometimes prostitute, sometimes con woman), were published. Each of these books makes some attempt to analyze the economic conditions that urge confidence women on. In the 1920s, too, brief analyses like *Confessions of a Gold Digger* appear as relatively straightforward statements of the games women play. Early-twentieth-century fiction also participated in the new explicitness. One of the clearest examples of the new confidence woman in fiction is Edith Wharton's Undine Spragg, the seriously flawed heroine of *The Custom of the Country*. Although Undine never considers herself to be anything but a commodity, she consistently demands the right to speak.

Undine Spragg: Lillie Ellis Re-created

To underscore the ways in which Undine is "new," I will compare her to a close precursor, Lillie Ellis in Harriet Beecher Stowe's *Pink and White Tyranny*. The similarities between the two stories are amazing, considering that Stowe wrote her novel in 1871 and Wharton wrote hers in 1913, forty-two years later. But the differences are more significant, indicating a major shift in the way women, and confidence women in particular, were understood.

Lillie Ellis in the Stowe novel is surprisingly like Undine Spragg. She is beautiful and knows it. The first sentence of the book sets the entire argument: John Seymour, her future husband, asks about Lillie, "Who *is* that beautiful creature?" Immediately Lillie is reduced to her appearance, and the "creature" foreshadows John's inability to see Lillie as a human being; his question could as easily have been asked concerning a woman in a painting. The reverse side of this view follows directly: Lillie is "sylphlike," "divine," able to "enchant" John. She is both less than and more than human, never a woman. John's first sight of her is a "vision," an analogue to the repeated visions of Undine that Wharton's Ralph Marvell will have: "The vision that [John] saw was of a delicate little fairy form; a complexion of pearly white, with a cheek of the hue of a pink shell; a fair, sweet, infantine face surrounded by a fleecy radiance of soft golden hair.

The vision appeared to float in some white gauzy robes; and, when she spoke or smiled, what an innocent, fresh, untouched, unspoiled look there was upon the face!"[2]

Later in the story we discover what lengths Lillie has to go to in order to achieve her various effects; we learn that she even "paints." Wharton shows Undine at her toilet, too, practicing the artless looks that will increase her value. The difference is that Stowe moralizes about Lillie's selfish pretenses while Wharton makes us rather admire Undine for her skill.

Both Lillie's and Undine's parents center their lives on their daughters because of their beauty. Both sets of parents are an "extremely common sort of people" who use their daughters' "wonderful beauty" as "a sort of stock in trade." Both Lillie and Undine consider their ability to "hook" men a profession, or business: "Miss Ellis was a belle by profession, and she understood her business perfectly." Wharton similarly compares Undine to her father, the businessman, and likens her manipulations to financial "strokes." In the perpetration of one of her schemes, Wharton describes Undine's thinking: "The business shrewdness which was never quite dormant in her suggested that this was not the moment for such scruples." Stowe is equally forthright about Lillie: "She saw through all the illusions of fancy and feeling, right to the tough material core of things. However soft and tender and sentimental her habits of speech and action were in her professional capacity of a charming woman, still the fair Lillie, had she been a man, would have been respected in the business world as one that had cut her eye-teeth, and knew on which side her bread was buttered."[3]

Both Lillie and Undine understand the function of a husband: he is "the man who [undertakes] to be responsible for his wife's bills." Similarly, both John and Ralph are enamored of their own "idea of a wife" as one who is to be molded, transformed by the husband. In Stowe's novel, John is sure he can "bring [Lillie] to all his own ways of thinking," turning her into a domestic angel who likes to read the moral philosophers. Likewise, in the Wharton book Ralph feels that he is "to defend [Undine] from [her own weakness] and lift her above it," to "draw her half-formed spirit from its sleep," and to "lift her to the height of his experience." He says to her half-angrily, "you foolish child . . . it's my affair to look after you, and warn you when you're on the wrong track."[4] John and Ralph

---

2. Harriet Beecher Stowe, *Pink and White Tyranny: A Society Novel,* 1–2.
3. Ibid., 28, 8; Edith Wharton, *The Custom of the Country,* 854; Stowe, *Tyranny,* 52.
4. Stowe, *Tyranny,* 52, 36, 60; Wharton, *Custom,* 739, 823, 728.

are both disappointed in their desire to transform a wife-child into their version of the ideal woman, disappointed because Lillie and Undine have very different visions of their own.

With so many similarities between the two books, it would seem inappropriate to call Undine Spragg "new." But in fact Lillie and Undine represent two quite different views of womanhood and woman's position in patriarchal society. Although the two characters are similar in personality, the narrative voices that present them are nearly a century apart. Stowe consistently passes a negative moral judgment on Lillie, calling her selfish and heartless, at last letting her die in illness and pain, a pettish old woman whose looks have been ravaged, leaving her nothing but a deathbed transformation into the loving wife John wanted all along. Lillie is constantly shown in contrast to the long-suffering, domestically perfect Grace Seymour, who achieves a perfect marriage and a comfortable home because of her honesty and plainness. Wharton, on the other hand, makes the reader so sympathetic to Undine's case, her desires, that we feel wretched when Undine fails and is reduced to haunting resorts alone because she has lost both Van Degen and Ralph. There is no righteous condemnation of Undine in the narrative voice, although we see Undine's selfishness clearly. Unlike Lillie, Undine at the end is victorious, a millionaire many times over, although still yearning. It is as if Wharton read *Pink and White Tyranny* and decided to retell the story from Lillie's point of view. Oddly enough, in the last scene of Stowe's book, Lillie refers to the water sprite of the German opera who at last becomes human through love, her name "Undine": "You remember that story of Undine you read me one day? It seems as if most of my life I have been like Undine before her soul came into her."[5] Wharton's novel shows that Undine had a soul all along, a soul of her own creation, not her husband's.

That "soul" is the main difference between the two novels and indicates a transformation in the view of women between the two time periods. In *Pink and White Tyranny*, Stowe refuses to allow Lillie full consciousness of her own actions, despite the implications of the story's rhetoric. What is in one moment a "profession" is in the next—in a typical nineteenth-century naturalistic fashion— a mere instinct. Stowe uses a quotation she says is from "de Balzac" to instruct us how to think about Lillie even though Lillie's actions have already shown us how to think about her quite differently. "De Balzac" says that "*Every woman lies—*

5. Stowe, *Tyranny,* 329.

obliging lies—venial lies—sublime lies—horrible lies—but always the obligation of lying. . . . And woman is so naively impertinent, so pretty, so graceful, so true, in her lying! . . . lying is to them the very foundation of language, and truth is only the exception. . . . they often finish by lying even to themselves. . . . their deception flows as softly as the snow falls from heaven." According to Balzac, deception is to be expected from women; it is natural to them, as natural as the snow. Stowe leaps at this reduction of the confidence woman's art to explain away Lillie's skill: "Lillie," she says, "was as precisely the woman here described as if she had been born and bred in Paris."[6]

Repeatedly, Stowe backs away from the implications of her own character's actions and words. One good example is when Lillie is determined that not only will *she* not go out to the poor workers' Sunday school, but neither will John. Lillie had used "all her womanly graces and fascinations" to convince John to stay at home with her. His only argument at last "was immediate and precipitate flight." Lillie watches her husband and Grace drive off; then Stowe tells us, " 'Well,' she said to herself, 'he shan't do that many times more,—I'm resolved.' " But in the very next line, Stowe takes it back: "No, she did not say it" and then plunges on into a paragraph moralizing about how we ought to articulate our own desires to see how bad they really are. Time and again *Pink and White Tyranny* deconstructs in such manner. Lillie's deathbed salvation is not the least of Stowe's backpedaling. Lillie's actions and decisions certainly seem highly conscious; she manipulates and deceives in the manner of confidence women. But the narrator tries to tell us that Lillie "was, my dear sir, what you suppose the true woman to be,—a bundle of blind instincts."[7] That "dear sir" and the Balzac quotation are significant, for Stowe bows to the patriarchal definition of womanhood, agreeing that confidence women are a sham, no threat at all because they have no purposive premeditation, just instincts. In effect, Stowe reduces Lillie from a confidence woman to an everyday pretender.

By the twentieth century, the emphasis has shifted. Rather than pointing out how really brainless confidence women like Lillie are, writers like Betty Van Deventer in *Confessions of a Gold Digger* both warn about and wonder admiringly at such women: "Only, remember this, their little heads are simply buzzing with ideas, and plans innumerable are taking delightful form in their

6. Ibid., 92–93, 94.
7. Ibid., 82–83, 84.

seemingly frivolous minds. Can anything hold more interest for the student of human behavior?"[8]

In *The Custom of the Country,* Wharton never lets us doubt Undine's conscious decision to live and act as she does. Undine understands the market value of her beauty and is rather shocked to discover that other people are not willing to acknowledge the business relationships she sees. At the Dagonets', she pains the company by talking about divorce as if it were a business deal: "Out in Apex, if a girl marries a man who don't come up to what she expected, people consider it's to her credit to want to change." Ralph laughingly responds, "If I were only sure of knowing what you expect!" And Undine answers, "Why, *everything!*" The last line of the chapter validates Undine's perception of her own value, for Mr. Dagonet says, "My child, if you look like that you'll get it."[9]

Wharton never backs away from the dual thesis that Undine is a commodity and that she knows it. On their honeymoon, Ralph holds her hand "as if it had been a bit of precious porcelain or ivory . . . to be fondled and dressed in rings." The fingernails are "smooth as rose-leaves," and when Ralph lifts the fingers, Undine is careful to let them fall back "only far enough to show the dimples."[10] The scene points up Ralph's inability to perceive Undine as a human being with desires of her own. His idyll is her torture, for while he wants to dream in seclusion, she wants to be where the "best society" is. It also points up the fact that Undine, like a businesswoman, is always working: the perfect fingernails and the dimples do not happen on their own. When Undine goes to the art gallery, much later in the book, she imitates the intellectual women she sees; when she goes to the opera, she spends her time studying the lead singer's toilet. She consistently tries to make herself more saleable, knowing that she can draw the best bids only when she is herself top of the line.

Undine has been practicing her confidence arts since she was a girl. Where Lillie as a child of eight makes a straight business deal—kisses for "papers of candy"—and "thus early acquired the idea that her charms were a capital to be employed in trading for the good things of life," Undine goes a step further. To get away from Apex in the summer, mainly because all her friends did, and because she did not wish to be outdone, the young Undine "secretly sucked lemons, nibbled slate-pencils and drank pints of bitter coffee to aggravate her look of

8. Van Deventer, *Confessions of a Gold Digger,* 30.
9. Wharton, *Custom,* 685.
10. Ibid., 714.

ill-health." Undine's childhood actions call to mind Kitty Adams sticking pins in her lips so she could cough blood and be released from jail and Sheeny Mike drinking soapsuds and ulcerating his skin for the same purpose. Undine herself later uses a similar ruse to get Ralph to send her to Europe: she has a "nervous attack" that only a change of scene can cure.[11] Undine does not work on so-called blind instinct. She plans her ruses and carries them out with a ruthlessness that is "fiercely independent."

Undine's name is suggestive in the book of her dual role as commodity and saleswoman. Named after one of her father's products, a hair curler, Undine herself is *"Diverse et ondoyante";* Wharton remarks on her "youthful flexibility. . . . She was always doubling and twisting on herself." But her flexibility is not the "malleability" Ralph thinks it is. Undine shapes herself, "adapting herself to whatever company she [is] in," in order to proceed with her plans. When Ralph tries to catch her in her lie about being with Van Degen, he discovers that her flexibility is part of her art: "She would go on eluding and doubling, watching him as he watched her; and at that game she was sure to beat him in the end."[12]

It is remarkable how similar Undine's world is to the world described by Thorstein Veblen in *The Theory of the Leisure Class.* Veblen emphasizes "ownership of the woman" as the fundamental form of "pecuniary emulation" in the economic power struggle men engage in. The more women a man "owns" and the more expensive the women are, the more a man has proven his worth. The woman participates in "conspicuous leisure" and "conspicuous consumption" by learning to follow rules of good breeding and by spending inordinate amounts of time and money at the dressmaker's; she becomes a "vicarious" symbol of the man's wealth, since the man actually *does* have to work to afford his wife.[13]

One can easily analyze *The Custom of the Country* in terms of conspicuous consumption and conspicuous leisure: it is the new prevalence of consumption over leisure that is at the heart of the war between the old families of New York, who calculate their worth by their ability to show good breeding and, using Veblen's terminology, to "engage in formal and ceremonial observances generally," and the nouveaux riches, who consider worth to be determined by one's ability to spend. Veblen explains that the rise of the nouveaux riches and

11. Stowe, *Tyranny,* 46; Wharton, *Custom,* 656, 791, 633.
12. Wharton, *Custom,* 676, 625, 727, 768.
13. Thorstein Veblen, *The Theory of the Leisure Class: An Economic Study of Institutions,* 22–29, 36–59 (chapters 2 and 3).

their belief in conspicuous consumption was a result of the expanding cities, with their transient populations. Extravagant spending is the only way to spread one's reputation for wealth efficiently. Veblen's suggestion that successful "pecuniary emulation" depends upon a "predatory" attitude explains both Elmer Moffatt's increasing success and Ralph's slow demise, insofar as pecuniary emulation depends on "freedom from scruple, from sympathy, honesty, and regard for life." Such "freedoms," Veblen says, "may, within fairly wide limits, be said to further the success of the individual in a pecuniary culture." If an upper-class person "reverts" to "non-predatory ways," he is thrown back, so that he won't dilute the stock.[14] Ralph in effect is discarded because he is not predatory enough, has too much scruple for the new economic system.

But *The Custom of the Country* is not a fictional restatement of Veblen's satire. Rather, it extends it and shows Veblen's limitations. For Veblen explicitly excludes women from his analysis of the predatory attitude common to the rising capitalist middle class. He states that girls are less "predaceous" than boys even as they grow up. He defines the "predaceous temper" as comprised of "the two barbarian traits, ferocity and astuteness. . . . both are highly serviceable for individual expediency in a life looking to invidious success." Women are, according to Veblen, "non-invidious" because they cannot go into business. Rather, they go into "service of other interests than the self-regarding one." Wharton's Undine and her various counterparts in the novel are not the malleable, tender-spirited women Veblen would have them be. Undine's astuteness, for instance, is highly developed. She has every bit as much "strategy or cunning . . . finesse and chicane," to use Veblen's words, as Moffatt does.[15] Her field of play is different from his, but the temperament is the same.

Undine is a confidence woman who sells herself as a commodity, repeatedly. The story she tells about herself changes, depending on the desires of her customer: to Ralph she is a woman he can mold, to Van Degen she is a woman of passion equal to his, to Raymond she is a graceful addition to his tapestries. Madame de Trezac makes Undine's status as a commodity absolutely clear: concerning Raymond's "set," she says, "It's not that they don't admire you—your looks, I mean; they think you beautiful; they're delighted to bring you out at their big dinners, with the Sèvres and the plate." Undine consistently considers

14. Ibid., 45–46 (old money and new), 86–91 (expanding cities), 223 (freedom from scruple), 235 (being thrown back).
15. Ibid., 251, 274–75, 342, 273–74.

herself merchandise, thinking about her "setting" as if she were a gem and getting a "sense of well-being" when she sees herself in the mirror: her beauty is something she can always trade on.[16] Only Moffatt sees Undine for who she is, not mere merchandise but an astute and ferocious saleswoman besides, because Moffatt is a con man who understands the confidence woman in her. Their love match is an ironically fitting end for the book.

The epitome of Undine's confidence art occurs when she tries to get Van Degen to say he will marry her. References to her "game," and her "victory" run throughout the scene: "It was hard so to temper the rebuff with promise that the game of suspense should still delude him." Undine is in control, very consciously making her moves, "but she now saw what port she had half-unconsciously been trying for. If she had striven so hard to hold him, had 'played' him with such patience and such skill, it was for something more than her passing amusement and convenience: for a purpose the more tenaciously cherished that she had not dared name it to herself. In the light of this discovery she saw the need of feigning complete indifference." And finally, "It was time to play her last card," for "she thought she trembled on the edge of victory."[17]

This particular game takes a long time to complete. When Undine goes to live with Van Degen, an audacious act at the turn of the century, the narrator remarks: "She had done this incredible thing, and she had done it from a motive that seemed, at the time, as clear, as logical, as free from the distorting mists of sentimentality, as any of her father's financial enterprises. It had been a bold move, but it had been as carefully calculated as the happiest Wall Street 'stroke.' "[18] It is clear that Wharton's treatment of Undine Spragg and Stowe's treatment of Lillie Ellis are far apart. Wharton does not say "no, she didn't think this," because the point is that such calculations are what make Undine Spragg special. Whether one considers Undine morally reprehensible is not the issue, for she is participating in a reprehensible world. Her daring and her strategy are Wharton's focus, in part because Undine's ability to engage so well in the typically male economic enterprise must by its very nature subvert it.

Undine is not just merchandise; she has a "soul." Like her father and like Moffatt, she is caught up in the "chronic dissatisfaction" Veblen argues is a result of "pecuniary emulation" and the "invidious comparison" it invites. But Undine's

16. Wharton, *Custom,* 979, 1013.
17. Ibid., 774, 774, 776, 775.
18. Ibid., 861.

"restless straining" is not for more goods, more wealth, but for something she cannot quite define. Undine is in a sense a visionary. She goes beyond wanting to be the richest woman and the most sought after; she strives for an elusive state she calls "the 'real thing.' " Undine is shocked at her father when he suggests that she stay with Ralph until she finds a richer man: "Did he suppose she was marrying for *money*? Didn't he see it was all a question, now and here, of the kind of people she wanted to 'go with'?" Undine eventually discovers that it is not other people who will satisfy her, either, since she finally reaches the height of what she thought she was pursuing by marrying into the old French aristocracy, and yet she feels empty. What Undine's "restless straining" is after, Wharton does not name. Undine has "pioneer blood" and the daring to walk down Main Street with Moffatt after his temperance-meeting con game explodes. She says, "I mean to have the best, you know; not just to get ahead of the other fellows, but because I know it when I see it." Moffatt understands her and responds, "It was what you were always after, wasn't it?" That "it," the "best," hovers over Undine's life from the moment she overhears Miss Wincher and an acquaintance from Boston talking at a hotel in Virginia: "Undine, straining her ears behind a column of the long veranda, obtained a new glimpse into the unimagined." At the end of the novel, Undine is still straining, still unable to identify what "the best," the "unimagined" might be: "Even now, however, she was not always happy. She had everything she wanted, but she still felt, at times, that there were other things she might want if she knew about them."[19]

Wharton, however, suggests an answer to the question "What does Undine (a woman) want?" in the moment that Undine and Moffatt face each other in the de Chelles mansion: "They were looking at each other with challenge and complicity in their eyes. . . . Here was some one who spoke her language, who knew her meanings, who understood instinctively all the deep-seated wants for which her acquired vocabulary had no terms; and as she talked she once more seemed to herself intelligent, eloquent and interesting."[20] What Veblen forgot in his analysis of the leisure class is that women are not passive game pieces to be used or discarded by men, even if the men wish to so view them; women have a personal desire, a "self-regarding," that will work itself out in indirect ways if no straightforward channels offer. Undine Spragg's desire is to find herself, to

19. Veblen, *Theory of the Leisure Class*, 31; Wharton, *Custom*, 687, 703, 976–77, 657, 1012.
20. Wharton, *Custom*, 974–75.

be "intelligent, eloquent and interesting" in her own eyes as well as in the eyes of someone who really knows her; she wants to be a self-fulfilled human being. Because of the limitations put on her by the society that she lives in and that she is not imaginative enough to transform, Undine never achieves her desire of self-fulfillment, but she comes as close to it as she can by being, instead, a confidence woman.

Listening to the Confidence Woman at Last

Who were the confidence women in nineteenth-century America? They were the women who used disguise, deception, and manipulation to become human. When the commodity speaks, she is no longer a commodity. When a woman sells an image of herself or takes herself off the market, she is no longer product, ornament, symbol, merchandise. The confidence woman asserts her individual womanhood over her "womanliness" and thereby begins to invent a society different from the one she was born into. It has been my task to find the confidence woman as she appeared in the history, autobiography, and fiction of the nineteenth century and to try to continue the invention of her America as it was begun there. The confidence woman, however, has not been easy to find. Whereas the confidence man is an accessible figure, prominent in history books and in the comic literary tradition, the confidence woman has been well hidden, in both the nineteenth century and the twentieth. Because the confidence woman vigorously inhabits a world of deceit, disguise, and manipulation, she is dangerous to the stereotypes of both the submissive, pure "true woman" and the altruistic, hard-working, independent "new woman." The confidence woman is the reverse side, the alter ego of the two stereotypes and as such has been silenced by men and women alike.

If one wishes to find the confidence woman, one cannot look where one finds the confidence man. For at the same time that the confidence man was striking out on his own, beginning to feel the power that money could bring and the power of his own inventiveness in the 1830s and 1840s, women were finding themselves stripped of their economic worth, relegated to domestic concerns as the sexual division of labor solidified. Men went off to the factory and the marketplace to earn the money that had become the dominant means of exchange; women stayed at home, living out the new domestic ideology that made women an influence rather than a force. Confidence men "speculated": selling bogs as prize real estate, swapping horses, putting through "deals." A woman normally could do none of these things. She could not be a Captain Simon Suggs starting a church, nor a P. T. Barnum, nor could she be a Jay Gould, the financier turned con man whose financial swindles were big news in the 1860s, for her role was helpmate, mother, marriageable daughter, but seldom entrepreneur. As the nation of men surged forward, woman was pushed back, her role to be a refuge for men.

There are, of course, exceptions to the rule that women were not financiers in the nineteenth century. Jay Robert Nash, in *Zanies: The World's Greatest Eccentrics,* 155–64, tells the story of Hetty Green (1835–1916), "the Witch of Wall Street" (the name of a biography by Boyden Sparks). With her inherited wealth of $5 million, she married a millionaire, bought government bonds when they were down and sold them when they were up, bought railroads, and lent money to cities and states and other financiers. Once she succeeded in withdrawing her money from a bank just before it failed by throwing a tantrum: "She pulled at her clothes, cried, screamed, and stamped the floor, finally squatting on the floor and threatening to remain in that position until she was given her money" (p. 156). Green inherited her money in 1865 and was wildly prosperous by the 1890s. It was in 1900 that she was given the tag "witch." But Green was not a confidence woman. She came by her money legitimately, although she had a penchant for avoiding tax collectors by living in cheap boarding houses under assumed names. Her histrionics were perhaps eccentric, but they were not a trick.

To say that a woman could be neither Captain Simon Suggs nor Jay Gould, both confidence men, is not to say that she could not be a confidence artist. Her world was different from the con man's; the typically separate spheres also made a separate art. The confidence woman, as we have seen, is often found in male disguise. Where a man could go easily, without deception, a woman often could not. Ragged Dick of the Horatio Alger fantasy is not a con man when he shines boots. But Capitola Black in boy's clothing is akin to a con woman when she does so. When a young Southern gentleman joins the Confederate Army to fight the Yankees, he is not a confidence man. When Loreta Janeta Velazquez does the same, disguised as Harry T. Buford, she is a confidence woman.

You will not find a confidence woman being a James Fisk, selling fraudulent stocks worth millions, but you will find her being a Cassie Chadwick, pretending to be Andrew Carnegie's bastard daughter, heiress to millions. Because the confidence woman is expected to be a lady, she often plays the lady, but she is neither pious nor domestic nor submissive, and seldom enough pure. Undine Spragg, who plays the lady as well as she can, knows the value of tears, a pressure of the hand, elegant dresses, and a beautiful figure as she makes her "carefully calculated" decisions. You will find resonances of the confidence woman in the black woman who passes for white, the poor woman who passes for a millionaire, the clairvoyant who tells the future for pay, the prostitute who pretends to be a virgin for the twenty-third time. If you look, you will find the confidence woman in literature and history, but she will not be merely a female version of the confidence man.

Yet it is also clear that in many ways the confidence woman *is* like the confidence man. Both depend on intelligence and their ability to pretend to be someone they are not to get out of scrapes or to pull off schemes. Both enjoy the disguises, the machinations, the victory. Both subvert the established order, although in different ways. And both, in their own times at least, were a force. The influence of the confidence man on American history and on our imaginations has been thoroughly discussed by people like Susan Kuhlmann, Gary Lindberg, and William Lenz. The influence of the confidence woman, on the other hand, has been little examined. How great an influence the confidence woman has been is debatable, for she was not clearly seen in her own time and is not remembered now. In the 1850s, people flocked to hear about Ellen Craft's daring escape from slavery in the dress of a middle-class white male, but they did not come to hear her. Ellen herself was silenced, brought on stage as a curiosity after her husband's lecture. William Craft wrote the narrative of their escape, although it was Ellen's quick intelligence and self-control that made the escape possible, and William Wells Brown wrote the novel *Clotel* using Ellen Craft's story as the base, but he has Clotel make a fatal mistake, so that she must leap to her death to avoid her captors, a muting of Ellen Craft's true genius. In the 1860s and 1870s, the memoirs of Loreta Velazquez, Emma Edmonds, Belle Boyd, and Rose Greenhow were best-sellers, but the exploits of these soldiers and spies were muted too, made acceptable under the rubric of patriotism. Although Louisa May Alcott's Jean Muir and V. V. of her "blood and thunder" stories and E. D. E. N. Southworth's "madcap" Capitola Black of *The Hidden Hand* lived in the imaginations of millions, they were sanitized versions of real confidence women, distorting the unacceptable truth to fit at least partially the acceptable stereotype. Today, the silencing has been even more effective: the names of the historical confidence women are barely remembered and the best-selling books are now hardly read, so that to us, an Undine Spragg seems a twentieth-century creation, appearing out of nowhere, whereas in reality she is the culmination of a long line of confidence women we have been unable to or have refused to see. Because the confidence woman was muted, and often enough silenced in the nineteenth century, she could not shape the American imagination the way a confidence man could, and as long as we erase her from our memories, she cannot help us understand our own past.

The confidence woman was silenced in her own time because there was no place for her in the cultural paradigms of "true womanhood" or the "new woman." Being a woman of intelligence but little conventional morality, a woman of disguise, of daring, of foresight, of egocentrism, she was too elusive to be easily labeled, almost too dangerous to be imagined. Moreover, the confidence woman participated in her own silencing. Because she needed to use the prevailing stereotypes as her disguise and because she needed to avoid prosecution, she was the first to deny her own existence, the first to insist upon her innocence of any deceit. However, the persistence into the 1980s of the silence concerning the confidence woman is somewhat bewildering. The Alcott thrillers, Southworth's books, and the memoirs of gold diggers and spies are now available, yet the story of the confidence woman has not been written. Maybe she is still considered too dangerous to handle.

Such a reaction to her is understandable in some ways, however, for the confidence woman, at least in her criminal forms, is often quite unsavory. If she defies the old female psychology that describes women as infantile, incapable of genius or originality, able to lie or commit crime on a whim only but never out of premeditation, perhaps she defies the new female psychology, too, as Carol Gilligan, a major spokeswoman for the new psychology, argues that women are more connected to other human beings than men are and have less need for personal independence. The confidence woman disrupts the old and the new psychological formulations, for she is a woman of originality who separates herself from society, always looking for a way to work her will on it.

We have to confront the confidence woman, precisely because she disturbs our theories. Being a product of the hypocrisies and prejudices of the late nineteenth century, she is a part of our national consciousness and cannot be denied with impunity. Mark Twain showed in "The Facts Concerning the Recent Carnival of Crime in Connecticut" the danger of denying one's other self, one's conscience, no matter how grotesque it might be. If we fail to see the confidence woman, to take her into our national imagination, we deny a part of ourselves, a part of our own strength as well as a part of our own limitations. We need to see the confidence woman as the rebel she was, as a woman who played with the rules in order to break them and to break out of them, as a woman who often enough won; we need, too, to recognize the courage of writers like Alcott and Wharton who tried to confront the confidence woman in all her complexity, facing her unpleasant side even as they praised her strength. It is time now to bring the confidence woman out of hiding and to listen to what she is trying to say.

Bibliography

Abelson, Elaine S. *When Ladies Go A-Thieving: Middle-Class Shoplifters in the Victorian Department Store.* New York: Oxford University Press, 1989.

Adams, Henry. *The Education of Henry Adams: An Autobiography.* Boston: Houghton Mifflin, 1918.

Adler, Freda. *Sisters in Crime: The Rise of the New Female Criminal.* New York: McGraw-Hill, 1975.

Alcott, Louisa May. *Alternative Alcott.* Ed. Elaine Showalter. New Brunswick: Rutgers University Press, 1988.

———. "Behind a Mask; or, A Woman's Power." 1866. Reprint, in *Behind a Mask: The Unknown Thrillers of Louisa May Alcott,* edited by Madeleine Stern, 1–104. New York: Quill, 1984.

———. *Little Women.* 1868–1869. Reprint, New York: Grosset and Dunlap, 1947.

———. "A Marble Woman; or, The Mysterious Model." 1865. Reprint, in *Plots and Counterplots: More Unknown Thrillers of Louisa May Alcott,* edited by Madeleine Stern, 131–237. New York: Morrow, 1976.

———. "Pauline's Passion and Punishment." 1863. Reprint, in *Behind a Mask: The Unknown Thrillers of Louisa May Alcott,* edited by Madeleine Stern, 105–52. New York: Quill, 1984.

———. "V. V.; or, Plots and Counterplots." 1865. Reprint, in *Plots and Counterplots: More Unknown Thrillers of Louisa May Alcott,* edited by Madeleine Stern, 41–129. New York: Morrow, 1976.

Armitage, Susan, and Elizabeth Jameson, eds. *The Women's West.* Norman: University of Oklahoma Press, 1987.

Asbury, Herbert. *The French Quarter: An Informal History of the New Orleans Underworld.* New York: Pocket Books, 1949.

————. *Gem of the Prairie: An Informal History of the Chicago Underworld.* Dekalb: Northern Illinois University Press, 1986.

Auerbach, Nina. *Communities of Women: An Idea in Fiction.* Cambridge: Harvard University Press, 1978.

Avrich, Paul. *The Haymarket Tragedy.* Princeton: Princeton University Press, 1984.

Banta, Martha. *Imaging American Women: Idea and Ideals in Cultural History.* New York: Columbia University Press, 1987.

Barth, John. *Chimera.* New York: Random House, 1972.

Bataille, Gretchen M., and Kathleen Mullen Sands. *American Indian Women Telling Their Lives.* Lincoln: University of Nebraska Press, 1984.

Baym, Nina. *Woman's Fiction: A Guide to Novels by and about Women in America, 1820–1870.* Ithaca: Cornell University Press, 1978.

Beauchamp, Virginia Walcott, ed. *A Private War: Letters and Diaries of Madge Preston, 1862–1867.* New Brunswick, N.J.: Rutgers University Press, 1987.

Bell, Michael Davitt. *The Development of American Romance: The Sacrifice of Relation.* Chicago: University of Chicago Press, 1980.

Bennett, Lerone, Jr. *Before the Mayflower: A History of the Negro in America, 1619–1964.* Baltimore: Penguin, 1966.

Blair, John G. *The Confidence Man in Modern Fiction: Rogue's Gallery with Six Portraits.* New York: Barnes and Noble, 1979.

Blair, Walter. *Horse Sense in American Humor.* Chicago: University of Chicago Press, 1942.

Blumenthal, Walter Hart. *Brides from Bridewell: Female Felons Sent to Colonial America.* Westport, Conn.: Greenwood Press, 1973.

Boyd, Belle. *Belle Boyd in Camp and Prison.* With an introduction by George Augustus Sala. New York: Blelock, 1865.

Brown, William Wells. *Clotel; or, The President's Daughter.* Upper Saddle River, N.J.: Gregg, 1969.

Burton, Richard F., trans. *Tales from the Arabian Nights: Selected from the Book of the Thousand Nights and a Night.* 1885–1888. Reprint, ed. David Shumaker, New York: Avenel Books, 1978.

Butler, Becky, ed. *Ceremonies of the Heart: Celebrating Lesbian Unions.* Seattle: Seal Press, 1990.

Butler, Judith. "Contingent Foundations: Feminism and the Question of 'Postmodernism.'" In *Feminists Theorize the Political,* edited by Judith Butler and Joan W. Scott, 3–21. New York: Routledge, 1992.

Byrnes, Thomas. *Darkness and Daylight in New York: Criminal Life and Detective Experiences in the Great Metropolis.* Hartford, Conn.: Hartford, 1895.

———. *1886 Professional Criminals of America.* 1886. Reprint, New York: Chelsea, 1969.

Cary, Alice. "Uncle Christopher's." 1853. Reprint, in *Clovernook Sketches and Other Stories,* edited by Judith Fetterley. New Brunswick, N.J.: Rutgers University Press, 1987.

Cather, Willa. *A Lost Lady.* New York: Knopf, 1923.

———. *O Pioneers!* Boston: Houghton Mifflin, 1913.

———. *The Song of the Lark.* Boston: Houghton Mifflin, 1915.

Catherwood, Mary Hartwell. "Marianson." 1899. Reprint, in *Mackinac and Lake Stories,* 1–19. New York: Garrett Press, 1969.

Chopin, Kate. "Désirée's Baby." In *Bayou Folk.* Boston: Houghton Mifflin, 1894.

Christian, Barbara. *Black Women Novelists: The Development of a Tradition, 1892–1976.* Westport, Conn.: Greenwood Press, 1980.

Conrad, Earl. *Harriet Tubman.* New York: Paul S. Eriksson, 1943.

Conrad, Susan P. *Perish the Thought: Intellectual Women in Romantic America, 1830–1860.* Secaucus, N.J.: Citadel Press, 1976.

Craft, William. *Running a Thousand Miles for Freedom; or, The Escape of William and Ellen Craft from Slavery.* London: Tweedie, 1860.

Crane, Stephen. *Maggie: A Girl of the Streets.* 1893. Reprint, in *Stephen Crane: Bowery Tales: "Maggie" and "George's Mother,"* edited by Fredson Bowers. Charlottesville: The University Press of Virginia, 1969.

Crosbie, John S. *The Incredible Mrs. Chadwick: The Most Notorious Woman of Her Age.* Toronto: McGraw-Hill Ryerson, 1975.

Culley, Margo. "What a Piece of Work Is 'Woman'! An Introduction." In *American Women's Autobiography: Fea(s)ts of Memory,* edited by Margo Culley, 3–31. Madison: University of Wisconsin Press, 1992.

Davidson, Cathy N. *Revolution and the Word: The Rise of the Novel in America.* New York: Oxford University Press, 1986.

Defoe, Daniel. *Moll Flanders.* 1722. Reprint, Boston: Houghton Mifflin, Riverside Edition, 1959.

De Forest, John William. *Miss Ravenel's Conversion from Secession to Loyalty.* 1867. Reprint, ed. Gordon S. Haight, New York: Holt, Rinehart, and Winston, 1955.

De Lauretis, Teresa. "Desire in Narrative." In *Alice Doesn't: Feminism, Semiotics, Cinema,* 103–57. Bloomington: Indiana University Press, 1984.

De Pauw, Linda Grant. *Founding Mothers: Women in America in the Revolutionary Era.* Boston: Houghton Mifflin, 1975.

Derrida, Jacques. "Structure, Sign and Play in the Discourse of the Human Sciences." In *Writing and Difference,* translated by Alan Bass, 278–93. Chicago: University of Chicago Press, 1978.

Doyle, Arthur Conan. "A Scandal in Bohemia." 1892. Reprint, in *The Original Illustrated Sherlock Holmes,* Secaucus, N.J.: Castle, 1982.

Dreiser, Theodore. *Sister Carrie.* 1900. Reprint, in *Sister Carrie: An Authoritative Text, Backgrounds and Sources, Criticism,* edited by Donald Pizer, New York: Norton, 1970.

Durova, Nadezhda. *The Cavalry Maiden: Journals of a Russian Officer in the Napoleonic Wars.* Trans. Mary F. Zirin. Bloomington: Indiana University Press, 1988.

Edmonds, S. Emma. *Nurse and Spy in the Union Army.* Hartford, Conn.: Williams, 1865.

Ewen, Elizabeth. *Immigrant Women in the Land of Dollars: Life and Culture on the Lower East Side, 1890–1925.* New York: Monthly Review, 1985.

Faderman, Lillian. *Surpassing the Love of Men: Romantic Friendship and Love between Women from the Renaissance to the Present.* New York: Morrow, 1981.

Franklin, Benjamin. *The Autobiography of Benjamin Franklin.* New York: Lancer, 1968.

Franklin, H. Bruce. *Prison Literature in America: The Victim as Criminal and Artist.* New York: Oxford University Press, 1989.

Fraser, Antonia. *The Warrior Queens.* New York: Knopf, 1989.

Freeman, Mary E. Wilkins. "A Gala Dress." In *A New England Nun and Other Stories.* New York: Harper, 1891.

———. *Jane Field.* 1892. Reprint, Upper Saddle River, N.J.: Literature House, 1970.

———. *The Shoulders of Atlas: A Novel.* New York: Harper, 1908.

Freibert, Lucy M., and Barbara A. White, eds. *Hidden Hands: An Anthology of American Women Writers, 1790–1870.* New Brunswick, N.J.: Rutgers University Press, 1985.

Friedman, Edward H. *The Antiheroine's Voice: Narrative Discourse and Transformations of the Picaresque.* Columbia: University of Missouri Press, 1987.

Fromm, Eric. "Disobedience as a Psychological and Moral Problem." In *On Disobedience: And Other Essays,* 16–23. New York: Seabury Press, 1981.

Fuller, Margaret. *Woman in the Nineteenth Century.* 1845. Reprint, New York: Norton, 1971.

Garber, Marjorie. *Vested Interests: Cross-Dressing and Cultural Anxiety.* New York: Routledge, 1992.

Giddings, Paula. *When and Where I Enter: The Impact of Black Women on Race and Sex in America.* Toronto: Bantam, 1984.

Greenhow, Rose O'Neal. *My Imprisonment and the First Year of the Abolition Rule at Washington.* London: Bentley, 1863.

Grimké, Sarah M. "Letters on the Equality of the Sexes and the Condition of Women." 1837. Reprint, in *Feminism: The Essential Historical Writings,* edited by Miriam Schneir, 39–47. New York: Vintage, 1972.

Hall, Richard. *Patriots in Disguise: Women Warriors of the Civil War.* New York: Paragon House, 1993.

Halttunen, Karen. *Confidence Men and Painted Women: A Study of Middle-Class Culture in America, 1830–1870.* New Haven, Conn.: Yale University Press, 1982.

Harper, Frances E. W. *Iola LeRoy or Shadows Uplifted.* 1892. Reprint, edited and with an introduction by Hazel Carby, Boston: Beacon, 1987.

Harrentsian, Dale. "The Nature of Female Criminality." In *Psychology of Women: Selected Readings,* edited by Juanita H. Williams, 413–28. New York: Norton, 1979.

Harris, Katherine. "Homesteading in Northeastern Colorado, 1873–1920: Sex Roles and Women's Experience." In *The Women's West,* edited by Susan Armitage and Elizabeth Jameson, 165–78. Norman: University of Oklahoma Press, 1987.

Harrison, Martha. "Narrative." In *The Female Experience: An American Documentary,* edited by Gerda Lerner, 11–14. The American Heritage Series. Indianapolis: Bobbs-Merrill, 1977.

Harte, Bret. "An Ingenue of the Sierras." In *The Writings of Bret Harte,* vol. 9 of the Standard Library Edition, 453–74. Boston: Houghton Mifflin, 1896.

Hartman, Geoffrey H. *Saving the Text: Literature/Derrida/Philosophy.* Baltimore: Johns Hopkins University Press, 1981.

Hawthorne, Nathaniel. "My Kinsman, Major Molineux." 1832. In *The Celestial Railroad and Other Stories,* 29–48. New York: Signet, 1963.

Hellerstein, Erna Olafson, Leslie Parker Hume, and Karen M. Offen. *Victorian Women: A Documentary Account of Women's Lives in Nineteenth-Century*

England, France, and the United States. Stanford: Stanford University Press, 1981.

Holley, Marietta. *My Opinions and Betsey Bobbet's: Designed as a Beacon Light to Guide Women to Life Liberty and the Pursuit of Happiness but Which May Be Read by Members of the Sterner Sect, Without Injury to Themselves or the Book.* 1872. Reprint, Hartford, Conn.: American Publishing, 1888.

Hooper, Johnson Jones. "The Captain Attends a Camp Meeting." In *Some Adventures of Captain Simon Suggs, Late of the Tallapoosa Volunteers: Together with "Taking the Census," and other Alabama Sketches.* Philadelphia: Carey and Hart, 1846.

Hopkins, Sarah Winnemucca. *Life among the Piutes: Their Wrongs and Claims.* Ed. Mrs. Horace Mann. Boston: Putnam, 1883.

Irigaray, Luce. *This Sex Which Is Not One.* 1977. Reprint, trans. Catherine Porter and Carolyn Burke. Ithaca: Cornell University Press, 1985.

Iser, Wolfgang. *The Act of Reading: A Theory of Aesthetic Response.* Baltimore: Johns Hopkins University Press, 1978.

Jameson, Elizabeth. "Women as Workers, Women as Civilizers: True Womanhood in the American West." In *The Women's West,* edited by Susan Armitage and Elizabeth Jameson, 145–64. Norman: University of Oklahoma Press, 1987.

Jastrow, Joseph. *Error and Eccentricity in Human Belief.* New York: Dover Publications, 1935.

Jewett, Sarah Orne. *A Country Doctor.* 1884. Reprint, Boston: Houghton Mifflin, 1912.

Johnson, Susan L. "Sharing Bed and Board: Cohabitation and Cultural Difference in Central Arizona Mining Towns, 1863–1873." In *The Women's West,* edited by Susan Armitage and Elizabeth Jameson, 76–94. Norman: University of Oklahoma Press, 1987.

Johnston, Johanna. *Mrs. Satan: The Incredible Saga of Victoria C. Woodhull.* New York: Putnam, 1967.

Jordan, Winthrop D. *White over Black: American Attitudes toward the Negro, 1550–1812.* Baltimore: Penguin, 1968.

Katz, Jonathan Ned. *Gay American History: Lesbians and Gay Men in the U.S.A., A Documentary History.* 1976. Reprint, Revised Edition, New York: Meridian, 1992.

Kelley, Mary. *Private Woman, Public Stage: Literary Domesticity in Nineteenth-Century America.* New York: Oxford University Press, 1984.

Kinchen, Oscar A. *Women Who Spied for the Blue and the Gray.* Philadelphia: Dorrance, 1972.

King, Florence. *Confessions of a Failed Southern Lady.* Toronto: Bantam, 1985.

Kinney, James. *Amalgamation! Race, Sex, and Rhetoric in the Nineteenth-Century American Novel.* Westport, Conn.: Greenwood Press, 1985.

Kirkland, Caroline M. *A New Home—Who'll Follow.* 1839. Reprint, ed. William S. Osborne, New Haven, Conn.: College and University Press, 1965.

Kirkland, Frazar. *The Pictorial Book of Anecdotes of the Rebellion; or, the Funny and Pathetic Side of the War, Embracing the Most Brilliant and Remarkable Anecdotical Events of the Great Conflict in the United States . . . with Famous Words and Deeds of Women.* St. Louis: J. H. Mason, 1889.

Kuhlmann, Susan. *Knave, Fool, and Genius: The Confidence Man as He Appears in Nineteenth-Century American Fiction.* Chapel Hill: University of North Carolina Press, 1973.

Kurtz, Paul. *The Transcendental Temptation: A Critique of Religion and the Paranormal.* New York: Prometheus, 1986.

Laclos, Chaderlos de. *Les Liaisons dangereuses.* 1782. Reprint, Garden City, N.Y.: Doubleday, 1961.

Lenz, William E. *Fast Talk and Flush Times: The Confidence Man as a Literary Convention.* Columbia: University of Missouri Press, 1985.

Leonard, Eileen B. *Women, Crime, and Society: A Critique of Theoretical Criminology.* New York: Longman, 1982.

Lerner, Gerda. *The Female Experience: An American Documentary.* The American Heritage Series. Indianapolis: Bobbs-Merrill, 1977.

Lindberg, Gary. *The Confidence Man in American Literature.* New York: Oxford University Press, 1982.

Lombroso, Caesar, and William Ferrero. *The Female Offender.* New York: Appleton, 1899.

Longstreet, Augustus Baldwin. "The Horse Swap." In *Georgia Scenes, Characters, Incidents, etc, in the First Half Century of the Republic.* Augusta: S. R. Sentinel Office, 1835.

Lott, Eric. *Love and Theft: Blackface Minstrelsy and the American Working Class.* New York: Oxford University Press, 1993.

Lyons, Sophie. *Why Crime Does Not Pay.* New York: Ogilvie, 1913.

Madeleine: An Autobiography. 1919. Reprint, with a new introduction by Marcia Carlisle, New York: Persea Books, 1986.

Mann, Herman. *The Female Review: Life of Deborah Sampson, the Female Soldier in the War of Revolution.* Boston: J. K. Wiggin and W. Parsons Lunt, 1866.

Maurer, David W. *The American Confidence Man.* Springfield, Ill.: Charles C. Thomas, 1974.

————. *The Big Con: The Story of the Confidence Man and the Confidence Game.* Indianapolis: Bobbs-Merrill, 1940.

May, Henry F. Introduction to *Oldtown Folks,* by Harriet Beecher Stowe, 3–43. Cambridge: Belknap, 1966.

McNeal, Violet. *Four White Horses and a Brass Band.* Garden City, N.Y.: Doubleday, 1947.

Melville, Herman. *The Confidence-Man: His Masquerade.* 1857. Reprint, in *Herman Melville: "The Confidence-Man: His Masquerade": An Authoritative Text, Backgrounds and Sources, Reviews, Criticism, and an Annotated Bibliography,* edited by Hershel Parker, New York: Norton, 1971.

Mills, James. *The Underground Empire: Where Crime and Government Embrace.* Garden City, N.Y.: Doubleday, 1986.

Moers, Ellen. *Literary Women.* Garden City, N.Y.: Doubleday, 1976.

Murphy, Mary. "The Private Lives of Public Women: Prostitution in Butte, Montana, 1878–1917." In *The Women's West,* edited by Susan Armitage and Elizabeth Jameson, 193–205. Norman: University of Oklahoma Press, 1987.

Nadler, Susan. *Good Girls Gone Bad.* New York: Freundlich, 1987.

Nardo, Anna K. *The Ludic Self in Seventeenth-Century English Literature.* New York: State University of New York Press, 1991.

Nash, Jay Robert. *Bloodletters and Badmen: A Narrative Encyclopedia of American Criminals from the Pilgrims to the Present.* New York: Evans, 1973.

————. *Look for the Woman: A Narrative Encyclopedia of Female Poisoners, Kidnappers, Thieves, Extortionists, Terrorists, Swindlers, and Spies from Elizabethan Times to the Present.* New York: Evans, 1981.

————. *Zanies: The World's Greatest Eccentrics.* Piscataway, N.J.: New Century, 1982.

Patrick, G. T. W. "The Psychology of Women." In *Psychology of Women: Selected Readings,* edited by Juanita H. Williams, 3–11. New York: Norton, 1979.

Pearson, Carol, and Katherine Pope. *The Female Hero in American and British Literature.* New York: Bowker, 1981.

Phelps, Elizabeth Stuart. *Dr. Zay.* 1882. Reprint, edited and with an afterword by Michael Sartisky, New York: The Feminist Press, 1987.

Pierce, Jane Louise Runner. "Marietta Holley's (Josiah Allen's Wife) Techniques of Humor." Master's thesis, Kansas State College, 1961.

Pinkerton, Allan. *Thirty Years a Detective: A Thorough and Comprehensive Exposé of Criminal Practices of All Grades and Classes . . .* 1884. Reprint, New York: Chelsea, 1983.

Pollak, Otto. *The Criminality of Women.* Philadelphia: University of Pennsylvania Press, 1950.

Pratt, Annis V. "The New Feminist Criticisms: Exploring the History of the New Space." In *Beyond Intellectual Sexism: A New Woman, A New Reality,* edited by Joan I. Roberts, 175–95. New York: McKay, 1976.

Reynolds, David S. *Beneath the American Renaissance: The Subversive Imagination in the Age of Emerson and Melville.* Cambridge: Harvard University Press, 1989.

Rich, Adrienne. *On Lies, Secrets, and Silence: Selected Prose, 1966–1978.* New York: Norton, 1979.

Riley, Glenda. *The Female Frontier: A Comparative View of Women on the Prairie and the Plains.* Lawrence: University Press of Kansas, 1989.

Riviere, Joan. "Womanliness as a Masquerade." In *Formations of Fantasy,* edited by Victor Burgin, James Donald, and Cora Kaplan, 35–44. London: Methuen, 1986. Originally published in *The International Journal of Psychoanalysis* 10 (1929).

Robinson, Harriet H. "Fourteenth Annual Report of Massachusetts Bureau of Statistics of Labor, 1883." In *Feminism: The Essential Historical Writings,* edited by Miriam Schneir, 48–56. New York: Vintage, 1972.

Rosen, Ruth, and Sue Davidson, eds. *The Maimie Papers.* Old Westbury, New York: The Feminist Press, 1977.

Rowson, Susanna. *Charlotte Temple: A True Tale.* 1794. Reprint, New Haven, Conn.: New College University Press, 1970.

Ryan, Mary P. *Womanhood in America: From Colonial Times to the Present.* New York: New Viewpoints, 1975.

Schneir, Miriam, ed. *Feminism: The Essential Historical Writings.* New York: Vintage, 1972.

Schur, Edwin M. *Labeling Women Deviant: Gender, Stigma, and Social Control.* Philadelphia: Temple University Press, 1983.

Scott, Anne Firor. *The Southern Lady: From Pedestal to Politics, 1830–1930.* Chicago: University of Chicago Press, 1970.

Sedgwick, Catharine Maria. *Hope Leslie; or, Early Times in the Massachusetts.* 1827. Reprint, New Brunswick, N.J.: Rutgers University Press, 1987.

Sharpe, May Churchill. *Chicago May: Her Story.* New York: Macaulay, 1928.

Showalter, Elaine. *The Female Malady: Women, Madness, and English Culture, 1830–1980.* New York: Pantheon, 1985.

———. *A Literature of Their Own: British Women Novelists from Brontë to Lessing.* Princeton: Princeton University Press, 1972.

Smart, Carol. *Women, Crime, and Criminology: A Feminist Critique.* London: Routledge and Kegan Paul, 1977.

Smith, Gene, and Jayne Barry Smith. *The Police Gazette.* New York: Simon and Schuster, 1972.

Smith, Sidonie. *A Poetics of Women's Autobiography: Marginality and the Fictions of Self-Representation.* Bloomington: Indiana University Press, 1987.

———. "Resisting the Gaze of Embodiment: Women's Autobiography in the Nineteenth Century." In *American Women's Autobiography: Fea(s)ts of Memory,* edited by Margo Culley, 75–110. Madison: University of Wisconsin Press, 1992.

Southworth, E. D. E. N. *The Hidden Hand; or, Capitola the Madcap.* 1859. Reprint, edited and with an introduction by Joanne Dobson, New Brunswick, N.J.: Rutgers University Press, 1988.

Spacks, Patricia Meyer. *The Female Imagination.* New York: Knopf, 1975.

Spofford, Harriet Prescott. "Mrs. Claxton's Skeleton." In *A Scarlet Poppy and Other Stories.* 1894. Reprint, American Short Story Series, no. 76, New York: Garrett, 1969.

Sterling, Dorothy. *Black Foremothers: Three Lives.* Old Westbury, New York: The Feminist Press, 1979.

Stern, Madeleine B. *Louisa May Alcott.* Norman: University of Oklahoma Press, 1950.

Stoddard, Elizabeth. *The Morgesons and Other Writings, Published and Unpublished.* 1862 *[The Morgesons].* Reprint, edited and with a biographical and critical introduction by Lawrence Buell and Sandra A. Zagarell, Philadelphia: University of Pennsylvania Press, 1985.

Stowe, Harriet Beecher. *Dred: A Tale of the Great Dismal Swamp.* Boston: Houghton Mifflin, 1856.

———. *Oldtown Folks.* 1869. Reprint, edited and with an introduction by Dorothy Berkson, New Brunswick, N.J.: Rutgers University Press, 1987.

———. *The Pearl of Orr's Island: A Story of the Coast of Maine.* 1862. Reprint, Boston: Houghton Mifflin, 1884.

———. *Pink and White Tyranny: A Society Novel.* 1871. Reprint, with an introduction by Judith Martin, New York: New American Library, 1988.

———. *Uncle Tom's Cabin.* 1851–52. Reprint, New York: Signet Classic, 1981.

Tannahill, Reay. *Sex in History.* New York: Stein, 1980.

Taylor, Susie King. *Reminiscences of My Life in Camp with the 33rd U.S. Colored Troops, Late First South Carolina Volunteers: A Black Woman's Civil War Memories.* 1902. Reprint, edited by Patricia W. Romero, with an introduction by Willie Lee Rose, New York: Wiener, 1980.

Thompson, C. J. S. *The Mysteries of Sex: Women Who Posed as Men and Men Who Impersonated Women.* New York: Causeway, 1974.

Tompkins, Jane. *Sensational Designs: The Cultural Work of American Fiction, 1790–1860.* New York: Oxford University Press, 1985.

Twain, Mark. *Adventures of Huckleberry Finn.* 1885. Reprint, in *Samuel Langhorne Clemens: Adventures of Huckleberry Finn: An Authoritative Text, Backgrounds and Sources, Criticism.* New York: Norton, 1977.

———. *Following the Equator: A Journey around the World.* Hartford, Conn.: American Publishing, 1897.

———. *Pudd'nhead Wilson and Those Extraordinary Twins.* 1894. Reprint, a facsimile of the first edition, San Francisco: Chandler Publishing, 1968.

Van Deventer, Betty. *Confessions of a Gold Digger.* Little Blue Book no. 1392. Girard, Kans.: Haldeman-Julius, 1929.

———. *How New York Working Girls Live.* Little Blue Book no. 479. Girard, Kans.: Haldeman-Julius, 1928.

Van Kirk, Sylvia. "The Role of Native Women in the Creation of Fur Trade Society in Western Canada, 1670–1830." In *The Women's West,* edited by Susan Armitage and Elizabeth Jameson, 53–62. Norman: University of Oklahoma Press, 1987.

Veblen, Thorstein. *The Theory of the Leisure Class: An Economic Study of Institutions.* 1899. Reprint, New York: Viking Press, 1945.

Velazquez, Loreta Janeta. *The Woman in Battle: A Narrative of the Exploits, Adventures, and Travels of Madame Loreta Janeta Velazquez . . .* Edited and with a preface by C. J. Worthington. 1876. Reprint, New York: Arno Press, 1972.

Ward, Artemus. "The Octoroon." In *The Complete Works of Artemus Ward: With a Biographical Sketch (by Melville D. Landon, "Eli Perkins") and Many Humorous Illustrations,* 43–47. New York: Carleton, 1883.

Warner, Susan. *The Wide, Wide World.* 1892. Reprint, edited and with an afterword by Jane Tompkins, New York: The Feminist Press, 1987.

Welter, Barbara. "The Cult of True Womanhood: 1820–1860." *American Quarterly* 18 (Summer 1966): 151–74.

Wharton, Edith. *The Custom of the Country.* 1913. Reprint, in *Edith Wharton Novels,* 621–1014. New York: Library of America, 1985.

Wheelwright, Julie. *Amazons and Military Maids: Women Who Dressed as Men in the Pursuit of Life, Liberty, and Happiness.* London: Pandora, 1989.

Wilson, Harriet E. *Our Nig; or, Sketches from the Life of a Free Black, in a Two-Story White House, North. Showing that Slavery's Shadows Fall Even There.* 1859. Edited and with an introduction by Henry Louis Gates Jr. New York: Random, 1983.

Worthington, C. J., ed. Preface to *The Woman in Battle . . . ,* by Loreta Janeta Velazquez. Richmond: Gilman, 1876. Reprint, New York: Arno Press, 1972.

Wulffen, Erich. *Woman as a Sexual Criminal.* Trans. David Berger. New York: American Ethnological Press, 1934.

Index

Actresses: confidence women as, 13, 28, 32, 37, 79, 90, 97, 98, 100, 112, 138, 147, 155, 157, 165–66, 175, 181; cross-dressing and, 105, 106, 118, 130; in *Police Gazette*, 111, 111*n6*; in fiction, 165–66, 167, 169, 175, 176, 181, 183; mentioned, 20
Adams, Henry, 30–31
Adams, Kitty, 80, 185, 241
Adler, Irene, 20
Adventuresses: as gold diggers, 15, 28, 93; types of, 15, 93; definition of, 18, 93; in the South, 43; discussion of, 92–96; in fiction, 93, 162, 164–70, 180
African Americans: *See* Cassy; *Clotel;* Craft, Ellen; Fiction as game: novels that are games, *Iola LeRoy;* novels that are not games, *Our Nig;* Moore, Flossie; Slavery; Tubman, Harriet
Allen, Samantha, 202–6
Anthony, Susan B., 51
Antihero: confidence man as, 1, 6, 33; criminal as, 69; confidence woman as, 69, 71, 187; need to confront, 187. *See also* Rebels
Armstrong, Kate, 82
Asbury, Herbert: on Chicago's growth, 38–40; on Flossie Moore, 40; on Moll Hodges, 40; on panel houses, 40; on strong-arm women, 40; on voodoo queens, 41; on Kitty Adams, 80; on Kate Armstrong, 82
Assassins, female, 140

Augustine, 79
Autobiography: as con game, 108, 113–14, 142, 144, 188; theories of, 109–10; rhetoric in, 110, 113–14, 116, 174; influences on fiction, 111, 174; historical accuracy of, 114, 136, 142, 145, 152; as fiction, 201; in the twentieth century, 236

Babcock, Elizabeth and Emily, 184
Badger game: Chicago May as Badger Queen, 18, 91–92, 152; definition of, 39; Sophie Lyons's game, 62–63; mislabeling of, 85, 91–92; in fiction, 162–63; mentioned, 17
Bank robbers: 2, 150–51; Sophie Lewis/Lyons as, 4, 72, 146–47, 150–51; anonymous female, 150; mentioned, 2
Bannock War, 129–30
Barry, Dr. James, 17, 124–25
Beauty: of confidence women, 4, 60, 66, 71, 131, 145, 149, 156; in fiction, 159, 163–64, 223, 225, 232, 235, 236–37, 242, 243. *See also* Confidence woman, appearance of; Confidence woman, commodity status of
Beck, Sophie, 17–18, 65, 181
Black, Capitola: attitude of, 170, 171, 174, 182; in boy's clothes, 170, 235, 246; story of, 170–75; fast talk, 172; strategies of, 172; as heroine, 172–73; compared to soldiers and spies, 182; mentioned, 247